SANTA FE
AND TAOS
THE WRITER'S ERA

SANTA FE AND TAOS

THE WRITER'S ERA
1916-1941

MARTA WEIGLE
◆
KYLE FIORE

ANCIENT CITY PRESS / SANTA FE

Grateful acknowledgment is made for permission to reprint:

"Morning Walk—Santa Fe" from *The Iron Dish* by Lynn Riggs. Copyright 1930 by Howard E. Reinheimer. Reprinted by permission of Doubleday & Company, Inc.

"The Santa Fe Group" by Elizabeth Shepley Sergeant. Copyright © 1934 by *Saturday Review*. All rights reserved. Reprinted by permission.

"Taos" from *Phoenix I*, the Posthumous Papers of D. H. Lawrence. Edited with an Introduction by Edward D. McDonald. Copyright 1936 by Frieda Lawrence. Copyright © renewed 1964 by the Estate of the late Frieda Lawrence Ravagli. All rights reserved. Reprinted by permission of Viking Penguin Inc.

International Standard Book Number
0-941270-79-3
Library of Congress Catalog Number
81-71485

Designed by Emmy Ezzell
Cover illustration by Willard Clark
Cover design by Connie Durand

10 9 8 7 6 5 4 3 2 1

CONTENTS

PREFACE

Both Santa Fe and Taos are well known as important twentieth-century American art colonies. However, their fame rests more upon the reputations of resident and visiting artists than the contributions of the writers, playwrights and poets who visited, lived and worked side-by-side with those artists in the same inspiring land, shared equally civic responsibilities, and also enjoyed the liberating atmosphere of these Southwestern Bohemias. Although literati are mentioned throughout the spate of work on individual artists and their "colonies," except for D. H. Lawrence and his Taos entourage, Willa Cather, Mary Austin and perhaps Witter Bynner, the activities, attitudes and achievements of literary New Mexicans have remained for the most part poorly chronicled. By focusing on "Literary New Mexico" between World War I and World War II, in many respects a Periclean time for *all* the arts in the state, this book complements the more extensive literature on "Artistic New Mexico."

Santa Fe and Taos: The Writer's Era, 1916-1941 is patterned after Van Deren Coke's 1963 study of *Taos and Santa Fe: The Artist's Environment, 1882-1942*, with the cities' names reversed to indicate the state capital's greater importance to the literary scene. This volume is more an exhibition catalogue than a strict literary or social history. We have not attempted to interview persons with firsthand knowledge of these times but have chosen instead to consider their written record—the way they presented themselves then—in books, magazines, newspapers and all manner of printed ephemera, and the memoirs they have published since.

The history and ambience of the art colonies at Santa Fe and Taos are sketched in "A Chronicle." This introductory overview is followed by the two main "exhibits": "Portraits and Self-Portraits, Contemporary and Retrospective"—a collection of photographs, pictures, poems, articles and selected quotations from fiction and non-fiction describing the inspiration and quality of life in New Mexico, especially Santa Fe and Taos; and "Publications Ephemeral and Exemplary"—certain examples of contemporary printing, much of it executed locally. Because of the enormous number of writers who have been associated with New Mexico in various ways, we have chosen to compile a directory of those who identified themselves or were identified as New Mexico writers only during the 1930s, when both the academic community and the growing tourist industry began to define the state's artists and literati. A brief "Bibliographic Note" supplements the sources cited in notes following each chapter of "A Chronicle."

Every section of the book has been indexed. Some individuals appear infrequently; others are noted again and again—by their contemporaries, by scholars, and by their chroniclers. The index thus forms an integral part of the story of each writer's involvement in the literary and social history of New Mexico during the formative and flourishing years of the art colonies at Santa Fe and Taos.

* * * *

In addition to formal notices on the copyright page, we would like to acknowledge and sincerely thank the following persons and publishers for permissions to reprint and for support in the preparation of this book:

Nancy Applegate, The Villagrá Book Shop, Santa Fe, for items from her collection and for continuing counsel and encouragement.

John Atlee, Albuquerque, for his photographs of items in Albuquerque collections.

Laughlin Barker, Santa Fe, for "Santa Fe in the Twenties," by his mother, Ruth Laughlin.

Emily Otis Barnes, Santa Fe, for information about and the photograph of her brother and sister-in-law, Raymond and Bina Otis.

Roberta Benecke, Albuquerque, for assistance with typing.

Willard F. Clark, Santa Fe, for making available items in his collection, for sharing his considerable knowledge of printing and of these times, and especially for designing the jacket on this book. Illustrations for the part-titles in this book were designed by Mr. Clark during the 1930s and are reproduced here through the courtesy of Nancy Applegate and Mrs. Philip C. Duschnes.

Philip C. Duschnes, Inc., and Mrs. Philip C. Duschnes, New York, for "The Rydal Press of Santa Fe New Mexico," from *Colophon: The Annual of Bookmaking*, Volume I.

Emmy Ezzell, Albuquerque, not only for her design of this book but also for patiently teaching the intricacies of the profession in which she is so skilled.

Farrar, Straus & Giroux, Inc., New York, for selections from Paul Horgan, *Approaches to Writing*.

Donald Farren and his staff, Special Collections, Zimmerman Library, University of New Mexico, Albuquerque, for help in locating obscure and crucial sources.

Francis Fergusson, Kingston, New Jersey, for selections from *Home in the West: An Inquiry into My Origins*, by his brother, Harvey Fergusson.

Devon Ferster, Albuquerque, for her constant support these several years.

Elizabeth Hadas, University of New Mexico Press, Albuquerque, for her critique of earlier drafts of this book.

David Holtby, University of New Mexico Press, Albuquerque, for assistance in various editorial and technical matters.

Clark Kimball and Charlotte J. Stone, The Great Southwest Books, Santa Fe, for generously donating many photographs, for invaluable information and counsel, and especially for sharing the richness and excitement of these literary times and places.

Alfred A. Knopf, Inc., New York, for selections from Carl van Vechten, *Spider Boy: A Scenario for a Moving Picture,* and Edith Lewis, *Willa Cather Living: A Personal Record.*

Henry S. Monroe, Santa Fe, and the editor of *Poetry,* Chicago, for selections from Harriet Monroe, "In Texas and New Mexico," copyrighted in 1920 by the Modern Poetry Association.

Museum of New Mexico, Santa Fe, for photographs and publications in their collections, with special thanks to Arthur Olivas and Richard Rudisill of the Photo Collections and Sharon Smith-Gonzales of the History Library.

New Mexico State Records Center and Archives, Santa Fe, for photographs, films, and documents in their collection, with special thanks to Kay Dorman and Sallie Wagner for locating and identifying photographs.

The North American Review, Cedar Falls, Iowa, for selections from Erna Fergusson, "Crusade from Santa Fé," quoted with permission from *The North American Review* (1937) and the University of Northern Iowa.

Mary A. Powell, Santa Fe, for her photographs of items in Santa Fe collections.

Jack Rittenhouse, Albuquerque, for invaluable assistance during the early stages of this project.

Mrs. Edgar L. Rossin, Tesuque, for selections from *Red Earth,* by her mother, Alice Corbin Henderson.

Roswell Museum and Art Center, Roswell, New Mexico, for the photograph of "New Mexico Gate," painted by Stuart Davis.

Southwest Review, Southern Methodist University, Dallas, for Witter Bynner, "Desert Harvest," and selections from May Sarton, "The Leopard Land: Haniel and Alice Long's Santa Fe."

Stark Museum of Art, Orange, Texas, for the photograph of "Ourselves and Taos Neighbors," painted by Ernest L. Blumenschein.

Diana and Joe Stein, Los Artesanos, Las Vegas, New Mexico, for locating resource materials and for sharing their considerable knowledge of books in this area.

Frank Waters, Taos, for the selection from his novel, *People of the Valley*.

This book would not have been possible without the knowledge, guidance and abiding concern of the founder of Ancient City Press, Robert F. Kadlec. It is dedicated to him.

A CHRONICLE

PROLOGUE

I can hardly imagine how [Santa Fe] is supported. The country around it is barren. At the North stands a snow capped mountain while the valley in which the town is situated is drab and sandy. The streets are narrow. In the morning this place is crowded with men, women and children who come in from the country with articles for sale. A Mexican will walk about the town all day to sell a bundle of grass worth about a dime. They are the poorest looking people I ever saw. They subsist principally on mutton, onions and red pepper.

—Letter from a traveler with the
Little Rock Company, printed in
The Arkansas Banner, 31 August 1849.

The Taos and Santa Fe art colonies can be traced to a heterogeneous group of nineteenth-century Anglo-American travelers and settlers. During New Mexico's Territorial period (1850-1912), government and military personnel, journalists, illustrators, novelists, scholars, health seekers and tourists attempted to depict the strange and novel New Mexican land, climate and cultures from many different perspectives.

Despite more than two decades of trade between Mexico and the United States, the Mexican Department of New Mexico, which Brigadier-General Stephen Watts Kearny claimed for the United States in Santa Fe on August 18, 1846, was almost entirely unknown to the forces of occupation and the new government. In 1856, when William W. H. Davis, former United States District Attorney for the new Territory, wrote up his personal observations and historical research undertaken "during a residence of two and a half years in New Mexico," he could rightfully claim:

There is no country protected by our flag and subject to our laws so little known to the people of the United States as the territory of New Mexico. Its very position precludes an intimate intercourse with other sections of the Union, and serves to lock up a knowledge of the country within its own limits. The natural features differ widely from the rest of the Union; and the inhabitants, with manners and customs of their Moorish and Castilian ancestors, are both new and strange to our people. For these reasons, reliable information of this hitherto almost unknown region can not fail to be interesting to the public.[1]

As part of determined efforts to assert their economic, political and cultural dominance, the small but powerful newcomer minority al-

3

most immediately established an English-language press. The first such journal, the Santa Fe *Republican*, was announced on January 1, 1847. A military paper owned and printed by the United States Army, the *Republican* began regular publication on September 10 of that year. In 1849 the Army sold its printing plant to the founders of the *Santa Fe New Mexican*, which was published sporadically until 1850, and resumed as a weekly in January 1863. June of 1851 marked the debut of New Mexico's first longstanding newspaper, the Santa Fe *Weekly Gazette*.

Despite these brave journalistic ventures, between 1847 and the arrival of the railroads in 1879, comparatively few English or Spanish newspapers were published for any appreciable length of time in the Territory of New Mexico, and often "their editors became exceptionally important and influential."[2] In an impoverished, isolated region with a predominantly illiterate populace, most of whom spoke Spanish or Native American languages, these frontier editors anticipated political and financial gains following rail connections rather than immediate journalistic success. Nevertheless, their papers contained occasional literary features, mostly poetry and humor.

During these years the Anglo experience in New Mexico was also portrayed with increasing frequency in Southwestern novels. These stories of action and romance were often set at least partially in New Mexico. One of the earliest was Timothy Flint's *Francis Berrian*, published in 1826. However, the authors of most such yarns—"adventurers, archeologists, colonists, cowboys, doctors, housewives, politicians, preachers, and soldiers . . . ventured from the more civilized areas of the East and South . . . [and] after brief visits or short periods of residence in the Southwest, more often than not . . . returned home to write."[3] The first novelist to feature a Santa Fean as a major character was Irishman Thomas Mayne Reid. Charles St. Vrain, a protagonist in Reid's 1851 novel *The Scalp Hunters*, was "a real-life Santa Fe trader."[4] While such literature did little to stimulate indigenous New Mexico writing, it did provide a number of Americans with a fictional image of the Southwest.

Southwestern dime, historical, local color and cowboy novels developed after the Civil War. The dime novel's eventual popularity prompted an editorial on "Literature for Children" in the *Santa Fe New Mexican* of April 7, 1900:

Parents should know what their children are reading. It will be news to many parents in Santa Fe that considerable literature of the blood and thunder kind is being read in this city. This is undoubtedly true in every other town in this territory. There is plenty of good literature, interesting to children published nowadays at low prices and there can be no excuse for children being allowed to read dime novels and wild, wooly west stories.

One of the first historical novels was out-of-state author Elizabeth [Williams] Champney's 1888 *Great-Grandmother's Girls in New Mexico,* while cowboy/range novelist Eugene Manlove Rhodes, an intermittent New Mexico resident between 1881 and 1906, made his literary debut with a poem, "Charlie Graham," in 1896.

The first locomotive entered Santa Fe on February 9, 1880. General Lew Wallace, governor of New Mexico from 1878 to 1881, spoke at the Santa Fe Railroad's opening ceremonies. Already the author of *The Fair God* (1873), an historical romance set in Mexico at the time of the Spanish Conquest, Wallace finished writing the final chapters of his classic novel *Ben Hur* (1880) in the Palace of the Governors on the Santa Fe Plaza and is thus one of the first colonist writers.[5]

The advent of the railroad brought a great increase in the number of health seekers journeying to New Mexico. Convalescents from many parts of the United States had begun arriving in early Territorial days, seeking dry, clean air and sunshine. Nestled high in the piñon-spotted foothills of the Sangre de Cristo mountains, Santa Fe was proclaimed to have the ideal weather for sufferers from consumption and other lung ailments.[6] An advertisement in the *New Mexican Review* of April 12, 1900, reads:

It is safe to estimate that there are over 300 sunshiny days in the Taos Valley. The tourist and the health seeker will find here many things to interest them, particularly the Taos Pueblos, called by Lummis, "The American Pyramids." Here one can study the customs of centuries ago, folklore, and try to fathom out the secrets of the 'kivas' or Council Chambers, and many ceremonial functions and mystic dances. Here one can find rest from the daily monotony of an active life and recuperate his grey matter. It is an ideal spot for a summer's outing, and will compare favorably with a trip to Egypt, while not taking up so much time and being less expensive.

Journalists and illustrators also found the Southwest a rich source for new material. Charles F. Lummis's 1893 *Land of Poco Tiempo* set the tone for such hortatory description:

Sun, silence, and adobe—that is New Mexico in three words. . . . It is the Great American Mystery—the National Rip Van Winkle—the United States which is *not* United States. Here is the land of *poco tiempo*—the home of "Pretty Soon." Why hurry with the hurrying world? The "Pretty Soon" of New Spain is better than the "Now! Now!" of the haggard States. The opiate sun soothes to rest, the adobe is made to lean against, the hush of day-long noon would not be broken. Let us not hasten—*mañana* will do. Better still, *pasado mañana* (p. 3).

Its visual counterpart appears in the work of travelling illustrators—adventuring artists out to capture exotica for Eastern viewers. They frequently portrayed Southwestern Indian and Hispanic cultures with varying degrees of realism for periodicals such as *Harper's Weekly*.[7] Impressed by the light, the land and the cultures they discovered, some of them returned to live and work in New Mexico after their commissioned travels. Artists Bert G. Phillips and Ernest L. Blumenschein's return to Taos in 1898 is now legendary, and the broken wagon wheel which Blumenschein carried into Taos Plaza on September 4 came to symbolize the beginnings of the Taos art colony.

The period between the coming of the railroad and statehood in 1912 also saw the influx of many scholars. The ancient and contemporary Indian cultures surrounding Santa Fe and Taos attracted archeologists, ethnologists and linguists. Their scholarly work became more widely known in part through a foray into literature by Adolph F. Bandelier, an inveterate explorer-ethnologist-archeologist who first came to Santa Fe in 1880 under the auspices of the new Archaeological Institute of America. Bandelier prefaced his 1890 novel, *The Delight Makers*, by claiming:

I was prompted to perform the work by a conviction that however scientific works may tell the truth about the Indian, they exercise always a limited influence upon the general public. . . , [so] by clothing sober facts in the garb of romance I have hoped to make the "Truth about the Pueblo Indians" more accessible and perhaps more acceptable to the public in general.

In 1909 the establishment of the School of American Archaeology and the Museum of New Mexico in Santa Fe further helped to attract scholars and to popularize their work.[8] During the early 1900s these two institutions formed a cultural hub for local society.

New Mexico's "foreign" culture, which so delighted scholars, journalists and artists, was a source of continuing concern to Anglo settlers. Due in part to their feeling of estrangement from the values of Eastern culture and their desire to transplant that culture in New Mexico, Anglos formed a variety of voluntary societies or culture groups during the late nineteenth and early twentieth centuries.[9] The organization of the Fifteen Club, a woman's literary group, for example, was quaintly described by Mrs. Mary Houghton Harroun in the 1915 Souvenir Edition of the *Santa Fe New Mexican:*

Once upon a time there were some good women in Santa Fe who were sad and longed intensely for the pleasant things in the homes they had left behind them. Of course, this could not be the case, now, but the old Santa Fe of 1891 (and that is the year of which I am writing) was entirely unlike the Santa Fe of today. That Santa Fe was as much a foreign city as if some genii had snatched it out of old Spain and dropped it down here in its valley in the mountains for the delectation of those who should "see America first."

So what more natural than that these women should organize a club on the same lines as the dear old clubs at home; do some studying, some literary work, "and last but not least" learn to appreciate each other.

And so, on October 14th, 1891, was formed the Fifteen Club.

This group continued into the twentieth century and in 1917 sponsored publication of a twelve-page pamphlet by Mary Catherine Prince, "The Literature of New Mexico—Written for the Fifteen Club of Santa Fe on the Occasion of Its Twenty-Fifth Anniversary, October, Nineteen Seventeen." However, most of the works Prince listed under "Historical," "Scientific," "General," and "Curiosities" categories were published before 1912.

Thus, on the eve of statehood New Mexico was a land of contrasting cultures and conflicting images. While many citizens were hard at work molding a state which would reflect their experiences in the towns and cities back East, Southwestern fiction writers, journalists and illustrators were portraying New Mexico as the homeland of aboriginal Indians, an outpost enclave of Spanish-Mexican culture, and the frontier heartland of the Anglo cowboy and outlaw. It was during this era (1900-1915) that "bona fide" Anglo artists and finally writers began to migrate and establish their colonies in the territory-turned-state. Unlike the businessmen and settlers before them, they were not hoping to create a replica of the towns and cities they had fled. They sought instead new vistas and new experiences to inspire their work. Fascinated by the sky, the mountains, the desert, and the Indian and Hispano cultures they discovered, they used brushes and pens to tell the nation and the world about the unique qualities of an American place which seemed so strikingly not American at all.

Notes

1. W. W. H. Davis, *El Gringo; or, New Mexico and Her People* (New York: Harper & Brothers, 1857), p. 57.

2. Porter A. Stratton, *The Territorial Press of New Mexico, 1834-1912* (Albuquerque: University of New Mexico Press, 1969), p. 2. According to Stratton: ". . . Only sixty-three newspapers were published in New Mexico [between 1847 and 1879, and] . . . many survived for only one issue and others for only a few weeks, so that in January,

1879, fifteen newspapers, seven of them relatively stable and long lived, were being published in the New Mexico territory" (ibid). Also see Pearce S. Grove, Becky J. Barnett, and Sandra J. Hansen, eds., *New Mexico Newspapers: A Comprehensive Guide to Bibliographical Entries and Locations* (Albuquerque: University of New Mexico Press, 1975).

3. Edwin W. Gaston, Jr., *The Early Novel of the Southwest* (Albuquerque: University of New Mexico Press, 1961), p. 31.

4. Ibid., pp. 223-24.

5. According to Mabel Major and T. M. Pearce, Susan Wallace joined her husband early in 1879, and: "While the governor was writing *Ben Hur*, she was recording the Southwest scene, the people, their history and legends. These articles were published in magazines, among them *The Atlantic*, and later, in 1889, collected and republished in *The Land of the Pueblos*" (*Southwest Heritage: A Literary History with Bibliographies*, 3d ed. [Albuquerque: University of New Mexico Press, 1972], p. 54).

6. Billy M. Jones, *Health Seekers in the Southwest, 1817-1900* (Norman: University of Oklahoma Press, 1967), p. 56. Such advertisements were given official help through an Act of February 15, 1880, which established a Territorial Bureau of Immigration whose object was "to prepare and disseminate accurate information as to the soil, climate, minerals, resources, productions and business of New Mexico, with special reference to its opportunities for development; and the inducements and advantages which it presents to desirable immigration and for the investment of capital; to have prompt replies sent to all inquiries relative to such subjects that may be addressed to it, and to publish and distribute such pamphlets and documents as in its judgment shall tend to promote the objects of the organization." See Herbert H. Lang, "The New Mexico Bureau of Immigration, 1880-1912," *New Mexico Historical Review* 51 (1976): 193-214.

7. For examples, see Andrew K. Gregg, *New Mexico in the Nineteenth Century: A Pictorial History* (Albuquerque: University of New Mexico Press, 1968).

8. Archeologist Jesse Nusbaum's recollections of his colleagues and the fledgling Museum, Santa Fe, Taos, and New Mexico throughout this "writer's era" have been published by his widow, Rosemary Nusbaum, as *Tierra Dulce: Reminiscences from the Jesse Nusbaum Papers* (Santa Fe, New Mexico: The Sunstone Press, 1980). Also see Russell S. Saxton, " 'The Truth about the Pueblo Indians': Bandelier's *Delight Makers*," *New Mexico Historical Review* 56 (1981): 261-84.

9. In 1859, e.g., citizens in Santa Fe organized the Historical Society of New Mexico. See James T. Stensvaag, "Clio on the Frontier: The Intellectual Evolution of the Historical Society of New Mexico, 1859-1925," *New Mexico Historical Review* 55 (1980): 294.

1916-1920

I'm in love with Santa Fe;
Like it better every day;
But I wonder, every minute,
How the folks who aren't in it,
Ever stand it, any way,
Not to be in Santa Fe.

—Mae Peregrine, "Santa Fe" (1915).

In their search for alternatives to the growing standardization of twentieth-century America, many artists and writers turned to the country's rural regions for congenial surroundings and unique and natural sources of inspiration. Journeying into the hidden recesses of America, they rediscovered New Mexico. There, behind uneven walls of adobe, they created the small, vibrant art colonies of Santa Fe and Taos—productive communities of artists, literati and involved citizens strongly influenced by the native Hispanic and Indian cultures among them.

Young and underpopulated, New Mexico was eager for the business that could be generated by tourists and new residents. After 1912, citizens of the new state capital mounted a vigorous campaign to attract visitors and future inhabitants. Proclaiming themselves residents of the oldest city in America, promoters emphasized a unique climate and a variety of cultural assets: Spanish-Pueblo architecture, the Museum and the School of American Archaeology, the art colony, and the surrounding Indian and Hispano villages.

The two publications most active in broadcasting the city's charms were the *Santa Fe New Mexican*, the capital's daily newspaper, and *El Palacio*, a weekly journal published by the New Mexico Archaeological Society.[1] Although ostensibly an archeological publication, *El Palacio* editors took great care to advertise the artistic and cultural charms of the region, and their pages occasionally carried poems of tribute to New Mexico written by local citizens. These homegrown verses foretold the fascination which the "Land of Enchantment" would hold for better writers in the years to come.[2]

In 1915, Santa Fe's campaign for tourists and residents received a neighborly boost from the Panama-California Exposition in San Diego. That year, throngs of people came through the city on their way to the West Coast, while many more learned of Santa Fe and New Mexico at the Exposition. To advise them properly of the city's many virtues, the *Santa Fe New Mexican*, in cooperation with the Women's Board of Trade and the Chamber of Commerce, published a souvenir

9

edition praising the wonders of Santa Fe in poetry, prose and photographs. The cover sported a light ode to the city written by Mae Peregrine. Inside, articles by citizens such as W. N. Townsend extolled the grandeur of New Mexico's scenery and proclaimed Santa Fe the Granada of America, the "City of a Thousand Wonders." Writing of more quotidian concerns, Mrs. N. B. Laughlin, State chairman of the Civic Department of the Federation of Women's Clubs, described Santa Fe's positive attributes as a place of residence which combined "climate and health, a good place to earn a living and recreation." Mentioning the "virgin soil" the city offered for good investments, Laughlin observed that "gas is badly needed to cook with, a winter garden would pay as all vegetables are shipped in during the winter months."[3]

Less than a year after this diversified publicity blitz, the first of New Mexico's literary colonists began to arrive. Among these twentieth-century immigrants was Alice Corbin, a Chicago poet who moved to New Mexico in the spring of 1916, accompanied by her artist husband, William Penhallow Henderson, and her young daughter, Alice.[4] As associate editor of *Poetry: A Magazine of Modern Verse* since 1912, Corbin had spent the preceding years writing editorials, soliciting and editing poems, and giving advice to poets such as Carl Sandburg, Ezra Pound, Vachel Lindsay and Witter Bynner. Stricken with tuberculosis, she had come to New Mexico more in search of health than culture, and, upon arrival in the capital city, both she and her family went to stay at Sunmount Sanitorium, a rest hospital for the cure of "chronic pulmonary complaints."

Established as Tent City in 1902, Sunmount had become a respected sanitarium under the direction of Dr. Frank E. Mera, who promoted it as a "health resort" rather than a hospital. Dr. Mera organized many social events for his patients in addition to providing good physical care. Writing of Sunmount in later years, Wayne Mauzy recalled how "Thespian groups produced small plays for festive occasions; the poetic minded gathered for tea in cottages and enjoyed and criticized each other's verses. A local artist of some renown held local classes on the grounds."[5] Alice Corbin was a patient at Sunmount on several occasions, and her sojourns there greatly influenced this lively atmosphere. She invited poets Carl Sandburg, Vachel Lindsay and Witter Bynner, among others, to give readings, and herself obliged appreciative audiences.

Two other literary figures also came to New Mexico in 1916—Willa Cather and Mabel Dodge Sterne (later Luhan). Cather had first visited New Mexico in the summer of 1915, when she and friend Edith Lewis made an extended tour of the Southwest and spent a month riding horses around Taos and the surrounding Hispano mountain villages.

The two returned in 1916 for a longer visit, during which they travelled to Santa Fe, Española and Santa Cruz. On this trip, Lewis recalls, Cather was "intensely alive to the country . . . continually receiving strong impressions from the things she saw and experienced."[6]

A controversial figure among her contemporaries, Mabel Dodge Luhan was responsible for the journeys that hundreds of famous people made to New Mexico during the twenties and thirties. When she first arrived from New York in the winter of 1916, Dodge had already achieved notoriety as the hostess of weekly Greenwich Village salons for radical artists, writers and politicians. A wealthy woman bored by her life of leisure, she was in a state of acute ennui and depression when her third husband, artist Maurice Sterne, wrote to her from Santa Fe suggesting that she develop an interest in Indians:

Dearest Girl.
Do you want an object in life? Save the Indians—their art, culture—reveal it to the world.[7]

Dodge found Santa Fe's cultural society "quite tiresome" and fled north to Taos after a day or two.

There, on the "edge of Taos desert," she joined a well-established community of artists, many of whom gravitated toward the Ledoux Street home of artist E. Burrit Harwood and his wife, Elizabeth Case.[8] Nevertheless, Dodge later recalled how she felt removed from the pretense and artificialities which had always seemed inevitable in society. "For the first time in my life I heard the world singing in the same key in which my life inside me had sometimes lifted and poured itself out."[9] Settling into an old adobe hacienda, she began to publicize the "spiritual qualities" of New Mexico and its Indian cultures to artists and writers all over the world.

Santa Fe could not boast a single champion so vigorous and vocal. Alice Corbin's efforts were quieter. Nevertheless, during the war years of 1916 and 1917, the city's popularity burgeoned. Articles praising its unique beauty and its proximity to ancient Indian civilizations appeared in *Scribner's*, *House Beautiful*, and *Sunset* magazines.[10] As its fame spread nationally, Santa Fe became more and more concerned with its age and appearance. Commenting on her city's increasing vanity, local chronicler Ruth Laughlin Barker pointed out that even "hard headed businessmen" had realized that Santa Fe's greatest attraction lay in its atmosphere of remote antiquity: "Accordingly, the ancient city . . . pulled a rusty black shawl over her head and posed for the world to come and see her as the oldest capital in the United States, the royal headquarters for the kingdom of Spain for one hundred and fifty years before the Mexican war."[11]

Alice Corbin eagerly espoused this studied return to antiquity. Leaving Sunmount in the spring of 1917, she moved into a small adobe house on Telephone Road with William Henderson and young Alice. Christened after the newly-acquired telephone poles that marched up it to Sunmount, Telephone Road was originally called Camino del Monte Sol, a name Corbin immediately and successfully petitioned the city fathers to reinstate.

Fascinated by New Mexico, Corbin had begun to write about the country and the people around her while still at Sunmount. In February of 1917, she joined poets Harriet Monroe, Carl Sandburg and others to present a special issue of *Poetry* which highlighted Native American chants as a source of inspiration for modern American poets.[12] This number also included a set of poems expressing Corbin's feelings about her new home. In "Four O'clock in the Afternoon," she compares the vitality of "desert" life in New Mexico with the sophisticated sameness of eastern cities:

> A stream of money is flowing down Fifth Avenue
> They speak of the fascination of New York
> Climbing aboard motor buses to look down on the endless
> play.
> From the Bay to the Bronx
> But it is forever the same:
> There is no *life* there.
>
> Watching a cloud on the desert,
> Endlessly watching small insects crawl in and out of the
> shadow of a cactus,
>
> A herd boy on the horizon driving goats,
> Uninterrupted sky and blown sand:
> Space—volume—silence—
> Nothing but life on the desert,
> Intense life.[13]

This contrast would become a *cause célèbre* for New Mexican poets and writers in the years to come.

New Mexico's rise to national literary fame was boastfully reported in *El Palacio*, which continued its dual archeological and arts focus by publishing news, poetry, book reviews and stories by and about the local artists and literati. Its back pages recorded the triumphs, comings and goings of the fledgling art colony in the chatty tones of a society reporter. Here the names of visiting and resident poets, authors and journalists were mentioned: Natalie Curtis, Ina Sizer Cassidy, Herbert Knibbs, Alice Corbin Henderson, Rose Henderson, John Curtis Underwood, and Ruth Laughlin Barker.[14] The editors also made frequent references to *Poetry*, remarking in one issue: "One cannot help being thrilled that more and more the men and the women of high ideals who love Santa Fe, who live here or have been here, have part in the making of American literature and art."[15]

On November 2, 1918, a modest notice in the back of El Palacio announced that "Mrs. Mary Hunter Austin, the noted playwright and author, has arrived in Santa Fe to investigate land laws and customs among Pueblo and Southwestern Indians and early Spanish and Mexican settlers."[16] The size and position of this item in no way prepared El Palacio readers for the plethora of articles, poems and announcements by or about Mary Austin which would be published in the months to follow. In addition to keeping a running tally of the frequent lectures she gave on literature and drama, El Palacio editors provided several biographies of the author and her work.[17]

Austin delivered a talk to the Santa Fe Women's Club on November 26, 1918, and offered to assist Santa Feans in establishing a "permanent community theater" similar to the one she had initiated in Carmel.[18] Her offer was accepted with alacrity, and she immediately set to work organizing local artists, writers and would-be thespians. During the next two and a half months the newly formed Community Theater put together a four-part production of plays and songs in Spanish and English with sets designed by Gustave Baumann, Kenneth M. Chapman, Carlos Vierra, Sheldon Parsons, and Warren Rollins. Nina Otero-Warren, a Santa Fean who in later years became a writer, also took an active part in this production.

Performed on February 14, 1919, the four-part production was grandly announced in the "olde Englishe" program as "Ye First Appearance of Ye Communitye Theatre of Ye Anciente La Villa de Real de Santa Fe de San Francisco de Assisi." In a curious blend of old world and new, the program notes claimed that the "aim of the first performance has been to get back to the very beginning of the drama," by adapting production customs popular in Shakespeare's time "to the primitive Indian conditions that exist in the adjacent pueblos."[19] They also lauded the Theater's founder and its home:

When . . . a community can command such talent as that of Mary Austin, the founder of the Community Theater, a writer of successful plays, a deep student of folk lore and human nature, and of a colony of noted artists, writers and musicians, then it is indeed fortunate. Santa Fe, by these tokens, possesses free of cost what neighboring communities would pay out fortunes to possess. If it makes wide use of such great opportunities, it is indeed on the road to fame and fortune.

The inaugural bill's highlight was a one-act skit entitled "Tranquilina, An Archaeological Absurdity in One Fragment, Discovered, Excavated and Decoded by Waldo C. Twitchell." Twitchell, a local playwright, not only wrote but also directed and played the lead role in this spoof of the Santa Fe archaeological community. Though written by the son of a Museum board member, the play was frowned upon by Museum authorities, who did not take kindly to the satirizing of their life's work. Despite this controversy, the Community Theater of Santa Fe received glowing reviews in *El Palacio* and the *Santa Fe New Mexican*.[20]

Three months later, the Santa Fe Players put on a second production. Directed once again by Austin, this performance featured a play by New Mexican Fayette Curtis. The drama must have met Museum approval because the entire script was printed in the néxt issue of *El Palacio*, together with photographs and a most congratulatory review.[21] Although Austin left town a few weeks later, the Community Theater continued to thrive.

The year that followed Austin's whirlwind visit culminated in several literary events. Prompted by Alice Corbin, nationally known poets Carl Sandburg, Vachel Lindsay and Harriet Monroe visited Santa Fe in 1920, adding some big-time glamour to the local writing scene. Noting that H. L. Mencken had designated Chicago as the literary capitol of the United States, *El Palacio* crowed: "For the nonce, that literary capitol has been transferred to Santa Fe—at least in part."[22]

In the spring of that year, Alice Corbin collected her own poems into a slim volume entitled *Red Earth: Poems of New Mexico*. Composed of verses written between 1912 and 1920, *Red Earth* is a detailed and delicate study of New Mexico. The first poems describe the state as seen by the newcomers—the conquistador and the cowboy. The second set records Corbin's memories of urban life and her love for the desert. These desert poems are followed by the Indian verses printed earlier in *Poetry* and a group of poems with Indian motifs.[23] After a few personal poems, Corbin ends her collection with translations of Hispano folk songs and several poems about Spanish-Americans. In many ways *Red Earth* summarizes the sources of literary inspiration which Corbin and other early poets and authors found in New Mexico and the Southwest:

> The noise of passing feet
> On the prairie—
> Is it men or gods
> Who came out of the silence?
>
> —Alice Corbin, "Listening."[24]

Notes

1. The Santa Fe Railroad was also a vigorous advertiser for the city. F. G. Gurley, president of the Santa Fe, later remarked: "The commerce of New Mexico's capital influenced the organization of our railroad and from the capital we derived our name" ("New Mexico and the Santa Fe Railroad," an address before the Newcomen Society meeting at Albuquerque, 1950, The Newcomen Society). Also see James Marshall, *Santa Fe: The Railroad That Built an Empire* (New York: Random House, 1945).

2. See, e.g., Abbie Frank Smith, "The Desert Twilight," *El Palacio*, January 1914, p. 4. Smith is identified as a resident of Saint Francis' Farm, Myndus, New Mexico.

3. Mrs. N. B. Laughlin, "The Charming Residential City of the Southwest," *Santa Fe New Mexican*, Souvenir Edition, 1915, p. 9.

4. William Penhallow Henderson had first visited New Mexico as an adult on a sketching trip in 1904. Thus, in addition to her interest in the state's curative climate, Corbin also knew of its artistic attractions (Edna Robertson and Sarah Nestor, *Artists of the Canyons and Caminos: Santa Fe, The Early Years* [n.p.: Peregrine Smith, 1976], pp. 39-40).

5. Wayne Mauzy, "Sunmount Vital Force in City Life," *Santa Fe New Mexican*, "Centennial Fiesta Edition," 1949, section 7, p. 2.

6. Edith Lewis, *Willa Cather Living: A Personal Record* (New York: Alfred A. Knopf, 1953), p. 81.

7. Mabel Dodge Luhan, *Movers and Shakers*, Intimate Memories, Vol. III (New York: Harcourt, Brace, 1936), p. 296.

8. The Harwood's arrived in Taos from Europe in 1915. In 1923, their house was transferred to a foundation and has served as a community cultural center ever since (Anne Hillerman, "The Harwood Foundation at Taos," *Santa Fe New Mexican*, 20 November 1977, p. 16). Also see Helen Greene Blumenschein, *Recuerdos: Early Days of the Blumenschein Family* (Silver City, New Mexico: Tecolote Press, 1979).

9. Mabel Dodge Luhan, *Edge of Taos Desert: Escape to Reality*, Intimate Memories, Vol. IV (New York: Harcourt, Brace, 1937), p. 32. An analysis of Luhan's behavior and her motivations for moving to New Mexico appears in Christopher Lasch, *The New Radicalism in America, 1889-1963: The Intellectual as a Social Type* (London: Chatto & Windus, 1966). Also see William Garland Rogers, *Ladies Bountiful* (New York: Harcourt Brace, 1968); and Emily Hahn, *Mabel: A Biography of Mabel Dodge Luhan* (Boston: Houghton Mifflin, 1977).

10. These references are: Ernest Peixotto, "The City of the Holy Faith," *Scribner's* 69 (September 1916):321; Ruth Laughlin Barker, "Old Spanish Doorways," *House Beautiful* 42 (April 1917):166; Ruth Laughlin Barker, "Keeping the Oldest Capitol Old," *Sunset* 37 (September 1916):34-35.

11. Barker, *Sunset*, p. 34.

12. Corbin's verses on the desert and her poems based on Native American chants were also included in Harriet Monroe and Alice Corbin Henderson, eds., *The New Poetry: An Anthology of Twentieth Century Verse in English* (New York: Macmillan, 1917).

13. Alice Corbin, *Red Earth: Poems of New Mexico* (Chicago: Ralph Fletcher Seymour, 1920), p. 20.

14. For example: "Art and Literary Colony," *El Palacio* 4, 3 (July 1917):87.

15. "December Poetry," *El Palacio* 5, 22 (28 December 1918):363.

16. *El Palacio* 5, 15 (2 November 1918):254.

17. "Mary Austin in Santa Fe," *El Palacio* 5, 16 (9 November 1918):262-63; "Mary Austin's Work (from the *New York Sun*)," *El Palacio* 5, 17 (16 November 1918):284. These biographies and autobiographies were collected from a number of sources, including a letter from Austin to Houghton Mifflin Company and an interview with the author.

18. *El Palacio* 5, 20 (9 December 1918):335.

19. Foreword, Community Theater of Santa Fe Program, 14 February 1919. Also see: "Drama and Pageantry: Santa Fe's Community Theater," *El Palacio* 6, 5 (22 February 1919):86; Phoebe Dechart, "Community Theater: Santa Fe's Oldest Surviving Drama Group," *Santa Fe New Mexican*, 19 March 1978, pp. 12-14.

20. Dechart, ibid.

21. A review of this second performance appeared in *El Palacio* 6, 12 (24 May 1919): 190. The text of the Curtis play and photographs of the production appear in *El Palacio* 6, 13 (14 June 1919):194ff.

22. *El Palacio* 8, 7 & 8 (July 1920):181. Other contributors to *Poetry* who were by then visitors to or residents of New Mexico included John Gould Fletcher, Mary Austin, Marsden Hartley, Glenn Ward Dresbach, and Arthur Winters.

23. Although Corbin's book was subtitled "Poems of New Mexico," the Indian verses she included were based on translations of Chippewa Indian chants.

24. Corbin, *Red Earth*, p. 23.

THE TWENTIES

Taos, San [sic] Domingo, Chimayo and the other pueblos, as well as the old capital itself, have colonized artists and poets of late, as everyone knows. At last the wisdom of the ages has opened our eyes to the wonderland beyond our western gates, and made us aware not only of nature's stark and gorgeous sublimities, but of immediate and vivid creations of primitive art—one of the rarest, remotest, and most precious things on earth. "This is ancient Greece," said William Vaughn Moody fifteen years ago, after watching a katchina dance in northern Arizona; but we Americans, who would travel by the many thousand, if we had the chance, to see a Homeric rite in Attica, or a serpent ceremony in old Egypt, are only beginning to realize that the snake-dance at Walpi, or the corn-dance at Cochiti, are also revelations of primitive art, expressions of that original human impulse toward the creation of beauty which modern civilization does so much to defeat and destroy.

* * *

But what has all this to do with modern poetry? Ah, much, and more, and still more! I was almost oppressed with the wealth of our inheritance—or our "tradition," if you will. Why go to Greece or China, O ye of little faith? This South-west, which is but one chapter of our rich tradition, is our own authentic wonderland—a treasure-trove of romantic myth—profoundly significant and beautiful, guarded by ancient races practicing their ancient rites, in a region of incredible color and startling natural grandeur.

—Harriet Monroe, "In Texas and New
Mexico," *Poetry*, September 1920,
pp. 326-27, 328.

The twenties saw artists and writers in Santa Fe and Taos established creatively and civically, both locally and nationally. The Taos Society of Artists was already well known, while in Santa Fe the School of American Archaeology, the Museum of New Mexico and the new Fine Arts Museum provided a focus for immigrant and transient artists. Mabel Dodge Luhan in Taos and Alice Corbin Henderson in Santa Fe continued to attract visiting literati, many of whom stayed to experience and benefit from the heady, haphazard ferment of the growing art colonies.

By the early 1920s health-seekers no longer dominated the increasing influx of visitors to New Mexico. Resorts like Bishop's Lodge near

Santa Fe proclaimed: "The Lodge positively does not entertain tubercular guests."[1] Nevertheless sanitariums continued to flourish and some, like Santa Fe's Sunmount, accepted both ailing and healthy guests.

Poet Witter Bynner arrived at Sunmount on February 20, 1922, to visit Alice Corbin Henderson, then a patient. "Though it troubled me at first to stay in a building which was half hotel, half sanitorium for tuberculars, I was soon persuaded that I was safer at Sunmount than in a New York trolley car and I remained beyond the six weeks needed for recovery from influenza."[2] In a seventy-fifth birthday tribute to Bynner, on August 10, 1956, Ruth Laughlin Alexander recalled this visit, which lasted until the poet's death on June 1, 1968:

The first memory is of the night you read your Chinese poems at Sunmount in February, 1922, when Dr. and Mrs. F. E. Mera invited Santa Feans to meet you. We were impressed with the beauty of your poems, your resonant voice and dramatic presentation, your wit, keen mind and dignity. You had stopped over the week-end. . . . At that time everyone quoted the lines, "If Witter comes, can spring be far behind?" Witter came and the spring has been long and fruitful.[3]

Bynner soon rented an adobe from artist Paul Burlin, later purchased it, and resided at the 342 Buena Vista Street address for the rest of his life.[4] In his 1923 travelogue, In Quest of El Dorado, Stephen Graham called this residence "a hermit's hut in the desert." Bynner's secretary-companion, Spud (Walter Willard) Johnson immediately protested that "if a house located on one of the principal paved boulevards of a capital city, within five blocks of the state house, with telephone, electric lights, hot and cold water (sometimes), taxi service to the door, five delivery boys, six Indians and seven casual visitors a day, to say nothing of an automobile and a cesspool in the back yard—I repeat that if that is a hermit's hut in the desert, then Stephen Graham is a rosy apple hanging by his twig to a pecan tree."[5]

Among Witter Bynner's first houseguests were D. H. and Frieda Lawrence, who arrived with Mabel Dodge Sterne and Tony Luhan during the Lawrences' first trip to New Mexico in September 1922.[6] The English author's visits were to prove the crowning glory in Mabel's relentless campaign to establish Taos as a world-famous art colony. Although he was only in New Mexico some eighteen months all told (1922-23, 1924-25), Lawrence amply repaid his daunting hostess by providing a lifetime of gossip, innuendo and anecdote—not only for Mabel but for self-made and occasional Taoseños through many years to come. Actually, Lawrence spent little time in the town itself, which he characterized as "so much artistic small beer."[7]

New Mexico played a comparatively small part in Lawrence's writings, although his essay "New Mexico," first published in the 1929 *Survey Graphic*, powerfully expresses the impact of the land and the Indians on the Englishman. Lawrence's grandiose perceptions and much-ballyhooed experiences, particularly with respect to Native Americans, make a remarkable contrast to those reported by another, much-less-heralded Taos visitor of the same time—Swiss psychologist Carl Gustav Jung, who visited the town and the Pueblo in January 1925.[8] Both men were deeply—and divergently—affected by their Taos encounters.

During the early 1920s, active efforts to secure Indian rights intensified. In 1922, the so-called Bursum bill shocked and galvanized many residents and sympathetic visitors. This Congressional legislation would have given Hispanos and Anglos clear title to Pueblo Indian lands. The New Mexico Association on Indian Affairs, later the Southwestern Association on Indian Affairs (SWAIA), was quickly formed. An elected committee of artists and writers drew up "The Artists and Writers Protest," carried nationally by the Associated Press. Among its signers were D. H. Lawrence, Carl Sandburg, Edgar Lee Masters, Zane Grey, William Allen White, Maxfield Parrish and Vachel Lindsay.[9] Erna Fergusson claimed that "never did a more articulate, vociferous, propaganda-minded lobby descend upon the Congress of these United States for any cause":

. . . Alice Corbin Henderson and Elsie [Elizabeth Shepley] Sergeant appeared simultaneously in the *Nation* and the *New Republic*. *Theatre Arts* and the *Christian Science Monitor* carried spreads. Witter Bynner wrote for the *Outlook*. Harvey Fergusson, then a newspaperman in Washington, wrote for a capital paper. Mary Austen [sic] lent her prestige as the final authority on Indians. Harriet Welles put her short stories aside and produced propaganda. Eugene Manlove Rhodes, shaken out of his sunny dreams of the past, wrote a piece for the Santa Fe *New Mexican*. And that village sheet, what with fiery editorials from Dana Johnson every day, went on sale at Forty-second street and Broadway, and has been ever since.[10]

The bill was defeated and an effective organization formed. Novelist Oliver La Farge later claimed: "I take the year 1923 as the nadir of the Indians," recalling how what "seemed at first a small thing with a large name, the New Mexico Association on Indian Affairs, a local group to fight a local Bill . . . [proved] competent and . . . found support throughout the country."[11]

After the Bursum bill's defeat, the New Mexico group was set to disband when chairperson Margaret McKittrick heard about the plight of San Ildefonso and Tesuque Pueblos, where drought had left residents without food for winter. Successful efforts to raise money to help these Indians solidified the organization, which continues today. A popular means of fund-raising then was to produce plays. One such drama, written by Alice Corbin's artist husband William Penhallow Henderson and *New Mexican* editor E. Dana Johnson, "featured Henderson in the part of a character called the 'Desert Whip-poor-will'—and thus he acquired the nickname 'Whippy'."[12]

Many Association members were also concerned with the preservation of Southwestern Indian material culture. Mary Austin was prominent among the "small group of artists, writers and other in Santa Fe, who, concerned over the fast disappearing arts of the neighboring Pueblo Indians, had banded together to save what could still be had of their material culture for a permanent collection to be housed in Santa Fe, for the benefit of the Indians themselves, and for the enjoyment of all interested in the arts." This organization was first known as the Pueblo Pottery Fund but soon expanded to other Southwestern tribes and incorporated as the Indian Arts Fund in 1925. Austin was instrumental in the group's development, "particularly in 1928 when the permanent cooperative agreement was perfected between the Indian Arts Fund and the newly incorporated Laboratory of Anthropology, an institution which was planned to extend the field of southwestern research beyond that covered by the Fund."[13]

In 1926, Mary Austin joined fellow literati, artists and other townspeople to oppose the Chamber of Commerce, which had convinced the Texas Federation of Women's Clubs to establish a summer cultural center in Santa Fe. The Chamber anticipated business from some three thousand women and their families (almost half the usual population of Santa Fe) from nine Southwestern states. Although not strictly a Chautauqua adult education program, the proposal had been so labeled in Texas and was so attacked in New Mexico. As Austin declared: "That institution known as the Chautauqua Circle is a pure American product, the outstanding characterization of our naïve belief and our superb faith that culture can, like other appurtenances of democracy, proceed by majorities."[14]

Many Santa Feans were concerned about the proposed cultural center's physical effects on the town, and they established the Old Santa Fe Association in April of 1926. On May 23, the *New Mexican* reported that "the line of demarcation between those striving to keep Santa Fe 'different' and those indifferent to what form the growth takes, is being more sharply drawn, but there is little doubt the far-sighted policy will prevail and sentiment will be adequately organized to prevent losing Old Santa Fe in the rush of progress." The paper had earlier (May 19) admitted that the summer visitors might not be necessary to growth because "the countless writers who have been here and the scores who are here are pouring out a stream of what becomes publicity for Santa Fe—whatever form it takes, letters, magazine and newspaper articles, books—and the artists cause a lot of talk about Santa Fe." In July, Austin could proclaim the successful campaign "against the banners of Main Street" thus:

There are, said Santa Fe, two types of cultural centre, the creative and the Chautauqua, and the two are incompatible in the same community. Having one, we prefer not to have the other. . . .
. . . Whatever discovery Santa Fe had made for itself, it proved, like so many discoveries, to be the unvoiced conviction of innumerable other small cities and large. There are two types of community culture, one in which the community works by individuals to produce definite achievement on a cultural plane, and the other in which the community exists chiefly to hear about what has been produced. And even towns which, if put to the test, might vote for the more popular and populous type, are agreed that it would be a relief to know that there is one town, preferably Santa Fe, made safe against it.[15]

Although a frequent visitor to New Mexico, Mary Austin did not settle in Santa Fe until late 1924. The town's art colony by then resembled the one at Carmel-by-the-Sea, California, where Austin had lived between 1904 and 1911. As in Carmel, she planned and supervised construction of her own house with advice from her neighbor, painter and sculptor Frank Applegate. The spacious adobe at 439 Camino del Monte Sol was completed in 1925 and became known as *Casa Querida* or "Beloved House." There, Austin lived with her niece Mary Hunter and held court for various resident and visiting literati, artists and other notables, many of them acquaintances or "referrals" from her Carmel and New York City days. Often, these visitors were on their way to or from Taos and a visit with Mabel, who had finally married Antonio Luhan of Taos Pueblo in April 1923. Austin herself "went there often, for while there is practically no likeness between Mabel and me, very little consenting approval, there is the groundwork of an intelligent approach to problems of reality, and a genuine affection."[16] In a 1944 memorial, Mabel expressed her own pleasure at these visits, recalling how "Mary loved to put on a big apron and go into our big old kitchen and toss a couple of pumpkin pies together" and how "she loved to hob-nob, to sit and spin out reasons for strange happenings, to hear and tell about all the daily occurrences in both our lives."[17]
The William Penhallow Henderson's were among Austin's neighbors

on the Camino. They too maintained ties with Taos, especially after their daughter Alice Oliver married Mabel's son John Evans in 1922. Thus, during the twenties, visiting or sojourning writers like Vachel Lindsay, Bliss Carman, John Gould Fletcher, Arthur Davison Ficke, John Galsworthy, Sinclair Lewis, Alfred Kreymborg, Carl Sandburg, Willa Cather and numerous others could conveniently visit any or all of these local literary *dueñas*.

Still other neighbors along the Camino called themselves Los Cinco Pintores, "The Five Painters." Artists Fremont Ellis, Willard Nash, Jozef Bakos, Will Shuster and Walter Mruk had exhibited together almost annually since their first show at Santa Fe's new Art Museum in December 1921. By 1925, poets Alice Corbin, Witter Bynner, Haniel Long, Spud Johnson and Lynn Riggs had formed their own group which met weekly, first at the Hendersons' studio and eventually at a nearby house he had built for the family residence. According to Johnson, the group acquired its name because "we seemed to lapse so often into a Rabelasian mood, that soon we were referring to ourselves as the Rabelais Club, which was quickly altered, since that sounded much too stodgy, to the simple informality of 'The Rabble'."[18] In 1938, Haniel Long fondly recalled their meetings and a related adventure:

I doubt whether any masterpieces resulted from our poetry discussions on the Camino; but we were certainly not too ceremonious or polite, and we certainly did not bar out ideas. Bynner and I went out one very cold November night and placarded the town with LaFollette propaganda. We had no brush for the paste, and so spread it on poles and walls with our bare hands. It was painful, and it was unavailing. . . . Bynner wrote his poem, "A Considered Farewell to Politics," as a result of this pasting experience. In that poem he refers to me as one who had been doing his small fishing at a hidden turn in the river, but now withheld from the current no longer. Which was quite true—it was a liberating fortnight for the lonely fisherman. I mention the incident to show that we shared more than the artistic life, could even wax enthusiastic.[19]

Witter Bynner had been instrumental in bringing both Lynn Riggs and Spud Johnson, the youngest Rabble members, to Santa Fe. Riggs was a college senior at the University of Oklahoma, suffering from a nervous breakdown and pulmonary tuberculosis, when he met Bynner during the latter's 1922 lecture tour. Riggs shortly followed Bynner to New Mexico to convalesce, working briefly as the latter's secretary and then at various jobs. He wrote a number of Santa Fe poems but soon made friends with Ida Rauh Eastman, a former member of the original Provincetown Players. Fired by Eastman's enthusiasm, Riggs wrote almost a dozen plays in five years. His first published drama, *Knives from Syria* (1927), was successfully presented by the Santa Fe Players in 1925, the year he wrote his first full-length play, *The Primitives*. Unhappy with this satire on life in Santa Fe, Riggs destroyed its script.[20] Interestingly, in the following year Witter Bynner himself wrote a satirical play, *Cake*, an unflattering portrait of *Taoseña* Mabel Dodge Luhan. According to Bynner's biographer James Kraft: "Mabel's possessive nature never forgave Bynner for going with Lawrence [and Spud in 1923] and for the affection Frieda felt for him, and she sought revenge by taking Spud [in 1927 to be her secretary in Taos] and by accusing Bynner, later in life, of having brought homosexuality to New Mexico—an accusation so marvelous in its imaginative vindictiveness as to be almost forgivable."[21]

While still Bynner's secretary-companion in Santa Fe, Spud Johnson printed and published a small literary magazine, *Laughing Horse*, which he moved to Taos in 1927.[22] Johnson had started this journal with James Van Rensselaer and Roy Chanslor in 1922, as "a horse-laugh at the university," Berkeley, where all three were students and once attended a poetry class taught by Bynner. The fourth issue of the fledgling publication gained notoriety after its suppression "for publishing an 'obscene' letter from D. H. Lawrence (with certain words deleted)."[23] The three former students drifted apart as the magazine's debts mounted. Issue Number 8 appeared in 1923 with the note: "It has been pastured at Chapala, Jalisco, Mexico, under the care of Willard Johnson, saddled and bridled at Guadalajara, Mexico, by Gallardo y Alvarez del Castillo, and will be stabled in Santa Fe, New Mexico, U.S.A., untill further notice." Johnson had been travelling with Bynner and the Lawrences in Mexico when:

. . . I "inherited" the magazine and converted it into a journal of, by and for New Mexicans. Unearthing a Navajo legend about the sungod riding a turquoise horse with "a joyous neigh," it seemed a natural transition to keep the title (which had proved wonderfully rememberable) and to change its nature to suit the new environment.[24]

Johnson's efforts earned him a small, devoted following, but it was fellow Rabble member Alice Corbin who secured a place for New Mexico poets on the national literary scene. She edited *The Turquoise Trail: An Anthology of New Mexico Poetry*, published by Houghton Mifflin at The Riverside Press Cambridge in 1928. Of the thirty-seven contributors, only three (S. Omar Barker, Margaret Pond Church, and Eda Lou Walton) were born in the state. Thirteen (Mary Austin,

Witter Bynner, Alice Corbin, Paul Horgan, Willard Johnson, D. H. Lawrence, Haniel Long, Mabel Dodge Luhan, Eugene Manlove Rhodes, Lynn Riggs, Lucy Sturges, N. Howard Thorp, and John Curtis Underwood) had resided in New Mexico for an extended period, while another nine (Willa Cather, Arthur Davison Ficke, John Gould Fletcher, Marsden Hartley, Henry Herbert Knibbs, Maurice Lesemann, H. J. Spinden, Glenway Wescott and Yvor Winters) stayed for lesser periods. Badger Clark, John Galsworthy, Alfred Kreymborg, Janet Lewis, Vachel Lindsay, Harriet Monroe, James Rorty, Carl Sandburg, William Haskell Simpson, Stanley Vestal, and Edith Wyatt paid briefer visits; Edgar Lee Masters was an acquaintance from Henderson's Chicago days. The volume was announced in the 1928 program for the Santa Fe Fiesta thus:

THE TURQUOISE TRAIL
Edited by
Alice Corbin Henderson
+
A collection of Contemporary Verse
by more than thirty poets who live
or have spent some time in New Mexico and the Southwest—the old Spanish province of *"Nuevo Mexico"*.
+
Houghton-Mifflin Company

Just off the Press
On Sale at Santa Fe Book Stores
$2.25

Santa Fe's first bookstore, started by Roberta Robey in the early 1920s, occupied a corner of Healy's Stationery Store, then located on a corner of the Plaza across San Francisco Street from La Fonda Hotel. According to Spud Johsnon's recollections: "Besides a small rental library, those initial shelves offered the very first opportunity for local folks to buy books—except for a limited few volumes on southwestern subjects that were occasionally found among blankets and Indian silver at one or two of the Plaza curio stores." In 1927, Robey moved to the Sena Plaza, then newly remodelled, and opened Villagra Bookshop, while "the Healys moved to the corner of Don Gaspar and San Francisco and changed their name to The Santa Fe Book and Stationery Company, having been taught by Miss Robey that books, amazingly enough, were actually merchandise that at least a few people were willing to buy."[25] Both stores prospered, but by 1933 Alice Corbin Henderson dubbed Roberta Robey the "Bookseller to Santa Fé":

The fundamental secret of Miss Robey's success is, in fact, the very personal interest that she takes in her work, and in the predelections of her clientele. Over and above this, her unfailing hospitality makes of the Villagra Bookshop an inevitable Half-way House for all down-town shopping. One is practically sure, too, of meeting some of one's friends there, and sharing the latest book gossip. The Villagra Bookshop is, in fact, one of the landmarks of old, and new Santa Fé.[26]

After Robey sold the shop to Clifford McCarthy in 1936, Spud Johnson managed it for a short time.[27]

Johnson later recollected that among those who had occupied the Bookshop's "armchair near the corner fireplace (which Roberta claimed sold more books than she did!)" was Willa Cather. Cather's *Death Comes for the Archbishop*, then and perhaps still one of the best and most widely known Southwestern novels, had appeared in 1927, much to the dismay of Mary Austin, who claimed that Cather had used her *Casa Querida* to write the novel, in which: "She had given her allegiance to the French blood of the Archbishop; she had sympathized with his desire to build a French cathedral in a Spanish town. It was a calamity to the local culture. We have never got over it."[28] Despite Austin's repeated claims and Cather's own inscription in the former's copy of *Death Comes for the Archbishop* ("For Mary Austin, in whose lovely study I wrote the last chapters of this book. She will be my sternest critic—and she has the right to be. I will always take a calling-down from my betters"), Elizabeth Shepley Sergeant describes Willa Cather as "exasperated" when told of Austin's assertions, which soon became local legend.[29]

When Edith Lewis, Cather's longtime companion, later wrote a "personal record" of her friend, she recounted their visits to New Mexico in the summers of 1925 and 1926, remarking only that upon their return in the fall of 1925, "Willa Cather went straight to Jaffrey; and it was there that she wrote—at a sitting, as it seems to me now—the magnificent introduction to *Death Comes for the Archbishop*." Mary Austin is not mentioned at all in these reminiscences, while Mabel Luhan, whom they visited both summers, is very favorably characterized as: "Essentially an artist herself—[who] knew the conditions that contribute to an artist's work, and was able to create them . . . [and who] had, too, a large, ungrudging generosity toward people she admired; one felt that she enjoyed helping them toward their aim and seeing them realize their desires."[30] Ironically, however, Cather receives almost no notice in Luhan's writings, while she seems to have loomed as an unwitting rival in Austin's scheme of literary affairs.

During one of Cather and Lewis's summer visits, the young writer Paul Horgan, who some fifty years later would complete a Pulitzer Prize-winning biography of Archbishop Lamy, chanced to encounter the two women at work in La Fonda. While not specifically mentioning that particular encounter, Horgan later recalled how "intoxicating" it was for him as an "artistic aspirant" to "encounter writers and painters in the flesh" in Santa Fe. He maintains that "I then uncritically accepted the idea of a 'colony' of artists and writers at Santa Fe and Taos, but it was not long until some of the individuals who were locally called 'sensitives' began to seem somewhat grotesque, self-advertising, and responsive to opportunities for envy and competition."[31]

The annual Santa Fe Fiesta was one place where such "self-advertisements" were both condoned and cultivated. The first fiesta, which commemorated Don Diego de Vargas's 1692-93 reconquest of Santa Fe after the Pueblo Revolt of 1680, was established as an "annual" event in 1712. Scarcely observed with such regularity, Fiesta was revived in 1919 by a group which included School of American Research Director Dr. Edgar L. Hewett. However, it "did not get its feet firmly on the ground until 1926-27, when Edgar L. Hewett . . . produced a collection of papers for fiesta use . . . [which] laid the groundwork for Santa Fe pageants and were intended to root the drama in the history and culture of Indians, Hispanos and Anglos from prehistoric times to the time of the annexation by the United States." This was in part the direction suggested in 1925 by Thomas Wood Stevens's pageant, a "two-and-a-half-hour presentation [which] covered the period from conquest to settlement and concluded with a masque in which the Spirit of the Land called upon the spirits of gold, air, water, and fire to destroy the invading explorers and missionaries."[32]

The Fiesta's increasingly tricultural emphasis was given a boost in the mid-twenties when "artists of the Modern School, with poets and writers, decided about 1926 that the historical parade was not typically Santa Fe, since it might be staged anywhere, so they instituted their own fiesta and named it El Pasatiempo [which] immediately . . . proved a 'howling success,' producing rhythms of laughter as it proceeded among the crowded lines of spectators."[33] El Pasatiempo parade was for years led by Witter Bynner and Dolly Sloan, wife of noted Santa Fe artist John Sloan. A staunch Fiesta supporter from the beginning of his Santa Fe residency, Bynner paid tribute to the "Artists and Fiesta" in the Official Program of the August 30-September 1, 1928 celebration:

Whether it be in the distinguished and harmonious decorations of the Plaza, in the ingenious, sometimes ludicrous and sometimes beautiful, features of the Hysterical Pageant, in the variegated and striking costumes worn on all occasions, or in the free and easy high spirits, the art colony has shown its ability and its appreciation of the spirit of the place. Their willingness to give thought and time and labor for the public gaiety is perhaps their best opportunity to make a concerted gesture expressing their sense of the privilege they enjoy through living in this most delectable of all American towns.

Celebrations in Taos were less highly organized and more often tied to observances at Taos Pueblo. However, artist and writer Blanche C. Grant devotes several pages in her 1925 description of *Taos Today* to activities on the downtown plaza:

If it is the fourth of July, a horse race may be on the program. Out on the desert flats to the east the crowd will go. That over, they will gather in the plaza again where a foot race may be planned for Indian and American contestants. Nearby, Spanish-Americans, Indians, cowboys in wide felt hats and leather chaps and Anglo-Saxon tourists, in the latest style or no style at all, will shade their eyes to see who wins. Then may follow an Indian dance on the dusty street or in the grassy plot within the fence. At such times, all sorts of vehicles line up in front of the stores from the high powered car to the cart behind the burro. People come and go, happy to be in town. The place is quite alive. No wonder that on such a day a little girl who had probably never been out of the valley in her life, was heard to say "It's just like a *real* city, isn't it?"[34]

New Mexico's burgeoning tourist industry was alert to capitalize on all such celebrations, as well as the artists, writers and assorted citizenry who participated in them. The first issue of *New Mexico Highway Journal* (July 1923) included the following among its dry notices about contracts and roadbuilding projects statewide:

While automobile tourists seek the attractions of local scenery, there is another big element in drawing them. That is the condition of the roads. A state that keeps its roads in good order is going to get a great deal more vacation travel from now on than it ever had before. This will go far toward paying for keeping the highways in good condition (p. 10).

By early 1927, this official publication of the State Highway Department began to print occasional verse such as "The Highway Blues" by Ladd Haystead and a more literary descriptive feature by Bertram C. Broome entitled "Highways and Byways." From then on, the editors published more and more "literary" poems, stories and articles by writers such as Eugene Manlove Rhodes, Orval Ricketts, Kyle Crichton, Frank Applegate, Margaret Page Hood, Blanche C. Grant, Elizabeth Willis De Huff and others too numerous to mention. In July 1931, the *New Mexico Highway Journal* merged with the State Game and Fish Department's organ, *The Conservationist*, changing its name to *New Mexico: The Sunshine State's Recreational and Highway Magazine*. On its fifteenth anniversary, according to a notice in the *Santa Fe New Mexican* of June 25, 1938, editor George Fitzpatrick, who encouraged literary contributors and book reviewers, oversaw a popular publication which printed some 8500 copies per issue.

The railroads also helped the growing literary/tourist scene. In 1928, for example, the Atchison, Topeka & Santa Fe Railway published a fifty-five-page pamphlet entitled *They Know New Mexico: Intimate Sketches by Western Writers*. It includes brief prose sketches by Charles F. Lummis, Alice Corbin Henderson, Mary Austin, Witter Bynner, Elizabeth Willis De Huff and Eugene Manlove Rhodes together with poems by Natalie Curtis, Mary Austin, Witter Bynner, Alice Corbin, John Gould Fletcher, Willard Johnson, Lucy Sturges, Henry Herbert Knibbs, Haniel Long, Harriet Monroe, William Haskell Simpson, Lynn Riggs, N. Howard ("Jack") Thorpe [sic], Margaret Pond, and John Curtis Underwood.

Another well-known New Mexico writer, Erna Fergusson of Albuquerque, also worked for the railroads. Fergusson had begun her career as a journalist, contributing a series of articles entitled "Do You Remember Old Albuquerque?" to *The Albuquerque Herald*. Together with a friend, Ethel Hickey, she then organized The Koshare Tours, taking "people out to see Indian dances, starting with Isleta and San Felipe, and gradually spreading out until we were taking people to the Snake Dance in Arizona and the Shalako at Zuni."[35] Koshare Tours influenced the organization of Fred Harvey's Indian Detours, for which Fergusson later worked.

Indian Detours, which was organized in 1925 and started its first trips in 1926, was billed as "an unusual outing-by-motor through the Spanish and Indian Southwest, available [at a cost of $50 per person] as a pleasant break in the long [transcontinental] all-rail journey" on the Santa Fe's California Limited or The Navajo. Couriers, "young women with intimate personal knowledge of the region supplemented by special training," accompanied each Harveycar.[36] Hired to organize and train these couriers, Fergusson issued the following statement about the requisite job qualifications:

Couriers are expected to be young women of education and some social grace, able to meet easily and well all kinds of people. They are expected to be intelligent enough to learn many facts about this country and to impart them in a way to interest intelligent travelers. They are selected also with an eye to their knowledge of Spanish, and any special knowledge or ability that will assist them in presenting this country properly.[37]

Among those who worked for Fergusson were writers (then or later) Elizabeth Willis De Huff, Emily Hahn,[38] Hester Jones and Farona Konopak.

Soon, not only the native Indian and Hispanic populations but the newcomer artists and writers themselves had become tourist attractions. Erna Fergusson even contributed a piece on this phenomenon to the 1928 Santa Fe Fiesta Program:

This year we are making a studied conscious effort not to be studied or conscious. Santa Fe now is one of the most interesting art centers in the world and you, O Dude of the East, are privileged to behold the most sophisticated group in the country gambolling freely to show you the untouched of Spanish and Mexican in Santa Fe at its best.

And Santa Fe, making you welcome, will enjoy itself hugely watching the dude as he gazes. Be sure as you stroll along looking for the quaint and the picturesque that you are supplying your share of those very qualities to this Santa Fe, the City Incongruous. Be sure that you are welcome. Remember that the essence of this, as of all western feast days and bonfire nights, is that each one should enjoy himself his way. You will see all New Mexico here having this kind of a good time. Santa Fe's welcome to you includes his cordial invitation to have your kind of a good time. Be yourself, even if it includes synthetic cowboy clothes, motor goggles and a camera.[39]

Whatever the delights and distractions of such public displays and their accompanying license, these occasions celebrated strong civic and creative commitments on the part of the art colonists. Their bonds were also forged on more intimate terms. In her dedication to The Turquoise Trail anthology, Alice Corbin Henderson marked that important private and spiritual community:

This book is dedicated to the poets included in the collection, and offered to them as a record of companionships—the covers of the book now taking the place of the low-roofed adobe houses within whose walls most of the poems have, at one time or another, been shared in manuscript form.

Notes

1. James R. Thorpe, *The Town of Santa Fe, New Mexico [A.D. 1604]: The Bishop's Lodge, Santa Fe* (Boulder, Colorado: The Taylor Company, 1921), p. 24. The Santa Fe Canyon resort of Los Cerros proclaimed in the 1924 Santa Fe Fiesta Program that: "Sick people are not desired. But it's a wonderful place for tired people."

2. Witter Bynner, "Alice and I," *New Mexico Quarterly Review* 19 (1949): 36, 37.

3. Ruth Laughlin Alexander, "On Hal's Birthday," *The [Santa Fe] New Mexican*, 12 August 1956, p. 5A.

4. James Kraft, "Biographical Introduction," *Selected Poems, The Works of Witter Bynner*, vol. 1 (New York: Farrar, Straus, Giroux, 1978), pp. li-liv. Also see James Kraft, ed., *Selected Letters, The Works of Witter Bynner*, vol. 5 (New York: Farrar, Straus, Giroux, 1981), p. 95. For a discussion of the artists and writers who lived in this College Street (now Old Santa Fe Trail)-Buena Vista Street area, see Edna Robertson and Sarah Nestor, *Artists of the Canyons and Caminos: Santa Fe, The Early Years* (n.p.: Peregrine Smith, 1976), pp. 63-70.

5. Stephen Graham, *In Quest of El Dorado* (New York: D. Appleton, 1923), p. 89; "The Inquest of El Dorado," in Willard Johnson, ed., *Laughing Horse: Southwest Number*, Santa Fe, New Mexico, Number Nine, December 1923, n.p.

6. Kraft, "Biographical Introduction," pp. lv-lvi.

7. For a personal reminiscence see Joseph Foster, *D. H. Lawrence in Taos* (Albuquerque: University of New Mexico Press, 1972). For a later view of Lawrence and his three women—Mabel Dodge Luhan (1879-1956), Frieda von Richthofen Lawrence [Ravagli] (1879-1962), and Dorothy Brett (1883-1978)—and their influence on Taos, see Claire Morrill, "Three Women of Taos" and "Taos in D. H. Lawrence," in *A Taos Mosaic: Portrait of a New Mexico Village* (Albuquerque: University of New Mexico Press, 1973), pp. 106-28, where Lawrence's derogatory statement appears on page 127.

8. Both essays are reprinted in Tony Hillerman, ed., *The Spell of New Mexico* (Albuquerque: University of New Mexico Press, 1976), pp. 29-43. Jung's appears as "America: The Pueblo Indians," an "extract from an unpublished MS.," part ii of the "Travels" chapter of his autobiography, *Memories, Dreams, Reflections* (New York: Pantheon Books, 1961), pp. 246-52. Also see Aniela Jaffé, ed., *C. G. Jung: Word and Image*, Bollingen Series XCVII:2 (Princeton: Princeton University Press, 1979), pp. 155-57.

9. Erna Fergusson, "Crusade from Santa Fé," *North American Review* 242 (1937):377-78; "SWAIA founded to aid Indians," *Santa Fe New Mexican*, 13 August 1978, "Indian Market" section, p. 8. Also see Edward P. Dozier, *The Pueblo Indians of North America* (New York: Holt, Rinehart & Winston, 1970), p. 108; and S. D. Aberle, *The Pueblo Indians of New Mexico: Their Land, Economy, and Civil Organization*, Memoir No. 70 (Menasha, Wisconsin: American Anthropological Association, 1948), vol. 50, no. 4, part 2.

10. Fergusson, "Crusade," pp. 378-79.

11. Quoted in D'Arcy McNickle, *Indian Man: A Life of Oliver La Farge* (Bloomington: Indiana University Press, 1971), pp. 73, 75.

12. Robertson and Nestor, *Artists of the Canyons and Caminos*, p. 43.

13. Anonymous, "The Indian Arts Fund," in Willard Hougland, ed., *Mary Austin: A Memorial* (Santa Fe, New Mexico: Laboratory of Anthropology, September 1944), pp. 59, 60. Austin's own account is in her *Earth Horizon: Autobiography* (Boston: Houghton Mifflin, The Riverside Press Cambridge, 1932), pp. 360-62. For a delightful glimpse of another Indian Arts Fund founder, who later became curator of archeology at the new Laboratory of Anthropology, see Marjorie Lambert, "The Wonderful Wit of H. P. Mera," *El Palacio* 76, 4 (1970): 20-30. Novelist Raymond Otis also worked for the Indian Arts Fund after settling in Santa Fe in the late 1920s and wrote a pamphlet, *Indian Art of the Southwest: An Exposition of Methods and Practices*, distributed by the Southwestern

Indian Fair during the early 1930s (Marta Weigle, Introduction to Raymond Otis, *Miguel of the Bright Mountain* [1936; reprint, Albuquerque: University of New Mexico Press, 1977], p. xiv). Another Santa Fe writer associated with this and other Indian causes was Elizabeth Willis De Huff, who came to the Southwest in 1918, when her husband John was appointed as superintendent of the Santa Fe Indian School. She organized a class of previously unrecognized Indian artists whose work was later patronized by Mabel Dodge Luhan. One of her students was Fred Kavotie, who illustrated "one of her nine books, 'Taytay's Tales' [1922], the first collection of Indian lore for children and the first book to be illustrated by an Indian" (*Santa Fe New Mexican*, 23 September 1947).

14. Mary Austin, "The Town That Doesn't Want A Chautauqua," *New Republic*, 7 July 1926, p. 195.

15. Ibid., p. 196. We are indebted to Claudia Larcombe for her 1977 University of New Mexico history seminar paper, "Changing Images of Santa Fe," on the Chamber of Commerce in the 1920s.

16. Mary Austin, *Earth Horizon*, p. 354. For material about Austin in Santa Fe, see work by T. M. Pearce, notably: *The Beloved House* (Caldwell, Idaho: The Caxton Printers, Ltd., 1940), *Mary Hunter Austin* (New York: Twayne, 1965), and especially *Literary America 1903-1934: The Mary Austin Letters*, Contributions in Women's Studies, no. 5 (Westport, Connecticut: Greenwood Press, 1979).

17. Mabel Dodge Luhan, "Mary Austin: A Woman," in Hougland, ed., *Mary Austin*, p. 22. This memorial contains tributes by Houghton Mifflin Co., Jane Baumann, Henry Seidel Canby, Carl Van Doren, Mabel, Dudley Wynn, Erna Fergusson, Peggy Pond Church, Leonora F. Curtin, Elizabeth Willis De Huff, T. M. Pearce, Ina Sizer Cassidy, Ruth Laughlin, and Edgar L. Hewett.

18. Spud Johnson, "The Rabble," *New Mexico Quarterly Review* 19 (1949):74.

19. *The New Mexico Sentinel*, 19 January 1938. Also see Haniel Long, "The Poets' Round-Up," *New Mexico Quarterly Review* 19 (1949):68-69. A journalist, poet and teacher, Long had been a professor of English at Carnegie Institute of Technology since 1910. He spent 1924-25 in Santa Fe. In 1928, he was appointed department head. Stricken with ill health less than a year later, he moved to Santa Fe permanently with his wife and son in 1929. He died in 1956, and *The Santa Fe New Mexican* published a tribute to him, 15 June 1958, p. 23.

20. Thomas A. Erhard, *Lynn Riggs: Southwest Playwright*, Southwest Writers Series 29 (Austin, Texas: Steck-Vaughn, 1970), pp. 6-7.

21. Kraft, "Biographical Introduction," p. lviii. According to Ina Sizer Cassidy: "The outstanding play . . . was Witter Bynner's *Cake*, the lead played by Miss Lacy Van Wagonen, a season visitor from New York, magnificently staged and costumed from local trunks and Oriental collections, the necessary properties challenging the imaginative ingenuity of the stage director" ("The Little Theater in Santa Fe," *New Mexico Magazine*, October 1938, p. 25).

22. Tricia Hurst Richards, "Taos Profile—Living Myth," *The Santa Fe New Mexican*, 2 December 1959, p. 8; Kraft, "Biographical Introduction," p. lv; and Morrill, *Taos Mosaic*, pp. 133-35. Also see Spud Johnson, "Shall Taos Annex Santa Fe?," *Fiesta Program*, 1928, p. 28.

23. Spud Johnson, "Laughing Horse Awake from Sepen [sic] Year Siesta: Ready to Trot Off the Rumbling Press of Taos," *The New Mexico Sentinel*, 24 April 1938, p. 9.

24. Spud Johnson, "The Laughing Horse," *New Mexico Quarterly* 21 (1951):165. Here he lists as contributors: Witter Bynner, D. H. Lawrence, President Obregon of Mexico, Robert Herrick, Mary Austin, Mabel Dodge Luhan, Andrew Dasburg, Lynn Riggs, Alice Corbin, William Penhallow Henderson, Haniel Long, Eda Lou Walton, Frank Waters, Elizabeth Shepley Sergeant, John Evans, Willard Nash, Lincoln Steffens, Idella Purnell, Will Shuster, Paul Horgan, Carl Sandburg, Arthur Davison Ficke, Evelyn

Scott, Sherwood Anderson, Margaret Larkin, John Dewey, Harriet Monroe, Carl Van Vechten, Myron Brinig, Miguel Covarrubias, Maxwell Perkins, E. B. White and Alfred Knopf, "among others."

25. Spud Johnson, "The Santa Fe Gadfly: Pioneer Bookselling," *The Santa Fe New Mexican*, 11 August 1963, *Pasatiempo*, p. 12. In "A city tradition moves to a new location," Denise Kessler notes that Robey began operations in 1921, with a table of books in Boyle's Flower Store on the Plaza and then moved to the Thunderbird Shop across from La Fonda, from which "uniformed waiters arrived daily at 4 p.m. with trays of martinis" (*The New Mexican*, 31 May 1981, p. A-3).

26. Alice Corbin Henderson, "Bookseller to Santa Fé," *Publishers' Weekly* CXXIV (19 August 1933):495. Henderson had purchased the first Villagra Book Shop book (Kessler, ibid).

27. Julia M. Keleher, "Los Paisanos," *New Mexico Quarterly* 6 (1936):54. Among the Bookshop's publications is *The Early World and Other Poems*, by Robert Hunt, printed by Rydal Press in 1936. Later, when Robey served as librarian of the University of New Mexico's Harwood Foundation in Taos during the late thirties and early forties, she called on Johnson for help: "During one summer of her tenure in Taos, I happened to be in charge of the art gallery, upstairs above the library, and Roberta kept nagging me to 'Please stock some books.' She said that she was constantly being asked by library patrons and tourists WHERE they could buy Barbara Latham's, Mabel Luhan's, or Frank Waters' latest books. So she wanted me to Do Something About It. As a result, I commandeered an old trastero from Mrs. Harwood's living room, got permission from the Board of Directors to sell books as well as paintings, and set up a minute bookshop [Laughing Horse Bookstall], even smaller than the one which had started the Robey career in Santa Fe. My point, of course, is that Roberta Robey was not only the mother of both Santa Fe bookshops, but at least the step-mother of those in Taos!" (Johnson, "Gadfly").

28. Austin, *Earth Horizon*, p. 359.

29. Inscription quoted in T. M. Pearce, *Beloved House*, p. 176; Elizabeth Shepley Sergeant, *Willa Cather: A Memoir* (Lincoln: University of Nebraska Press, 1963), pp. 225-26.

30. Edith Lewis, *Willa Cather Living: A Personal Record* (New York: Alfred A. Knopf, 1953), pp. 144, 143.

31. Paul Horgan, *Approaches to Writing* (New York: Farrar, Straus and Giroux, 1974), pp. 220-21. According to Lawrence Clark Powell: "Paul Horgan . . . tells of coming inadvertently upon Miss Cather and Miss Lewis in lounging chairs on a La Fonda balcony, surrounded by books and papers, at work on the *Archbishop*. '. . . The nearer of the two ladies turned upon me a light blue regard of such annoyance and distaste at my intrusion that I was gone too quickly to take more than a sweeping impression of where I had been.' It was the only time he ever saw Willa Cather. Chagrin and respect mingled in an unfading memory of his intrusion" (*Southwest Classics: The Creative Literature of the Arid Lands, Essays on the Books and Their Writers* [Los Angeles, California: The Ward Ritchie Press, 1974], p. 131).

32. Ronald L. Grimes, *Symbol and Conquest: Public Ritual and Drama in Santa Fe, New Mexico* (Ithaca, New York: Cornell University Press, 1976), pp. 187, 188.

33. Elizabeth Willis De Huff, "The Santa Fe Fiesta," *The Santa Fean*, Fiesta Edition 1941, p. 30.

34. Blanche C. Grant, *Taos Today* (Taos, New Mexico: n. n., 1925), pp. 9-10.

35. Quoted in Barbara Young Sims, "Those Fabulous Fergussons," *El Palacio* 82, 2 (summer 1976):46-47. Also see David A. Remley, *Erna Fergusson*, Southwest Writers Series 24 (Austin, Texas: Steck-Vaughn, 1969), pp. 10-11. Unlike her brother Harvey, who lived most of his life outside the state, Erna maintained her home in Albuquerque.

For her brother's view of the state and his background, see Harvey Fergusson, *Home in the West: An Inquiry into My Origins* (New York: Duell, Sloan and Pearce, 1944).

36. *Roads to Yesterday: Motor Drives out from Old Santa Fe*, Harveycars, Atchison, Topeka & Santa Fe Railway, March 1927, pp. 21, 3.

37. Quoted in D. H. Thomas, *The Southwestern Indian Detours: The Story of the Fred Harvey/Santa Fe Railway Experiment in 'Detourism'* (Phoenix, Arizona: Hunter Publishing, 1978), p. 77.

38. Emily Hahn writes of her experiences as a Courier in *Times and Places* (New York: Pinnacle Books, 1971), pp. 87-100.

39. Erna Fergusson, "The City Incongruous," *Fiesta Program*, 1928, p. 19. Also see Evelyn Scott, "The Santa Fe Art Colony," *Wings*, October 1930, pp. 10-13; Paul Horgan, *The Centuries of Santa Fe* (1956; reprint, New York: E. P. Dutton, 1965), pp. 317-18.

1930-1935

Painters, writers, sculptors, dancers, drawn from a varied background of the world's art centers, come to Santa Fe for a two-day stop-over and remain here to build their homes. After that they become a hardy, thriving element in the life of Santa Fe. They not only add the bohemian note of studio life but give freely of their time and effort to make this a vital place to live. They accept in full measure that town consciousness which makes Santa Fe unique. They are as interested in paving and sewers, elections and talkies as the business men. Being articulate, their opinions are sometimes more effective than their number.

—Ruth Laughlin Barker, *Caballeros:
The Romance of Santa Fe and the
Southwest,* 1931, p. 114.

Ruth Laughlin Barker portrays her hometown as "The City of Contrasts," one in which the art colonists play an integral role. Her pride in them and in the town echoes theirs in having discovered an exotic land and a pastoral village in the midst of twentieth-century America. Through their literary and civic efforts they continued to proclaim this cultural mecca and to affirm their determination to preserve its uniqueness as a free-spirited community within a powerful natural and cultural setting.

This regional pride surfaced in Mary Austin's first New Mexico novel, *Starry Adventure,* the story of Gard Sitwell, an Anglo boy who moves to the state with his parents when his father contracts tuberculosis. Growing up at Rancho Arriba, Gard becomes attached to the New Mexico landscape. The wide starry skies of summer seem to promise him a "great adventure." Despite the death of his father and a series of economic hardships which cut short his education, Gard holds fast to his dream. In the final portion of the book, an older and wiser Gard comes to realize that his "starry adventure" is, after all, the life he has made with his wife Judy in the New Mexico mountains.

Writing of *Starry Adventure* in her autobiography *Earth Horizon,* Austin describes it as a novel "in which I gathered up the knowledge I had gained of the various levels of native life in New Mexico."[1] In 1930, she had collaborated with Ansel Adams to produce *Taos, Photographed by Ansel Adams and Described by Mary Austin.* Her fourteen-page introduction to this large folio, published by Grabhorn Press of San Francisco, provided a context for Adams's photo essay on Taos Pueblo.

35

Mary Austin also continued the work she had done with the Spanish Colonial Arts Society by becoming a principal backer of its Spanish Arts Shop, which opened at the Sena Plaza in May 1930.[2] She and neighbor Frank Applegate, a co-founder of the Society, were deeply involved in plans and notes for a book on the Spanish Colonial arts of New Mexico when the latter died on February 13, 1931. Although the planned volume remained unfinished, Austin did prepare Applegate's *Native Tales of New Mexico* for publication by J. B. Lippincott Company, Philadelphia, in 1932. A collection of stories about Indian and Hispano folklife, most of the tales had been gathered from the small villages and pueblos where Applegate had sought New Mexican arts and crafts. Although completing the book brought painful memories of her friend, Austin claimed that "we had worked together so long and so completely in each other's confidence, with such free interchanges of material that I did not find it at all difficult to do."[3]

Despite various financial and physical set-backs, Austin continued to write about life in New Mexico and Santa Fe with optimism and enthusiasm. An October 1932 article entitled "Why I Live in Santa Fe" informed *Golden Book* readers across the nation that, while there were other towns in the Southwest which offered "opportunities for association" with Indian and Hispanic folk cultures, only Santa Fe offered the "complete intellectual sophistication" that she found so necessary to her creative work:

For the very reasons which have led me to select [Santa Fe] there are gathered here, or visit for longer or shorter durations, people of the first rank of creative and intellectual achievement. There is no time of the year in which there are not to be found individuals of the rank of A. V. Kidder, Sylvanus Morley, John Galsworthy, Carl Sandburg, Willa Cather, Witter Bynner, John Sloan, Dr. Robert Millikan, Dr. William McDougall, William Allen White, Paul Kellogg, Sinclair Lewis, and other scores of welcome names.[4]

While Austin extolled the creative and intellectual advantages of the town, others capitalized on the art colonists as tourist assets. The *Santa Fe Visitor's Guide* of 1931 identified George Park's New Mexico Cafe at 125 San Francisco Street as the place "where the artists and writers go to dine and talk." Thirty writers were listed as residents: Mary Austin, Ruth Barker, Roark Bradford, Joseph Bursey, Witter Bynner, Kenneth Chapman, Elizabeth De Huff, T. T. Flynn, Seymour Hess, Bertram C. Broome, Raymond Otis, Camilo Padilla, Philip Stevenson, Paul Walter Jr., Wilber Wiswall, Withers Woolford, Lucy Bacon, Earl Scott, Marian Scott, Phyllis Crawford, Anna V. Huey, R. W. Bennett, Tait Farrell, Donald Clark, Mrs. J. B. McGovern, Mrs. William Nielsen, Alice Corbin, Katherine Chapman, Lenore Curtin, and J. C. Underwood.

Some of these writers contributed to a special issue of Spud Johnson's *Laughing Horse*, which returned temporarily to Santa Fe for its seventeenth number in February 1930. This was a special "Symposium of Criticism, Comment and Opinion on the Subject of Censorship," with contributions by Carl Sandburg, Maxwell Perkins, Edward C. Aswell, Will Irwin, John Dewey, Arthur Davison Ficke, Sherwood Anderson, B. W. Heubsch, William Allen White, Witter Bynner, Margaret Larkin, Ellery Sedgwick, Alfred A. Knopf, Mabel Dodge Luhan, W. W. Norton, Upton Sinclair, Mary Austin, E. B. W[hite], John Collier, Camilo Padilla, Harriet Monroe, Evelyn Scott, Henry Goddard Leach, Lincoln Steffens, John Metcalfe, Logan Clendening, Josie Turner, Cyril Kay-Scott, Haniel Long and Ward Lockwood. Johnson recalled its inception and reception thus:

When *Lady Chatterley's Lover* was refused entry into the country, *The Laughing Horse* appealed to Senator Bronson Cutting, got him interested enough to make a special fight to alter the censorship clause in the current tariff bill. A hurried Censorship issue of the *Horse* was printed, one edition exclusively for distribution in the United States Senate, and an amazing collection of articles and telegrams from celebrities all over the United States poured in. An odd angle to this effort was that a cartoon by Will Shuster scheduled for the censorship number, itself got censored by the Mayor of Santa Fe, and had to be released separately "by request only." And Senator Cutting dedicated the issue of the Congressional Record which contained his pleas on the subject "To the editor of *The Laughing Horse*, but for whom it might have read differently."[5]

The Santa Fe New Mexican continued to serve as the favored local forum, however, with E. Dana Johnson a sympathetic editor. Comment and criticism was also enacted, especially during Fiesta parades. Many art colonists participated in the Santa Fe Players. The group's 1931 Fiesta production, "Sure Fire: Episodes in the Life of Billy the Kid," was written by novelist Philip Stevenson. Ruth Laughlin Barker was a member of the costume committee. Barker, E. Dana Johnson, Witter Bynner, Alice Corbin, Haniel Long and Anna V. Huey were on the publicity committee, which launched a full scale advertising campaign. Barker, Long and Bynner also wrote glowing reviews of the drama for the *Santa Fe New Mexican*.[6]

Yet another local drama played to good-natured critical acclaim on Wednesday, January 6, 1932:

"A Day in Santa Fe" featuring the Santa Fe burro was shown to an audience of several hundred persons Wednesday night in the lecture room of La Fonda. The producers, Lynn Riggs and James Hughes, were assisted by Henway Rodakiewicz at the projector,

Mary Christine and Levi A. Hughes, Jr., Dorothy Belle Flanagan, John K. C. Andrews and John McMahon, who received and ushered.

Artistic shots of sky and trees combined with poetic captions written by Poet Riggs made this amateur motion picture one of unusual beauty. Character was delineated in feet and hands as well as in faces, an outstanding sequence being the march of variegated shoes, every type from high heels to Indian moccasins, past a Plaza well.

A large number of local persons made their motion picture debut in the film. Mrs. Gustave Baumann in Mexican blouse and skirt was seen in several sequences, her daughter Ann, in one. Mrs. Juan Sedillo and her Great Dane were photographed at play; Edwin Brooks diving and swimming in the White Tank; Norman McGee buying a ring from one of the best-known Plaza Indians; John Dorman at siesta; Josef Bakos at work, an unusual picture in silhouette; Raymond and Francès Otis at breakfast; Joseph H. Stevenson and Evie Stevenson's smile appropriate after the summer rain, Betty Galt, Mary Christine Hughes and a group entering a local curio store to see paintings by Ma-Pe-Wi; the Aztec parrot, Helen Wolfe, Ladd Haystead and others in typical attitudes.

A Fiesta scene introduces a Mariachi Jalisco players, groups of Indians dancing and crowds of natives on the Plaza.

Clever continuity was as much a factor in the success of the picture as the excellent photography. A musical score accompanied the picture under the direction of Mr. Hughes.

Ernest Knee and Gina MacDowell entertained with a party for the producers and cast after the second performance at the home of Mr. Knee on Canyon Road. Those who attended were Mr. Riggs, Mr. Hughes, Mr. & Mrs. Norman McGee, Mr. & Mrs. Clifford McGee of Plainfield, N.J., Mr. & Mrs. Raymond Otis, Mr. & Mrs. Juan A. Sedillo, Miss Henrietta Harris, Mr. & Mrs. Philip Stevenson, Miss Flanagan, Miss Hughes, Mr. Andrews and Mr. Hughes, Jr.[7]

The newspaper account does not mention one of the movie's highlights—Alice Corbin Henderson lounging in a chair while awaiting poetic inspiration, which arrives momentarily.

By far the most joyful dramatic productions were the New Mexico Poets' Round-Ups, performed each summer from 1930 to 1939 in one or another of Santa Fe's private gardens. Organized by Alice Corbin and various patrons and supporters of the arts, the Round-Ups combined two of the literati's major interests—poetry and Indian cultural welfare. Originally created as fund raisers for the New Mexico Association on Indian Affairs, these gatherings soon took on a life of their own. At the annual spectacles local and visiting poets, resplendent in bandanas and blue jeans, would dash out of cardboard chutes to recite their works for appreciative listeners. The poets, who often included performers such as Mary Austin, Witter Bynner, Langdon Mitchell and Ernest Thompson Seton,[8] were assisted by local musicians who played the guitar and sang Spanish and cowboy songs.[9] Many works so presented later appeared in print, some in the newly established *New Mexico Quarterly*.

The first issue of the *Quarterly* appeared in 1931. Published in Albuquerque by the University of New Mexico, it was a journal "designed to give to the faculty, advanced students and all others who may have something worthwhile to contribute to the literature and scholarly thought of New Mexico an outlet for their writing."[10] The *Quarterly's* premiere sparked sharp debate among various writers as to the proper purpose of the journal. Henry Nash Smith wanted it to be a regional magazine. Mary Austin thought that it needed to take a sophisticated literary stance, while Kyle Crichton praised it as a medium capable of "encouraging and publishing the work of the younger writer."[11]

The University of New Mexico and its newly established Press thereby joined the University of Oklahoma and its Press in publishing regional literature as well as other works.[12] Notable among the latter's publications was *Folksay: A Regional Miscellany*, edited by University of Oklahoma professor Benjamin A. Botkin, a frequent visitor to New Mexico. Issued once a year from 1929 to 1932, *Folksay* was dedicated to the idea that folklore is a natural source of strength and revitalization for literature. The authors approached it from both critical and creative perspectives. During its four years of publication, *Folksay* carried stories, poems and essays by New Mexicans Frank Applegate, Mary Austin, Witter Bynner, John Gould Fletcher, Paul Horgan,[13] Philip Stevenson, S. Omar Barker, Willard [Spud] Johnson, Alice Corbin, Haniel Long, Peggy Pond Church, and L.S.M. Curtin.

In 1932, Haniel Long, Alice Corbin, Peggy Pond Church and Witter Bynner, four among those who had been active in founding the Poets' Round-Ups, came together to establish a publishing house in Santa Fe. Committed to helping "good writing grow from native American soil" and believing that "regional publishing would foster the growth of American literature," they encouraged Walter L. Goodwin, owner and operator of the Rydal Press, to move his operations from Pennsylvania to the Santa Fe area.[14] Goodwin arrived in the summer of 1933, and set up his equipment in the dining hall of a defunct sanitarium in Tesuque. That year, Writers' Editions published its first three volumes: Alice Corbin's *The Sun Turns West*, Peggy Pond Church's *Foretaste*, and Haniel Long's *Atlantides*. Each author paid for the publication of her or his own book with the understanding that she or he would retain ninety per cent of the profits, the remaining ten per cent going to Writers' Editions, other members of which would help with mailing, bookkeeping and the like.

An undated news release about a year later proclaimed that these "Southwest Writers Renew Revolt Against East—Enlarge Self Publishing Venture—Ask Public Support":

Writers' Editions, the group of writers and poets in the Southwest who joined together last year to form the first self-publishing group in the entire country, are again carrying the literary battle forward by enlarging their ranks and listing for publication this year more than twice the number of volumes they sponsored in 1934.

This group which originally sought freedom from the dictates of the Eastern publishing clique that determines what shall or shall not be published, was composed of Alice Corbin of Santa Fe, Peggy Pond Church of Los Alamos, Haniel Long of Santa Fe, Raymond Otis of Chicago and Santa Fe, and Eugene Manlove Rhodes, late of Pacific Beach, California.

These writers, well-known to magazine and book readers, objected to the restraint placed upon them by Eastern editors. Eugene Manlove Rhodes (now deceased) had no difficulty selling fiction to the Saturday Evening Post, but they would not publish "Penalosa", which he considered a major effort. To overcome this situation, these regional writers founded a cooperative publishing venture of which the Southwest should be proud since it is unique in American annals.

This year their new program is on a much wider scale. They have invited to join their group John Gould Fletcher of Arkansas; Elizabeth Shipley [sic] Sergeant, who divides her time between New York and New Mexico; B. A. Botkin, the editor of *Space*, who hails from Oklahoma; Lynn Riggs, the playwright; Spud Johnson, the editor of *The Laughing Horse*; Dorothy Bell Flanigan [sic], and Witter Bynner, both well known in Southwest literary circles.

Writers living in this territory are watching the movement with great interest, as they also feel that Writers' Editions is an original method of correcting the unbearable publishing situation that exists at present for authors whose type of work has a more limited audience than such volumes as "Anthony Adverse" or "Trader Horn".

* * *

"Writers who are anxious to affiliate with our group and enter into our cooperative venture," said Haniel Long, one of the founders, "Are welcome to discuss their manuscripts with us. We impose no restraints that should be irksome to the working author." Mr. Long makes his headquarters at Santa Fe, New Mexico. He, with the others of the group, think that their movement should receive such recognition this year that similar groups will start in other sections where writers congregate. It will be interesting to see how the New York publishers frame their answer to this challenge.[15]

The success of this "challenge" is shown by the seventeen or more books published by Writers' Editions between 1933 and 1940, two of which—John Gould Fletcher's 1935 *XXIV Elegies* and Gustave Baumann's 1939 *Frijoles Canyon Pictographs*, with wood blocks printed by Baumann in his own studio and text printed by Willard Clark—were honored by awards from Fifty Books of the Year.[16]

Taos too made literary news in 1932, with the publication of Mabel Dodge Luhan's book about D. H. Lawrence, *Lorenzo in Taos*. Dedicated to Luhan's longtime friend and sometime visitor, poet Robinson Jeffers, the account details the author's impressions of and relationship with Lawrence. The book also includes a number of letters which the English author wrote Luhan. While it probably increased her national notoriety, Luhan's book received a sharply critical review from Santa Fe author Philip Stevenson:

. . . One's final thought about *Lorenzo in Taos* is that [Luhan] has been content to use it to record tittle tattle. A collection of blazing jewels, Lawrence's letters, have been placed in a setting of mud. Adobe mud, if you like. Taos adobe, capable of being molded into beauty, solidity, and usefulness, but most often inert with the evil inertness of gossip, and formless with the pathetic formlessness of cultish intellectual processes.[17]

The year 1933 proved one of introspection. Poets and authors across New Mexico devoted considerable thought to the nature of the state and how it affected their work. On July 1, the English Department of New Mexico Normal (now Highlands) University sponsored the first New Mexico Round Table on Southwestern Literature. Organized by folklorist B. A. Botkin, then a visiting professor at New Mexico Normal, and Chair Lester Raines and Professor Margaret J. Kennedy of the English Department, this conference:

. . . brought together at Las Vegas a representative gathering of Southwest writers whose essential identity and sympathy of aims, underneath a lively difference of opinion, proclaimed the birth of a genuine regional group. The presence of two leading Southern regionalists who were spending the summer in the state, John Gould Fletcher and John Crowe Ransom, made the group not simply regional but interregional. And in combining the cultural emphasis of the University of Virginia round table held in July, 1931, with the literary interest of the University of Montana conference of July, 1932, the New Mexico round table advanced the discussion in several directions.[18]

Many Santa Fe and Taos writers attended and/or spoke at these conferences. The enthusiasm generated by the first New Mexico Round Table spurred the Department of English to hold them annually for the next three years. In 1934 and 1935, students began collecting interviews and biographical information for a dictionary of "Writers and Writings of New Mexico." Edited by Lester Raines and mimeographed by him and other members of the English Department, *Writers and Writings of New Mexico* and *More New Mexico Writers and Writings* catalogue the lives and works of some one hundred writers who thought of themselves as New Mexican—either through residency or professional interest.[19]

The December 1933 issue of *Poetry* magazine featured a collection of Southwestern verse with poems by Alice Corbin, Paul Horgan, Haniel Long, Peggy Pond Church, Ina Sizer Cassidy and Axton Clark. John Gould Fletcher offered some final editorial comments on the state of Anglo-Saxon poetry in the Southwest, particularly New Mexico. Describing the state as an "old and settled" land of "singular aloofness, dignity and unhurriedness," Fletcher claimed that in spite of its majesty and cultural richness, it had "probably produced less [poetry] than any other part of America so far." He credited this lack to the nature of the "usual modern poet" who is "of the sort that has not time enough to stop and puzzle out a people in whose veins run one of the longest histories of resistance to outside innovation on record." Remarking that "the best books on the Southwest are still those in prose," Fletcher proposed that "the present poets of the Southwest are therefore more important for what they indicate than what they have said." In light of these comments, Fletcher's conclusion that the poets shared "a certain directness, a bald concreteness of statement" was but weak applause.[20]

Other writers also gave special consideration to the contemporary spirit of Santa Fe—a spirit which many feared was being changed through growing commercialism and the immigration of idle wealthy. Writing in the *New Mexico Quarterly*, Philip Stevenson and David L. Neuman offered conflicting views of the "City Different." Stevenson characterized it as an isolated outpost of the spirit of civilization. Tracing this isolation back to the time of the Spanish Conquest when Santa Fe was "a tiny node of civilization, lost in a vast semi-arid wilderness," Stevenson maintained that "it is this character which she has kept with a remarkable degree of integrity throughout her existence." Recalling that "one year not long ago, when the winners of the Pulitzer Prize were announced, New York was surprised to discover that the co-author of the winning play and the author of the winning novel were both residents (at that time) of Santa Fe," he argued: "If Santa Fe can continue to ignore the whims of her lotus eaters and the ballyhoo of her boosters, both commercial and artistic

. . . then she may . . . remain what she has always been, an outpost of the spirit of civilization."[21]

David L. Neuman's rejoinder to Stevenson appeared as a letter to the editor in the next issue. While stating that he did not intend "to combat Mr. Stevenson's thesis which is well taken and ably argued," Neuman contended nonetheless that "we of the Southwest are prone to lose our perspective in our remote province. The feeble light which Mr. Stevenson describes is too pitifully feeble." Neuman saw little intellectual future for Santa Fe, maintaining: "If you eliminate our modern group of alien talent (which includes Mr. Stevenson) . . . what have we? . . . [Nothing but] an ingrown stock whose artistic heritage lay overgrown and undiscerned until in very recent years it was exhumed and touted by university nourished gentlemen and ladies from the East of whom Mr. Stevenson himself is one." Neuman closed his letter with passion:

Whom do we nourish? Our political faith is in the hands of a New Yorker, our best novel was written by a stranger, Willa Cather, our poetry by a Harvard graduate, our painting is done by anyone but people suckled at the teats of our local bi-lingual culture. And who fosters (i.e. buys) our local cultural goods? Easterners and strangers. It is only an incident that Santa Fe is the residence of artists in paint, poetry or prose. What little cidevant glory this town has belongs to Oñate, DeVargas and Villagra, and they were as Spanish as Mr. Stevenson and his talent are Anglo-Saxon.[22]

In the years that followed, Santa Fe came into even sharper printed focus. Pages of prose, poetry and fiction were devoted to descriptions of its diverse inhabitants and unique characters. The death on August 13, 1934, of one of the town's pioneer authors, Mary Austin, prompted an outpouring of literary comment.[23] The September 8th issue of the *Saturday Review of Literature* featured a lengthy summary of Austin's life by Santa Fe author Elizabeth Shepley Sergeant. Claiming that Austin "had come into her own in Santa Fe," Sergeant described her as a "mystic" who knew " 'more' than she had ever expressed or could express in poetry, romance, play, article," yet who was "somehow tied . . . down to the mud and the granite and the sandhills of the Southwestern land."[24]

Austin also figures prominently in the first novel written about the city's art colonists—Raymond Otis's *Fire in the Night*, published in 1934 by Farrar and Rinehart of New York and by Victor Gollancz of London as *Fire Brigade*.

The Santa Fe Volunteer Fire Department's efforts to quell a large downtown blaze in 1931 provide the vehicle for a sometimes satiric depiction of small-town interrelationships. . . . According to reviewer Withers Woolford, "the characters and events are mostly easily recognizable, but those who attempt to identify their friends will find it somewhat confusing because of the crossing of characteristics by the author." Woolford believes that "some of those who appear in the book are Juan Sedillo, attorney; the late Ashley Pond, capitalist; Norman Magee [McGee], merchant; Edwin Brooks, advertising; Senator Tom Catron; John Evans, writer; Mabel Lujan, capitalist; Witter Bynner, poet; Bill Roberts, mortician; and Nathan Salmon, real estate owner and theatre operator." Reviewer Esther B. Hazen notes that "the Santa Feans are not fond of the book—perhaps because they find bits of themselves in it, and also because they do not like to admit, even in a novel, that anything could possibly be wrong with Santa Fe."[25]

Nevertheless, by the mid-thirties something was clearly "wrong" with Santa Fe, both in print and in life.

During the summer of 1935, Robert Frost came through New Mexico and stopped for two days in Santa Fe to give a poetry reading sponsored by members of Writers' Editions. Once a classmate of Haniel Long and Witter Bynner at Harvard, poet Frost had by then won Pulitzer Prizes and was acclaimed one of America's major poets. His brief visit brought to the surface the bitterness and neglect felt by at least one local bard. Bynner was keenly aware of the relative lack of national recognition for his own poetry and greatly resented Frost's success. Designated to introduce Frost's reading, he ignored this duty and arrived late. Then, having invited Frost to his house for lunch the next day, Bynner quarreled with him over a book of poetry and "without any apparent provocation" poured his glass of beer over the distinguished poet's head.[26]

This incident was passed over lightly at the time. However, Bynner's actions highlight the growing sense of dissatisfaction present in the works of other Santa Feans. While at the same time praising the beauties of their town away from the beaten path, they seem to have begun to suspect that serious and longlasting critical acclaim was eluding most of them.[27]

Such discontent also prevades Paul Horgan's 1935 novel, No Quarter Given. In his saga about the trials of Edmund Abbey, a tubercular composer deposited in Santa Fe by his rich gadabout wife, Horgan portrays a number of local social types with remarkable candor and very little romance. Recounting the dying composer's "last flare up of life and creative power," Horgan presents Santa Fe as a town peopled by second rate artists and parasitic hangers-on, while his description of the New Mexico landscape is a far cry from Mary Austin's "Starry Adventure." When Abbey leaves his heiress wife for a penniless young actress, the lovers are cast out of the town. Banished by financial circumstances to the dry and dust-filled city of Albuquerque, they find that for the artist in New Mexico there is "no quarter given."

Notes

1. Mary Austin, *Earth Horizon: An Autobiography* (Boston and New York: Houghton Mifflin, The Riverside Press Cambridge, 1932), pp. 357-58.
2. Sarah Nestor, *The Native Market of the Spanish New Mexican Craftsmen: Santa Fe, 1933-1940* (Santa Fe, New Mexico: The Colonial New Mexico Historical Foundation, 1978), pp. 8-9. Besides Austin and Applegate, the original membership included: Mrs. Ruth Laughlin Alexander, Mr. and Mrs. A. S. Alvord, Mr. George Bloom, Mr. and Mrs. Gerald Cassidy, Dr. Kenneth Chapman, Miss Leonora Curtin, Mrs. Thomas Curtin, Senator Bronson Cutting, Mr. Andrew Dasburg, Mr. and Mrs. John DeHuff, Mrs. Charles H. Dietrick, Mrs. Lois Field, Mrs. William Field, Mrs. Alice Corbin Henderson, Mr. Wayne Mauzy, Mr. and Mrs. Cyrus McCormick, Mr. George McCrossen, Mr. Preston Myers, Mr. Sheldon Parsons, Dr. Francis Proctor, Mrs. Marie Robinson, Mr. H. Cady Wells, Miss Mary C. Wheelwright, "and others sensitive to Spanish culture" (ibid, p. 6). Despite their untimely demise, both the Spanish Market and the Spanish Arts Shop provided an impetus for the Native Market of Spanish New Mexican Craftsmen which was organized in 1933 by Leonora Curtin and provided an outlet for New Mexican Spanish crafts until 1940. For an excellent study of Anglo patronage of Hispano folk arts, including a discussion of both Austin and Applegate's roles and philosophies, see Charles L. Briggs, *The Wood Carvers of Córdova, New Mexico: Social Dimensions of an Artistic "Revival"* (Knoxville: University of Tennessee Press, 1980).
3. Mary Austin, "Frank Applegate," *New Mexico Quarterly* 2 (1932): 217. In 1932, Austin also carried her promotion of Spanish colonial arts and crafts to the Casa de Armijo in Old Albuquerque, where she lectured at an exhibit of Spanish Colonial arts sponsored by the New Mexico Arts League and the newly founded (in 1931) New Mexico Folklore Society. The exhibition, from March 28 through April 3, was concluded by Austin's talk on the arts and crafts of the Spanish Southwest, followed by a costume *baile*. See T. M. Pearce, "History of the New Mexico Folklore Society," from the *1976 Program Honoring the Bicentennial Year of the United States*, University of Albuquerque, 8 May 1976; and idem, "The New Mexico Folklore Society," *The New Mexico Folklore Record* 15 (1980-81):5.
4. Mary Austin, "Why I Live in Santa Fe," *Golden Book*, October 1932, pp. 306-307.
5. Spud Johnson, "The Laughing Horse," *New Mexico Quarterly* 21 (1951): 165-66. See the reprint of Shuster's cartoon in the "Publications Ephemeral and Exemplary" section of this volume. For an account of Senator Cutting's fight, see E. P. Walkiewicz and Hugh Witemeyer, "Ezra Pound's Contributions to New Mexican Periodicals and His Relationship with Senator Bronson Cutting," *Paideuma* 9 (1980): 449-50. Pound himself never visited New Mexico, but he did contribute to the *Santa Fe New Mexican* and an Albuquerque literary quarterly entitled *The Morada*, the first number of which appeared in Autumn 1929, and promised "Stories, Essays, Poems and Articles by Southwestern and foreign writers." Poet Norman Macleod, a student at the University of New Mexico, teamed with his wife Catherine Stuart and another student, Donal McKenzie, to start this publication. "By virtue of his earlier contributions to other little magazines in the United States and Europe, Macleod already participated in the extensive network of personal contracts that existed among the avant-garde writers and editors of that day, [so that] through this 'mutual admiration society,' as McKenzie retrospectively describes it, he and Macleod solicited poems, short stories and translations from some major writers." Among them was Ezra Pound, who contributed pieces to the first, third and fifth numbers, and in November 1930 declared in *The English*

Journal: "Morada, edited at Albuquerque, New Mexico, by Norman Macleod, appears to me the best bet as a successor to the *Little Review* (and is, naturally, in the worst financial condition of any of the new reviews)." The fourth number never appeared, but Donal McKenzie, who left Albuquerque for Germany in June 1930, edited and published a fifth number at Lago de Garda, Italy, in February 1931 (ibid, p. 443).

6. Ruth Laughlin Barker, " 'Sure Fire' Rehearsals Exciting: Play Is Real Community Effort," *The Santa Fe New Mexican,* 29 August 1931, p. 2; Haniel Long, "Why Tribute to an Outlaw?" *The Santa Fe New Mexican,* 2 September 1931, p. 4; Witter Bynner, "Old-timers and New Comers United in Production of 'Billy the Kid,' " *The Santa Fe New Mexican,* 5 September 1931, p. 3. The playbill is reprinted in the "Publications Ephemeral and Exemplary" section of this volume.

7. "Santa Fe Picture at La Fonda Draws Large Audience Wednesday Night," *Santa Fe New Mexican,* 9 January 1932, p. 1. "A Day in Santa Fe," 1931, is part of the Historical Film Collection, New Mexico State Records Center and Archives, Santa Fe. Notes and interviews about the film are also part of the Archives.

8. Ernest Thompson Seton was a longtime friend of Mary Austin and a frequent visitor to Santa Fe. A world famous naturalist, Seton was better known for his books of prose and paintings of wildlife than for his poetry. Born in 1860, he moved to New Mexico in 1930 to establish Seton Village, a 2500 acre community dedicated to the study of nature and the promotion of recreation and the outdoor arts. See Julia M. Seton, *By a Thousand Fires* (Garden City, New York: Doubleday, 1967).

9. Haniel Long, "The Poets' Round-Up," *New Mexico Quarterly Review* 19 (1949): 69-71.

10. "Foreword," *New Mexico Quarterly* 1 (1931): n.p. Also see David William Pugh, "A Study in Literary, Social and University History: The Life and Often Hard Times of the *New Mexico Quarterly,"* unpublished doctoral dissertation, University of New Mexico, 1975.

11. "Letters from *Quarterly* Readers," *New Mexico Quarterly* 1 (1931): 287-89.

12. The University of New Mexico Press was established by the school's Board of Regents in 1929. In a cooperative arrangement with the Museum of New Mexico and the School of American Research in Santa Fe, the University hired Paul A. F. Walter, Jr., as Director of University Publications and Assistant Director of the Museum of New Mexico. Fittingly enough, Walter was the son of Paul A. F. Walter, Sr., the founding editor of *El Palacio.* On August 2, 1930, young Walter received authorization from the Museum of New Mexico to move the *El Palacio* printing plant to the University campus in Albuquerque, where the equipment would be used to print pamphlets and bulletins written by faculty scholars. They would also continue to publish journals produced in Santa Fe, primarily *El Palacio* and the *New Mexico Historical Review.* See Jack Rittenhouse, "A Condensed History of the University of New Mexico Press," unpublished ms. in possession of the Press, n.d.

13. One of *Folksay's* most consistent contributors, Paul Horgan of Roswell, New Mexico, was born in New York and first moved to New Mexico as a boy of eleven, when his father was stricken with tuberculosis. Much like Mary Austin's Gard Sitwell, Horgan had developed a strong attachment to the land and cultures of the state. Employed as a librarian at the New Mexico Military Institute, Horgan devoted much of his time to creating "folk stories" about life in the small Hispanic villages of New Mexico, as well as to writing novels. See, e.g., James M. Day, *Paul Horgan,* Southwest Writers Series 8 (Austin, Texas: Steck-Vaughn, 1967).

14. "The Rydal Press of Santa Fe New Mexico: A Brief Account of Its History and Its Purpose," *The Colophon: The Annual of Bookmaking* (New York: The Colophon, 1938), n.p. This illustrated article is reprinted in the "Publications Ephemeral and Exemplary" section of this volume.

15. Mimeographed document courtesy of Clark Kimball and Charlotte J. Stone, The

Great Southwest Books, Santa Fe. A contemporaneous mimeographed news release announced: "The Rydal Press Enters General Publishing Field—Southwest Bookmakers Celebrate 1st Anniversary—See Manuscripts." Rydal Press president Walter L. Goodwin, Jr., stated that "in addition to fine book printing and binding his group of craftsmen would also publish and distribute suitable book manuscripts. . . . [and any] submitted for publication will receive the attention of a special Editorial Board and if deemed unsuitable for publication by the Press will be directed toward the proper type of publisher wherever possible." The first "suitable" book was to be "a cookbook of Mexican receipts by Erna Fergusson of Albuquerque with decorations by Valentin Vidaurreta of Old Mexico" because, as Goodwin explained: "Our group is the only one exclusively manufacturing fine books in this vast territory and naturally we chose as native a product as we could for our first publishing venture." (A second edition of Fergusson's 1934 *Mexican Cook Book* was published by the University of New Mexico Press in 1945.) Goodwin also printed books for Arrow Editions of New York, notably *Tom*, by e.e. cummings, in 1935.

16. According to Jack Rittenhouse: "Apparently no complete checklist exists of Writers' Editions books. Aided by Walter L. Goodwin, Jr., we submit the following list of seventeen known titles . . . : Baumann, Gustave: *Frijoles Canyon Pictographs* (1939-40). Chavez, Fray Angelico: *Clothed with the Sun* (1939). Church, Peggy Pond: *Familiar Journey* (1936) and *Foretaste* (1933). Corbin, Alice: *A Child's Bouquet:* Fifteen Songs for Children (1935); and *The Sun Turns West* (1933). Davey, William: *Arms, Angels, Epitaphs & Bones* (1935). Fechin, Alexandra: *March of the Past* (1937). Fletcher, John Gould: *XXIV Elegies* (1935). Johnson, Spud: *Horizontal Yellow* (1935). Long, Haniel: *Atlantides* (1933); *Interlinear to Cabeza de Vaca* (1936); *Malinche* (1939); *Pittsburgh Memoranda* (1935); and *Walt Whitman and the Springs of Courage* (1938). Rhodes, Eugene Manlove: *Peñalosa* (1934). Storm, Marion: *The Life of Saint Rose:* First American Saint and the Only American Woman Saint (1937)" ("Southwest Imprints: Writers' Editions," *Book Talk*, New Mexico Book League, Albuquerque, December 1975, p. 4).

17. Philip Stevenson, "Dere Mabel," *Southwest Review* 17 (1932): xix.

18. B. A. Botkin, "The New Mexico Round Table on Regionalism," *New Mexico Quarterly* 3 (1933): 152.

19. Material from both these books has been incorporated into "A Directory of New Mexico Writers" in this volume.

20. John Gould Fletcher, "Comment: The Land of Enchantment," *Poetry: A Magazine of Verse* 43 (1933): 150-52.

21. Philip Stevenson, "Santa Fe: A Study in Integrity," *New Mexico Quarterly* 3 (1933): 125-32.

22. David L. Neuman, "Smoke Talk—A Commentary Re: 'Santa Fe, A Study in Integrity,' " *New Mexico Quarterly* 3 (1933): 249-51.

23. A number of publications carried tributes to Austin that fall. Among them was *Space*, a "little magazine" of creative works. Started in April 1934 by editor B. A. Botkin, who was then at the University of Oklahoma, *Space* came out once a month for a series of twelve issues. During those months it featured frequent contributions from New Mexican writers. Its September 1934 number dedicated to Mary Austin was exclusively New Mexican.

24. Elizabeth Shepley Sergeant, "Mary Austin: A Portrait," *Saturday Review of Literature*, 8 September 1934, p. 96.

25. Marta Weigle, "Introduction" to reprint edition of Raymond Otis, *Miguel of the Bright Mountain* (1936; Albuquerque: University of New Mexico Press, 1977), pp. xx-xxi. Established in 1922, Santa Fe's Volunteer Fire Company was manned by several members of the literary colony, including Raymond Otis, Witter Bynner, and John Evans. See Raymond Otis, "The Santa Fe Volunteer Fire Department: A History of Its Life and Reputation," no publication details given, but a copy is in the Vertical Files, History

Library, Museum of New Mexico, Santa Fe. Also see: "1921 Holocaust Was Start of Santa Fe Fire Department," *The New Mexican*, 29 October 1959, p. 14. A photograph and "A Christmas Ballad of the Fire Fighter's Family," by Ruth Laughlin Barker and Will Barker, appear in the "Portraits and Self-Portraits" section of this volume.

26. James Kraft, "Biographical Introduction," *Selected Poems, The Works of Witter Bynner*, vol. 1 (New York: Farrar, Straus, Giroux, 1978), pp. lxv-lxvi. Also see: "Robert Frost Pleases Large Audience with Readings and Witty Wisecracks Under Auspices of Writers' Editions," *The Santa Fe New Mexican*, 7 August 1935, p. 5; and James Kraft, ed., *Selected Letters, The Works of Witter Bynner*, vol. 5 (New York: Farrar, Straus, Giroux, 1981), pp. 80, 148-49, 156-57.

27. This sense of discontent is noticeably lacking in Ross Calvin's *Sky Determines: An Interpretation of the Southwest* (New York: Macmillan, 1934), in which he demonstrates how the physical characteristics of New Mexico have shaped its cultural and economic development. The Rector of the Episcopalian Church in Silver City, Calvin took particular comfort in the conviction that, despite problems arising from human frailties, "when the last Americano . . . follows the last Spaniard and the last red man into the shadows, this will still be the same poignantly unforgettable land of beauty" (p. 333).

1936-1941

In no other state of this union is the trend of life so clearly shaped by art as in New Mexico. Art has rescued this state from the commonplace and made it conscious of its own fine character. The arts have kept Santa Fe from becoming an "up-to-date burg" and made it unique and beautiful among the capitals of our country. In the monolithic Palace of the Governors, the Art Gallery, La Fonda, in many public buildings, business houses, and in countless residences, the fine old architectural tradition of the region has been preserved and population and values have increased amazingly. Santa Fe doesn't advertise for tourists or residents. They can't be kept away. Artists and writers constitute only a small percentage of the population, but their influence is wherever you look. Taos was a sordid little mud village when some of us first knew it. Now no one visits the Southwest without going to Taos. Its artists and writers are known throughout the world. The town is one of the jewels of New Mexico, and of this country. . . .

The conditions that bring forth great art are inherent in the soil, skies, wind, clouds, spaces of the great southwest. We who live in it have long felt the eternal character of these vast spaces, silent but vibrant with life and color—subtle, mysterious, elemental. Artists and writers are revealing this to the world. In arousing in the minds of our people consciousness of the beauty of this southwestern land, in restoring this heritage of history, tradition, poetry, folk life, a priceless service is rendered to our state and its people. Painters and poets and historians are helping to shape the trend of life here as few realize. There can be no finer education for any people than to be brought to know the beauty of their homeland; the nobility of their history; the dignity of the simple folk ways in which are rooted all the great spiritual forces of civilization. Our newspaper goes far beyond the ordinary service of the press when it dedicates a special edition like this to the artists and writers, a group of men and women who are devoting their lives to a fine public service with no hope of reward other than the joy of doing it.

—Edgar Lee Hewett, "Introduction" to "Artists and Writers: A List of Prominent Artists and Writers of New Mexico," edited by Alison Dana and Margaret Lohlker as a special issue of *The Santa Fe New Mexican*, 26 June 1940.

On January 16, 1936, Lynn Riggs's new drama, *Russet Mantle,* opened at New York's Masque Theatre. The play, which "deals with a group of NY escapists who have come to Santa Fe to get away from it all (only to find all of it here?)," had a successful run on Broadway, on national tour, and subsequently at Lawrence Langner's Theatre in Westport, Connecticut.[1] To Easterners viewing these productions, Santa Fe must have seemed naive and fatuous. A sense of desolation pervades the comedy; neither Santa Fe's setting nor its citizens, whether native or newcomer, offer a genuine escape from or a possible answer to the nation's plight. Indeed, the quote from *Hamlet* which gives the drama its title ("But, look, the morn, in russet mantle clad, /Walks o'er the dew of yon high eastward hill") would seem to mean that for Riggs at least, the East must now revive the West, as in many respects it did while President Franklin D. Roosevelt's New Deal unfolded.

Like the rest of the nation, New Mexico suffered acutely the aftereffects of drought and depression. The art colonists were no less affected than their fellow citizens, and they too sought government relief when it became available. Federal Project Number One, the first of six Works Progress Administration (WPA) white-collar relief projects, was officially announced on August 2, 1935. Four of its five subprojects—the Federal Art Project, the Federal Music Project, the Federal Writers' Project, and later the Historical Records Survey— directly or indirectly supported various New Mexico art colonists, since significant Federal Theater Project activities were never organized in the state.[2]

Poet, writer and lecturer Ina Sizer Cassidy was appointed state director of the New Mexico Federal Writers' Project (NMFWP), apparently at the recommendation of John Collier, Commissioner of Indian Affairs.[3] From October 14, 1935, she conducted FWP business first in her home at 924 Canyon Road, Santa Fe, and after Christmas in Room 9 of the Renehan Building, then just off the Plaza. The NMFWP was initially allotted thirty relief workers, but it was hard to fill that quota with persons qualified both for writing and for relief. On February 7, 1936, for example, state WPA administrator Lea Rowland addressed a despairing letter to national FWP director Henry G. Alsberg, claiming: "It is difficult for the people in the East to realize the illiteracy with which we have to cope in New Mexico, as the State which is large in area, sparsely populated (433,000 popul.) ranks second in the U.S. in illiteracy."[4]

Although New Mexico's FWP quota was raised to fifty-five relief workers in May 1936, a proposed curtailment of all the federal arts programs later that year prompted Santa Fe artists to meet at the Little Red Schoolhouse, 402 Canyon Road. According to a notice in the December 2, 1936, issue of *The Santa Fe New Mexican:* "All writers and those interested in the welfare of art in New Mexico are [also] invited to attend." Artist Will Shuster proposed a permanent organization patterned after the Taos Art Association, "to include in this group writers, painters, sculptors and musicians . . . also . . . the formation of a similar group in Albuquerque and the subsequent consolidation of the Taos, Santa Fe and Albuquerque groups in a state organization." A committee composed of McHarg Davenport, Will Shuster, Wyatt Davis, Carlos Vierra, Datus Myers, Ina Sizer Cassidy, and Harvey Breit met at Cassidy's home on December 3 to organize the Santa Fe Art Association and "to take immediate action to prevent the curtailment of any federal arts projects, by the complete support of the WPA and TRAP [Treasury Art Project] administrators to that end."[5] On December 5, they sent telegrams protesting the cut-backs to Governor Tingley and various arts project officials, including Cassidy.

Later protests were lodged using Santa Fe Arts Association letterhead, which lists Wyatt Davis as president, Katherine Gay as vice president, and Vivian Morris as secretary-treasurer. In February 1937, the Arts Association's welfare committee, under acting chair Helen Cramp McCrossen, launched a campaign to reinstate former New York City writer Paul Reeve and to remove novelist Raymond Otis, alleging that the latter was wealthy and thus undeserving of employment on the NMFWP. Otis answered these charges in a letter of February 24, 1937, itemizing outstanding debts on each of his three houses and proclaiming himself "property poor," as well as a hardworking writer who, since his graduation from Yale in 1924, had "written seven novels, two of which were published in England and one in America, many short stories, two plays and several articles."[6] McCrossen's committee countered with a letter to FWP director Alsberg, claiming that comparatively well off men like Otis should not be allowed to hold "jobs that should be available to men like Mr. Reeve, who is literally underfed." However, Ina Sizer Cassidy had already written Alsberg to explain poet Reeve's earlier unsatisfactory record with the NMFWP and to laud Otis's skill as a rewrite editor, who was also "assisting Mr. [John Gaw] Meem in the completion of the material on the architecture." She summarily dismissed the group she had helped organize:

The Santa Fe Arts Association is a new association, organized ostensibly to support the proposed Coronado Cuarto Centennial celebration in . . . 1940 and to protect the interests of resident New Mexico artists and writers, as against artists and writers imported from other states . . . as it seems was done in the Texas centennial. At the present time however, its entire attention and efforts seem to be directed against the Federal Art and Writers' Projects. . . .

Incidentally, it might be mentioned that the membership of the Santa Fe Arts Association does not include the real writers and artists of Santa Fe, but is composed mostly of the lesser known ones and amateurs, therefore they cannot be said to represent the real sentiments of the Santa Fe creative workers.

Otis retained his job, and Reeve was not rehired.

The first tangible results of the New Mexico FWP appeared in 1937. A thirty-two-page *Calendar of Events*, written by Project workers, illustrated by New Mexico Federal Art Project artists, and sponsored by the Santa Fe Civic League and Chamber of Commerce, was printed at Rydal Press in Santa Fe. Two numbers of what was to have been a mimeographed periodical, *Over the Turquoise Trail* ("Title suggested by Alice Corbin Henderson's *The Turquoise Trail*, an Anthology of New Mexico Poetry, to which acknowledgment is herewith made"), also appeared in the spring. These issues contain poems, stories, various items of folklore, historical notes, document translations, "Did you know that. . . ?" features, and miscellaneous notices. When the second number was sent to Washington on June 17, officials there forebade further publication without an outside sponsor, as required by new federal regulations.

At various times between October 1935 and August 1939, the NMFWP subprojects included: Coordinating (editorial work in the Santa Fe office), Translators' (primarily documents in the Museum of New Mexico, Santa Fe), Reporting, Folklore, and the American Guide—the latter three carried out in Santa Fe and four subdivisions of the state. Work on the all-important state guide proceeded very slowly, however, while the collection and translation of Hispano folklore and folklife flourished. Creative writing per se was discouraged, and some NMFWP writers' dissatisfaction with the more pedestrian editorial and journalistic tasks required of them may have spurred their involvement with a new literary magazine in the autumn of 1938. NMFWP offices housed the new publication, which was sponsored by the New Mexico Writers' Guild yet carried the same title as the earlier NMFWP mimeographed periodicals. *Over the Turquoise Trail* was introduced as:

. . . a publication of articles, stories, and poems by New Mexico writers, most of them young, all of them eager.

The future of any region depends on the enthusiastic pursuits of worth-while matters by its people. We believe that literature is signally worthwhile, and that its future in New Mexico depends on the concerted efforts of all those interested—the creative workers and recipients alike. To give expression to these efforts we offer this experimental periodical which we hope will establish a medium between these two groups. We trust that this publication will be reguarded [sic] as a notebook of work in progress. We call attention to the format. Far from being apologetic for its graphic modesty, we recommend it to any group inhibited by lack of funds. OVER THE TURQUOISE TRAIL demostrates [sic], we hope, the importance of offering contributions indigenous to New Mexico, to a public concerned in the future of the literature of the Southwest.[7]

This first and sole number contains articles by John Gould Fletcher, Mabel Dodge Luhan, and Alfred Morang; poems by Norman Macleod, Alfred H. Stoddard, Eleanor B. Pesonen, Ina Sizer Cassidy, William Pillin, and Vesta A. Kiker; "folklore" by Aileen Nusbaum and Cassidy; and stories by Roy A. Keech and B. W. Kay. The magazine, with a cover designed by Howard West, cost thirty-five cents.

Unrest within the NMFWP eventually focused on state director Cassidy. Poet Norman Macleod, a refugee from the New York City FWP briefly employed by the NMFWP during the summer of 1936, later included a section on his Santa Fe experiences with that "redoutable elderly woman . . . Mrs. Crotchety [Cassidy]—whose only claim to being literary resided in the fact that she had written several rather sketchy poems about lover come back to me, etc.," and her assistant, "Mrs. Alice Hendricks [Henderson], yes-woman . . . and a poet—a rather good one, in fact" in his unabashedly autobiographical novel, *You Get What You Ask For* (1939). Protagonist Gordon Graham soon quits his eighty-five-dollar-a-month job because:

Gordon decided that his life couldn't continue away from Sonja, in Santa Fe where the beer cost so much. He would have to return to New York!
There was nothing for him in Santa Fe—that entr'acte for escapists. Mecca for tuberculars, where death splintered wooden coffins into the crucifixes of defeat!
The life of Santa Fe was buried in the past.
The Trojan women on the Federal Writers' Project in New Mexico could have their astrology! D. H. Lawrence had said—the light blinds them. There was too much sunlight and they couldn't get out of the darkness.[8]

In March 1938, Thomas Files Bledsoe, journalist, poet and would-be novelist, and for ten months (until September 1937) a NMFWP rewrite editor, wrote a short article entitled "Why a Federal Writers' Project?" He sent a copy to FWP director Alsberg in Washington with the concluding note: "What I ask of you is no more than justice and that the Writers' Project in this state and other states be conducted for the benefit of those for whom they are created." Bledsoe laid the blame for the Project's failure to produce the crucial (in Washington eyes) state guide squarely on Ina Sizer Cassidy:

The Director of the Project on which I worked is a woman past middle age whose sole proof of literary ability has been the occasional publication of a poem and the publication in the State magazine of a monthly article, generally regarded as of inferior workmanship and content. She has not and probably could not support herself by any regular journalistic or creative writing. As her appointment could not be justified on the basis of qualifications as a writer, neither could it be defended because of actual need, for she owns choice residential property with two rent houses that provide a substantial monthly revenue.

He denounced Cassidy's criticism of others' work as "harsh and superficial" and objected to her "practice to sign her name as co-author to copy of any merit before sending it to the Washington office." However, it was not until January 31, 1939, when, despite strong letters of support from U.S. Congressman John J. Dempsey, Witter Bynner and Alice Corbin Henderson, Ina Sizer Cassidy was demoted to researcher at a salary of $100 a month, about half her director's pay of $191.60 monthly.[9] After several weeks' vacation, she supposedly returned to write a survey of New Mexico arts and crafts. Her refusal to cooperate and to produce was criticized repeatedly, and she was finally fired in May.

Meanwhile, writer Aileen Nusbaum, Cassidy's former assistant, served as Acting State Director until her resignation for health reasons on August 31, 1939. Her administration was enlightened quite literally by moving the NMFWP offices from the condemned Renehan Building to 418 College Street in El Parian Analco, "('the meeting place' in the old Indian district of Santa Fe, or 'Barrio Analco') . . . the recreation of a traditional New Mexican plaza, with entertainment, restaurants, and various services and booths as well as a shop for sale of crafts."[10] As Nusbaum wrote Alsberg on March 15, 1939: "The fact that we have proper light and ventilation alone proves the wisdom of the change."

With considerable help from "loaned" FWP writers, notably Jacob Scher from Chicago and Vardis Fisher from Idaho,[11] Nusbaum managed to finish the bulk of the state guide work before her resignation. The tours for the volume proved especially troublesome, and Nusbaum assigned Scher and Charles E. Minton to their revision and completion. On June 13, 1939, Alsberg wrote a lengthy critique and exhortation to Nusbaum:

Try to make the readers see the white mid-summer haze, the dust that rises in unpaved New Mexican streets, the slithery red earth roads of winter, the purple shadows of later afternoon, the brilliant yellow of autumn foliage against brilliant blue skies, the pseudo-cowboys in the tourist centers, the blank-faced Indians who are secretly amused by white antics, the patched and irregular walls of the older adobes; make him understand the social cleavages and jealousies, the strangely rotarianized "Indian dances," the life of the transplanted Oklahomans, Texans, Mexicans, Greenwich Villagers, and so on.

A letter of July 20 reiterates this request, pleading that "we want the type of visual description that Steinbeck would give—that is, descriptions of the types of buildings common to smaller New Mexican towns, mention of color, smells, sounds, signs, and above all, of the types of people seen along the streets." By this time, novelist Vardis Fisher had been in Santa Fe for two weeks, and he answered Alsberg on July 24: "Nobody knows any better than I how thin some of these are; but it is impossible at this late stage to give them the Steinbeck color and details asked for . . . [because] the person or persons who logged under Mrs. Cassidy did a rotten job of it—a job so bad that it is almost beyond belief." After his return to Boise, Fisher wrote Alsberg again, recommending tour editor Minton for promotion and remarking rather truculently: "While in Santa Fe, I saw nothing of the country, having had plenty to do in trying to edit the volume in three weeks."[12]

The 1939 Emergency Relief Appropriation Act reorganized the Works Progress Administration as the Work Projects Administration, in which the renamed and revamped Art, Music, and Writers' Programs were to be administered under the Community Service Division. Charles E. Minton directed the New Mexico Writers' Program until its termination in 1943. He supervised far fewer workers, most of them at the Santa Fe office. Their main task was to finish the myriad final details on *New Mexico: A Guide to the Colorful State*, finally published by Hastings House of New York in August 1940, but not received in the state until mid-September, after most of the Coronado Cuarto Centennial celebrations, various state and federally sponsored programs commemorating Francisco Vásquez de Coronado's 1540-42 expedition through the Spanish Southwest. The *Guide's* late publication date, its orange and blue cover and even the subtitle brought cries of dismay from both Minton and the volume's sponsors, the University of New Mexico and the Coronado Cuarto Centennial Commission.[13]

Only two other New Mexico Writers' Program books—*New Mexico, American Recreational Series No. 30* (Northport, New York: Bacon & Wieck, 1941), and *The Spanish-American Song and Game Book* (New York: Barnes, 1942)—were printed, although an ambitious publications program ranging from the nationally instigated "History of Grazing" and "Health Almanac" to local folk cultural studies such as those on the Hispano villages of Las Placitas and Cordova were planned. By that time, however, war-related concerns had usurped all others.

From a national perspective, Alice Corbin Henderson, Norman Macleod, Raymond Otis, Jacob Scher, and of course Vardis Fisher probably enjoyed the best literary reputations of those associated with the NMFWP. Both cowboy song and story writer-collector N. Howard ("Jack") Thorp, then of Alameda, New Mexico, and Taos artist and writer Blanche C. Grant, who were employed as field writers on the Project, received more modest notice outside the state. In retrospect, however, the strength of the NMFWP lay not so much in the Project-sponsored original work of such individuals as in their editorial contributions and encouragement of local field writers, particularly Hispanos from northern New Mexico.

Although the New Mexico guide includes materials from throughout the state and its various cultures, the bulk of the extant NMFWP manuscripts are devoted to Hispano folklore and folklife. Notable among these contributors, most of whom received scant contemporary notice, are Lorin W. Brown of Taos and Cordova; Bright Lynn, a junior at New Mexico Normal (now Highlands) University in Las Vegas, where contributor Dr. Lester B. Raines taught in the English Department; Lou Sage Batchen of Las Placitas; Annette Hesch Thorp, who joined the Writers' Program after her husband Jack's death on June 4, 1940; and Reyes N. Martinez of Arroyo Hondo, then a high school student who was actively encouraged by Alice Corbin Henderson when she was an editor from 1936 to 1937.[14] Both Nina Otero-Warren, who published *Old Spain in Our Southwest* in 1936, and Aurora Lucero-White (later Lea), most of whose work on the Hispanic folklore of New Mexico did not appear until after 1940, were briefly associated with the New Mexico Writers' Project.

Although her interest in local Hispanic folk culture had begun earlier, Cleofas M. Jaramillo was probably encouraged by her brother Reyes N. Martinez's NMFWP experiences. Influenced by J. Frank Dobie's invitation to join the Texas Folklore Society, Jaramillo had started La Sociedad Folklórica de Santa Fe in 1935, drafting organizational rules "that the society should be composed of only thirty members, all of whom must be of Spanish descent, and that the meetings must be conducted in the Spanish language, with the aim of preserving our language, customs and traditions."[15] Members, who included Aurora Lucero-White, participated in Santa Fe Fiesta and later the Coronado Cuarto Centennial. After reading an article in *Holland's Magazine* on Hispanic cookery by Mrs. Elizabeth Willis De Huff, Jaramillo marveled:

. . . It was a three-page article, nicely written and illustrated, but very deficient as to knowledge of our Spanish cooking. In giving the recipe for making *tortillas* it read, "Mix bread flour with water, add salt." How nice and light these must be without yeast or shortening! And still these smart Americans make money with their writing, and we who know the correct way sit back and listen.[16]

Neither Jaramillo nor her friend Aurora Lucero-White were content to "sit back and listen." Both published modest volumes of folklore with Marceil and Maurice Taylor's young Seton Village Press in Santa Fe.[17]

Another native Hispanic New Mexican, Fray Angelico Chavez, had by then established his reputation as a poet and short story writer who often used themes from local folklore. His first book of poems, *Clothed with the Sun*, was published by Writers' Editions in 1939, and his first collection of short stories, with his own illustrations, *New Mexico Triptych: Being three panels and three accounts: 1. The Angel's New Wings; 2. The Penitente Thief; 3. Hunchback Madonna*, came out in 1940 with St. Anthony Guild Press of Paterson, New Jersey.[18] Like many Anglo and Hispano writers of the twentieth century, Chavez portrays the Penitente Brotherhood as an important part of traditional Hispano culture in northern New Mexico. His portrayal of Brotherhood beliefs and practices is sympathetic and non-sensational, like Alice Corbin Henderson's non-fictional *Brothers of Light: The Penitentes of the Southwest* (1937). Unfortunately, this was not always the case in many contemporary fictional and non-fictional works.

Sensationalized misrepresentations of the Brotherhood proliferated following the murder of freelance journalist Carl N. Taylor on February 5, 1936, near Cedar Crest in the Sandia Mountains east of Albuquerque. Modesto Trujillo, Taylor's fifteen-year-old houseboy, committed the crime, apparently to rob his employer. However, since Taylor had been writing an article on the Brotherhood, his literary agent and editors in New York "told the Associated Press Thursday that they were not entirely convinced that robbery was the sole motive in the crime and that Taylor may have been the victim of some strange Penitente plot."[19] The case made good copy nationwide, prompting such lurid banner headlines as:

BOY SCOUT SAYS HE KILLED WRITER (*New York Times*, February 7)
BRUTAL MURDER OF WANDERING WRITER UNVEILS WEIRD NEW MEXICO
  TORTURE CULT RITES HE WAS ABOUT TO EXPOSE (*The Cleveland News*, February 8)
BOY'S CONFESSION IN KILLING OF WRITER FAILS TO CALM CULT
  VENGEANCE (*New York American*, March 1)[20]

A purported "documentary" entitled "The Penitente Murder Case" was quickly filmed, and its release brought a letter of protest from

Governor Clyde Tingley to Mr. Will Hays, chairman of the National Board of Censorship in Hollywood:

. . . I have been told also that advertisements show nude women being lashed by flagellants and are shown standing at a cross in the attitude of crucifixion. If the advertisements are an indication of what the picture itself is like it is a libel on the State of New Mexico and on the penitenties [sic] and is an appeal to cheap sensationalism.

The picture will be banned in New Mexico if I have to make use of my police powers to prevent it.[21]

Although investigation proved conclusively that the Brotherhood was in no way implicated, no retractions appeared nationally. The case provided a windfall for the pulps and yellow journals, as well as some more reputable publications.[22]

By the time of Taylor's slaying, literary agents and publishers of all kinds were accustomed to receiving work from New Mexico writers and often visited their clients in Santa Fe, Taos and Albuquerque. Publisher Alfred A. Knopf, for example—whose list included books by Willa Cather, Witter Bynner, Dorothy Thomas, Erna Fergusson, and Conrad Richter—and his wife Blanche were occasional visitors. The Macmillan Company also sent representatives regularly to Santa Fe.[23] In fact, a sixteen-page mimeographed "Southwest Book List for 1938'39," put out by Santa Fe Book and Stationery Company Incorporated, included some 280 adult and juvenile titles and names of 88 "Writers Living in and About Santa Fe."[24]

Other evidence for the recognition and institutionalization of the arts in Santa Fe and Taos (and in Albuquerque, where the University of New Mexico held sway) is found in Santa Fe's Arsuna School of Fine Arts and Taos's Harwood Foundation. Mary Austin's Camino del Monte Sol *Casa Querida* housed the Arsuna School and its gallery. According to a city guidebook of 1939:

The Arsuna School of Fine Arts in Santa Fe carries out the tradition of this cultural cross roads of the Southwest. The word Arsuna means ART IS ONE, and the school was founded three years ago with this in mind.

Maurice M. Lichtmann, Dean of the School and Head of the Music Department is a graduate of the Royal Conservatory and Meisterschule of Vienna, and has concertized in Europe and America. The faculty includes Alfred Morang, internationally known short story writer and art critic, in charge of the Writing Department; Raymond Jonson, one of the leading non-objective painters of this country, and other painting, writing and music instructors covering the entire range of contemporary art.

Mrs. Clyde Gartner, President of Arsuna, is a lecturer upon art and music, and her wide grasp of the problems confronting the student, enables her to select significant speakers for the lecture courses, which includes all the Arts, Archaeology, Philosophy and Science.

Among the lecturers who have appeared at Arsuna's AT HOMES on the first and third Sundays of each month are such world-known names as: Dr. Edgar L. Hewett, Kenneth Chapman, Dr. Reginald Fisher, Dane Rudhyar, Dr. H. P. Mera, Harold Butcher and John Gould Fletcher.

The student at Arsuna is in constant touch with the creative life of the world and he has the undeniable advantage of association with the best talent of Europe and America. The artistic tomorrows of any country depend upon its schools, and Arsuna is unique in that it offers the best in so many branches of the arts.[25]

In Taos, the Harwood Foundation program was less ambitious, but the library, gallery, Laughing Horse Bookstall, occasional lectures, classes, and even a Book Review Club stimulated the "organized" literary scene.

Local newspapers in Santa Fe especially had long reported literary activities and thus contributed to their local visibility and increasing organization. E. Dana Johnson served as editor of Bronson Cutting's *Santa Fe New Mexican* from 1913 to 1937, and he proved a steadfast supporter of the arts. In her obituary essay, Alice Corbin Henderson describes him as "a native New Mexican, in every sense except of having been born here, whatever concerned New Mexico concerned him—vitally, intimately, personally":

One remembers countless instances in which it was his pen that carried the day—as for instance the saving of the Sanctuario [sic] at Chimayo. . . . Similarly, he supported every cause and movement that tended to keep New Mexico, and Santa Fe its ancient capital, a symbol of the races that made it—to preserve its essential character and integrity. Not to keep it different in the sense of just being different, as a sales point, but to be itself; as it is, and was, and as he wanted it to remain. For the Santa Fe plaza and the road along the river-bed, and shade trees menaced by thoughtless, unnecessary destruction, he waged many a fight.

He "tied in" and was one of all the civic and social groups— merchants, archaeologists, artists and writers. His participation in The Poets' Round-Up was always one of the highlights of that summer event—where he invariably captured the audience with a piece of effective, sparkling light verse—written that morning, or the day before! Briefly, he was interested in life; and the essential gaiety of his spirit, united with an underlying deep seriousness of purpose, was an inspiring stimulus to any group and any cause.[26]

During the summer before his death, Johnson edited *The Santa Fe Plaza*, an eight-page weekly which made its debut on August 1, 1937:

The SANTA FE PLAZA will be
full of the atmosphere
and activities of
OLD SANTA FE
the first issue may
perhaps give you the general
idea. If you are a
Full-time or Part-time Santa Fean,
Here or Elsewhere,
there will be something of
interest to you here about the unusual
life of the Villa Antigua . . .

This short-lived paper was printed at The Rydal Press, which had just moved from Tesuque to 998 Canyon Road in Santa Fe. There, printer Walter Goodwin was able from time to time to join forces with Willard F. Clark of Clark's Studio, whose print shop had operated in town since 1928.

True to his word "to be the connecting link between extra-territorial Santa Feans and the old town," E. Dana Johnson reported news of current and erstwhile residents, visitors, and area artists and writers alike. Among the more illustrious visitors were:

Playwright-wifed, medium-heighted, dapper-dressed N.Y. journalistic sophisticate Editorial Tycoon Henry R. Luce of *Time* and also of *Life* and *Fortune*, etc., accompanied by Spouse-celebrity Claire Booth, creator of Broadway-thrilling theater-goer-wowing 50-women-and-no-men-cast current dramatic hit *Women* [who] Fondaed, touristed, Indian-detoured and weekended in Santa Fe. . . . Luce warms up about Fonda and Santa Fe; atmosphere mellows metropolitan protective aloofness of the great. (August 7, p. 7)

Johnson also published occasional verse, primarily humorous comments on the contemporary Santa Fe scene.

Spud Johnson (no relation) contributed a column entitled "The Perambulator," in which he and an imaginary alter named Jasper reported "literary gossip" from Taos and Santa Fe. In the August first column he described perambulations during which he saw page proofs for *Fantasy and Fugue*—poems by Marina Wister (Dasburg), *Edge of Taos Desert* by Mabel Dodge Luhan, *Midas of the Rockies* by Frank Waters, and *Little Valley* by Raymond Otis. He also noted the publication of Isis Harrington's short story about a Navajo boy, "Nah-le Kah-de," and Alice Corbin Henderson's *Brothers of Light*, as well as:

A new novel by D. J. Hall called "Perilous Sanctuary" [which] is laid in a Penitente community [in the Sandias] and discusses the brotherhood more or less learnedly. It is being quite popular here, although "Time" dismissed it snootily in a recent issue as "another example of the Southwest's inevitable incitement to mystical riot in English writers." Well, well! (August 1, p. 2)

Spud and Jasper's next column reported the new Writers' Edition publication, Marian Storm's *The Life of Saint Rose*, other Rydal Press news, and notes about Lynn Riggs and Evelyn Scott. Also:

To go with our list of new-as-possible literary gossip: Here's a new book we'll bet a red token none of you have read: "Hall of Mirrors," by Lenore Marshall. Neither have we. It isn't out yet. But it's by one of our newest New Mexico Writers. Lenore Marshall and her husband have been out at Bishops Lodge for only a few weeks, but they say they feel like natives already and are going to stay as long as they possibly can. (August 7, p. 3)

Perhaps their most interesting announcement concerned *The New Mexico Sentinel*, a weekly newspaper then published in Albuquerque:

New also, and arousing much interest in town, is the New Mexico Writers page in the *Sentinel*, which was inaugurated July 21st. Three issues have now appeared with articles and poems by Haniel Long, the editor of the page, Jean Toomer (who lives in New York but has spent much time here during the past few years—in fact he got married in Taos a year or so ago), Witter Bynner, (who is just back from several weeks in New York City), Robert Walker (who is sick-a-bed), Paul Horgan (who spent last week-end in town, but is spending most of the summer in Roswell writing a play), Orville [sic] Ricketts (who is one of our best-known New Mexico news editors), William Davey (who is summering in Taos), Dorothy Belle Flanagan (Mrs. Levi Hughes, Jr., who is now on the staff of the Santa Fe Plaza), Peggy Pond Church (whose latest book is "Familiar Journey"), Marina Wister (whose new book of poems we announced last week,), Paul Reeves (who is now in Chimayo and whose new book of verse may be published by Writers' Editions) . . . and others. ("Go on, mention yourself," prompts Jasper.) (August 7, p. 2)

The *Sentinel's* "New Mexico Writers: A weekly page of prose and verse contributed by New Mexicans, at home or abroad" soon came to be known simply as the Writers' Page. Editor Haniel Long was assisted by "associates" Witter Bynner, Erna Fergusson, Paul Horgan and Frieda Lawrence. The editor ended his brief inaugural contribution, a tribute to Carl Sandburg and his 1936 volume, *The People, Yes,* with a discreet paragraph:

The day he came into my workroom and offered me this literary page in *The Sentinel,* my friend Cyrus McCormick must have been astonished by my enthusiasm. As great a pleasure as any in being given such a page to edit, is the chance it affords to speak of somebody one admires, as I admire Sandburg, poet of an always new and trustworthy mysticism.

A photograph of Long by Ernest W. Knee accompanied the article. It appeared with a series of "Meditations: J. T. and P. B." by Jean Toomer, "Four Sketches" by Spud Johnson, a character sketch entitled "Hughie" by Witter Bynner, "It Didn't Rain: A Prose Poem" by Thomas U. Calkins, and a photograph of the words "There is nothing but the proof to make of that which one thinks presents serious obstacles. I continue therefore my studies," with the caption: "Robert Walker of Santa Fe translated this sentence from Cezanne's letters, and then cut it on wood, because he believes we should read more slowly and thoughtfully, the words of the great."

Cyrus McCormick moved his *New Mexico Sentinel* editorial offices from Albuquerque to Santa Fe, where the first issue was published on October 20, 1937. The Writers' Page thrived, despite misgivings which Long later voiced in his "Jottings in Farewell" of January 1, 1939:

As no American newspaper had attempted a literary page of this particular kind, to be devoted to prose and poetry written by persons in the locality, we were in the dark at first as to whether there would be enough material to keep the page going for more than a few months. Privately, I was afraid that a prejudice of mine against the forms of self-pity as one sees them in the magazines or book world might create a problem—for self-pity is often engaging and clever, or even has a certain boy-soprano-ish beauty from an ostensible desire to "save" mankind and the world by this or that panacea.

Knowing that my associate editors would stand by and help me out in case of need, I went ahead. It happened that there was no problem, no dearth of manuscripts. Here in New Mexico we are living on a volcano of expressiveness, and the lid may blow off any day. I once told H. B. Hening, walking across the Plaza with him, that every third New Mexican wrote verses, every fourth had a novel concealed in his desk, and every fifth was just finishing a four-act play. Mr. Hening laughed. He thought I was joking.

Besides publishing works by first-time and seasoned writers, the Page also carried controversies about the difficulties of writing in Santa Fe's easy-going ambience, about the quality of New Mexico art and writing, about local writers' philosophies of their art, and about women's role in the arts.

On Sunday, July 24, 1938, the Writers' Page celebrated its first anniversary by printing numerous, primarily laudatory "Letters on our Birthday" and mourned the passing of Raymond Otis—"good citizen, good writer, good friend"—on July 13. By October 9, the Page's logo was changed to read: "NEW MEXICO WRITERS: Homemade literature made by hand and contributed by New Mexicans, at home or abroad." The editor and his associates remained the same throughout, however.

Cyrus McCormick announced the demise of the Writers' Page in his New Year's Day editorial of 1939:

> To my mind the Writers' Page has been by all odds the most stimulating section of a newspaper that works to purvey only the best. It would have been pleasing if the appearance of literature week after week had drawn forth more comment from the potential array of supporters. . . .
> The Writers' Page should not be regarded as anything but an artistic success. It is unfortunate that it must now become one of the many literary ventures in the United States which have flourished for a time and have then been compelled to cease publication because of the lack of some element necessary for continuing prosperity. This fact I personally regret. The fact that I have been associated with Haniel Long in publishing New Mexico Writers for a year and a half will remain a deep satisfaction.[27]

Long ended his "New Mexico Writers" as he had begun it, this time with praise for *The Pajarito Plateau and Its Ancient People*—"a book, just published [University of New Mexico Press], by a most distinguished New Mexico writer, Dr. Edgar L. Hewett," and a tribute to its author:

> Long before I came to the southwest or knew anything of Santa Fe, I had read Dr. Hewett and admired his way of writing. I copied certain of his sentences into my notebook because I liked the turn of them. They had been put together by somebody who relished the difficulties of building a sentence so that its meaning would be as clear as possible.
> "The Pajarito Plateau and Its Ancient People" is a book by a man who knows how to build a phrase, a sentence, a paragraph, a

chapter, a philosophy of life. "I have tried to give you," says Dr. Hewett in his Introduction, "a picture from our Southwest, to lead you to contemplate the mighty forces which shaped it, to think of the subtle influences which abide in it, which moulded life in its myriad forms and shaped the destinies of the men who inhabited it. These are old, old trails over which we have walked in the Southwest in order to bring the experiences of the past into the life of today. Nature is our surest teacher, and man's place and part are fairly clear."

Not only do these unassuming words seem to me real writing but Dr. Hewett fulfills his promise and shows me this country as I have never seen it before, far richer, far more intricate in its hold on my imagination and my sympathy. I was conscious of his achievement yesterday afternoon, as I watched the sunset: the lilac color that deepened on the Jemez mountains and their preliminary plateaus and hills, was richly and freshly peopled for me by his book. He has performed the rare service of adjusting us better to our landscape and background. Who can do more?

New Mexicans "at home and abroad" who were disappointed by the demise of the Writers' Page could at least subscribe (at two cents a copy, one dollar per year) to *The Horse Fly: Smallest and Most Inadequate Newspaper Ever Published.* Spud Johnson had launched the one-sheet weekly in Taos on July 9, 1938. He printed it on his own press, announcing:

But it is frankly an experiment. Even a miniature publication has to have news and advertising gathered, has to have the copy written, has to have the type set up and has to have it printed, then distributed . . . and whether one lean fellow can do all of these things in the space of one week and still have time to eat and sleep has yet to be satisfactorily proved.

Even when its work force was incapacitated by influenza, the "miniature publication" prospered and eventually joined the county newspaper *El Crepusculo* and then *The Taos News* as a column.

The Horse Fly soon became a kind of headline news bureau, police blotter, weather report, society column and community bulletin board, especially when local artists and writers were concerned. Thus, Johnson included notices like:

NOVELIST Frank Waters, who spent last summer in Taos, is back in New Mexico again, staying in Mora. He was a visitor in town last week-end. (9 July 1938)

THORNTON WILDER, novelist and playwright of note, arrived in Taos Friday with his sister for a two-week visit. (23 July 1938)

Visitors from Santa Fe this week were GINA KNEE and Novelist OLIVER LA FARGE.[28] (30 July 1938)

Marina DASBURG has returned to her home near Ranchos. She was called east a month ago by the sudden death of her father, OWEN WISTER. (27 August 1938)

Bobby and Katherine Bright, who have spent the summer & fall on the Hawk Ranch, are leaving for California within the next few days.[29] (5 November 1938)

James and John Karavas are entertaining the artists & writers of Taos (what's left of them) at their annual elk dinner this evening in the lounge of their hospitable and popular hotel [El Greco]. (21 January 1939)

Novelist Myron Brinig is expected to arrive in Taos sometime early in June. He plans to rent Mabel Luhan's 'Pink House,' and to remain there throughout the summer. . . . Mr. and Mrs. Robert Bright have returned from California and are again at Del Monte ranch for the summer. . . . Clarice Short is expected to return home this week-end. (27 May 1939)

Some twenty Taosenos were the guests of Frank Waters & Mrs. G. E. Tinker at a chicken dinner in the old Butler Hotel in Mora, on Sunday afternoon.[30] (17 June 1939)

Occasional poems and stories were also published.

Doubtless due to his association with Mabel and Tony Luhan, Spud regularly reported news from Taos Pueblo in *The Horse Fly*, thereby making the Indians seem less tourist attractions than neighbors. If anything, Mrs. Luhan constituted the star attraction in and around "Mabeltown." Her sayings and doings filled newspaper pages there and elsewhere.

A $50,000 slander suit brought against Mabel by Dr. Charles D. Kanter in the summer of 1938 contributed to this notoriety. The Taos doctor claimed that at a September 1936 dinner party Luhan had declared: "I do not believe that Dr. Kanter even has a license to practice." The trial was attended by "everyone," but ended rather abruptly a month later before a second hearing. *The Horse Fly's* third number (July 23) noted that the "Dancing Doctor's Slander Suit Ends":

Although Dr. Charles Kanter claimed he was not physically well enough to attend court for the hearing of his $50,000 slander suit on Monday, H. A. Kiker cleverly imported a Santa Rosa attorney who testified that only a few days ago Kanter had attended a dance from the hours of 10 p.m. to 1 a.m.—and what is more, that he had danced! The Judge consequently decided Kanter should not be given the opportunity to re-open the suit at his convenience, and dismissed the case in favor of the defendant, Mabel Dodge Luhan.

Such goings-on earned the Taos *dueña* an important, thinly disguised role in Myron Brinig's 1941 novel, *All of Their Lives*. Central figure Florence Gresham is a headstrong, passionate, much-married woman with pretentions toward writing. Unlike her real-life counterpart, her stay "In the Shadow of the Mountains" is brief and violent, but her entourage—replete with Indians, Hispanos, artists, an ailing writer, and assorted audiences—is definitely "drawn to life."[31] Brinig's description of Taos is comparable to Edwin Corle's novel about Santa Fe from the perspective of twelve hours in the fictitious Blue Haven Cafe on Burro Alley. The Blue Haven's patrons include various recognizable types of locals and tourists, including a writer and playwright, but few specifically and readily identifiable individuals.[32]

Spud Johnson continued to publish sporadic issues of *Laughing Horse* during the late thirties, and in July 1940 his little magazine was joined by another in Santa Fe. Editors Alison Dana and Margaret Lohlker bravely inaugurated *The Santa Fean: A National Monthly* with these words:

TO OUR SUBSCRIBERS

In these insecure and troubled times it may seem strange that a new magazine should be launched. Some may feel that this magazine, should the United States be drawn beyond her present plan of defense only, may find it impossible to go on. We wish to assure you that this will not be the case. Beginning with this July issue we are convinced that you will be pleased with its excellence: stories, articles, format, paper and price. This form will be continued as long as our country remains at peace. But should this status change it may become necessary to reduce the cost of printing. We guarantee, however, that the standard of the Santa Fean's text will not be lowered.

The first number featured articles, short stories and poems by Lawrence Rand Bynon, Alfred Morang, P. H. Wistrand, John L. Sinclair, Jacob Scher, Margaret Lohlker, Alfred Hazen Stoddard, Alva Woodward, Lorin W. Brown, Elizabeth B. Fierlein, Harold Butcher, Jean Cady, Helen E. Cunningham, Mrs. George H. Danforth, W. Thetford LeViness, Roy A. Keech, and Madeline Gwynn, with art work by Willard F. Clark, Fritz Broeske and Harold E. West. *The Santa Fean* soon dropped its subtitle of "a national monthly" and was also forced to print in a smaller format in 1941, but it continued publication, first as a bimonthly and then more irregularly after Pearl Harbor.

In the holiday number of 1941, Taos poet Phillips Kloss sparked an impassioned controversy reminiscent of earlier exchanges in the Round Tables, the *New Mexico Quarterly*, the Writers' Page, and elsewhere. Kloss proclaimed:

Most of us who have settled or lived in the plateau region of New Mexico have felt a definite intimation of great things past, great things to come. There is a spirit to the land that arouses and awakes, stimulates and inspires. Thousands have felt it. It is a quite tangible thing. In a word it is a feeling of renascence, a feeling that a new culture, a new civilization might be born in this area which some have called the Tibet of America.[33]

He deplored the unfulfilled promise, however, challenging local artists and writers to work for a genuine "renascence" with a "regional universality":

Let us examine what we already have and what we need. We do have a few artists and writers of considerable power, and we are getting more. We do have excellent anthropologists. We do have a distinct regional architecture, very livable and very beautiful. We have a basic Indian culture more vital, more significant, more powerful than any other primitive culture anywhere else in the world; it is a culture to stimulate but not to imitate. And finally we have a good many genuine people who know how to live.

What we need first and foremost is sincerity. The pretense and pose that prevails among the majority of the so-called intellectuals of Santa Fe and Taos obviates a renascence before it begins. The silly Bohemianism, the false fronts and false faces, the ostentatious studios, the commercial rather than esthetic effort—these are the flaw of character that makes Santa Fe and Taos ridiculous. . . .

The second requisite, contingent on and reciprocal to the first, is economic outlet, or inlet, but mainly an outlet for ethical self-expression whether in business, art, or science. The best agency for achieving this is a comprehensive vigorous vital magazine. . . . What we need is a gargantuan magazine wherein all the arts and all the sciences shall be given full expression. . . .

As a regional magazine, it should have a definite editorial direction to make it coherent. Here in the Four Corners Country that direction should be a New Naturalism, for that is our essence, that is the spirit which is already here, the curative spirit of many of the world's sad ills.[34]

Pearl Harbor and World War II rendered this clarion the more poignant.

The Second World War drastically altered "literary New Mexico," but its art colonists had matured and consolidated their gains locally and nationally. Yet these expanded horizons never obscured the sense of person and place in Santa Fe and Taos. What endured and what compelled were still the land and its people, a natural and social fellowship found in few other places in the United States. As May Sarton later recalled:

I saw it first in December of 1940. . . . I was unprepared in every way, unprepared for the air itself, seven thousand feet up, thin and dry so there is a bubble of excitement in one's chest; unprepared for the huge bare landscape that reminded me of Chinese painting and of Northern Spain. For my target had been a friend rather than a city, a friend I had never seen, but one who had written me a letter when my first novel came out, Haniel Long, the poet.[35]

Notes

1. Julia M. Keleher, "Los Paisanos," *New Mexico Quarterly* 6 (1936): 56; Thomas A. Erhard, *Lynn Riggs: Southwest Playwright*, Southwest Writers Series 29 (Austin, Texas: Steck-Vaughn, 1970), p. 26. New Mexicans were given an opportunity to view the play when it was selected for the November 25, 1936, opening of the new building for the Little Theater in Albuquerque (Ina Sizer Cassidy, "Art and Artists of New Mexico: Albuquerque Little Theater," *New Mexico Magazine*, January 1937, p. 58).

2. A basic source on the national projects is William F. McDonald, *Federal Relief Administration and the Arts* (Columbus: Ohio State University Press, 1969). On the Federal Writers' Project see, e.g.: Jerre Mangione, *The Dream and The Deal: The Federal Writers' Project, 1935-1943* (Boston: Little, Brown, 1972); and Monty Noam Penkower, *The Federal Writers' Project: A Study in Government Patronage of the Arts* (Urbana: University of Illinois Press, 1977).

3. For a history of the New Mexico Federal Writers' Project, see: "Notes on Federal Project One and the Federal Writers' Project in New Mexico," in Lorin W. Brown with Charles L. Briggs and Marta Weigle, *Hispano Folklife of New Mexico: The Lorin W. Brown Federal Writers' Project Manuscripts* (Albuquerque: University of New Mexico Press, 1978), pp. 239-52; Marta Weigle with Mary Powell, "From Alice Corbin's 'Lines Mumbled in Sleep' to 'Eufemia's Sopapillas': Women and the Federal Writers' Project in New Mexico," *New America*, vol. 4, no. 3, 1981, in press.

4. The December 1935 issue of *New Mexico Quarterly* included one of the first official notices to writers about the NMFWP. According to Julia M. Keleher: "Work shall be given to writers, teachers, map draughtsmen, photographers, reporters, editors, journalists, librarians, research workers, etc., who are already on the relief rolls. The schedule of pay calls for 'subsistence wages' for any one qualified to help in compiling and editing of the [American Guide] Manual" ("Los Paisanos," *New Mexico Quarterly* 5 [1935]: 277). Rowland to Alsberg, 7 February 1936, is in Record Group No. 69: Records of the Work Projects Administration in the National Archives, Washington, D.C. (hereafter NA #69). State Professional and Service Projects director Mary B. Perry also wrote Alsberg about the difficulties in securing qualified personnel, forcing Cassidy to accept "teachers and other professional people not accustomed to writing or to research work" (10 January 1936). Henderson too commented on the field writers in a letter to Cassidy dated April 20, 1936, stating that "few, if any of them, are trained writers" and lamenting: "Our field workers in this vast area are few and far between, in addition to being inexperienced writers, and they have no travel expense to make personal investigations." Weigle's research in Washington, D.C., repositories was sponsored by a grant to her and William H. Wroth from the National Endowment for the Humanities

(no. RS-00056-79-0589) to document and analyze "Governmental Support of the Arts in New Mexico, 1933-1943."

5. "Organization Meeting Held by Local Artists," *Santa Fe New Mexican*, 3 December 1936, p. 3.

6. NA#69. Also see Marta Weigle, Introduction to reprint ed. of Raymond Otis, *Miguel of the Bright Mountain* (1936; reprint, Albuquerque: University of New Mexico Press, 1977), pp. v-xxx; idem, afterword to reprint ed. of Raymond Otis, *Little Valley* (1937; reprint, Albuquerque: University of New Mexico Press, 1980), pp. 274-83.

7. *Over the Turquoise Trail*, vol. 1, no. 1, New Mexico Writers' Guild, Autumn 1938, p. 2. The Guild occupied the same office as the NMFWP in #9 Renehan Building, Santa Fe. Membership cost $2.00 per year. Ina Sizer Cassidy was chair and announced that the Guild "is an association drawn together by regional ties and mutual craft interests. A broad program is planned, including the publication of a regional magazine, OVER THE TURQUOISE TRAIL, sponsoring publication of material, lectures, marketing advice, and other means of advancing New Mexico literature and art. The co-operation of the writers and artists of New Mexico is invited" (p. 52). According to Haniel Long's notice in *The New Mexico Sentinel* Writers' Page, 18 December 1938, poet William Pillin and Cassidy edited the first number, and: "There is a very definite place for a New Mexico literary magazine and I am glad that one has appeared for us to support both by subscription and by manuscripts."

8. Norman Macleod, *You Get What You Ask For* (New York: Harrison-Hilton Books, 1939), pp. 153-54, 185-86. According to Jerre Mangione: ". . . Macleod got a job on the New Mexico Writers' Project. . . . The director was Mrs. Inez [sic] Cassidy, a woman of matriarchal temperament with whom he got along famously. On one occasion when he wound up in jail after a drinking spree, she came to his rescue and had him released. 'The first time you go to jail,' she told him, 'we get you out. The next time we let you rot.' Despite his love for Santa Fe, he missed his friends in the East. Quitting his job, he returned to New York. . . " (*The Dream and The Deal*, p. 178).

9. NA#69. On May 4, 1938, Alice Corbin Henderson addressed copies of a letter supporting Cassidy to both Nancy Lane and Henry Alsberg, claiming that disputes which arose were "a part of the job—and, incidentally, intellectually stimulating!" She concluded: "I look back upon the year and a half that I spent on the project with Mrs. Cassidy as a delightful and invigorating experience in a work in which I was happy to share and of which I cherish happy memories." Bynner wrote Dempsey from Hollywood on January 20, 1939: "News comes from Santa Fe that there is some move on the horizon to demote Ina Cassidy for 'lack of administrative ability.' An outsider can know little about the insides of a situation like this; but I, for one, do know how well Ina handled a revolt some time ago which was definitely instigated by communistic elements and I should be inclined to trust her judgment and ability in managing ordinary people. At any rate I have been asked (not by her) to say a word to you and am saying it" (NA#69).

10. Sarah Nestor, *The Native Market of the Spanish New Mexican Craftsmen, Santa Fe, 1933-1940* (Santa Fe, New Mexico: The Colonial New Mexico Historical Foundation, 1978), p. 35. El Parian Analco complex opened officially on August 7, 1937. For two years its open air theater, El Teatro Analco, served various groups, including the Santa Fe Players, who performed the 1937 Fiesta melodrama there on September 9 and 10: " 'Nellie, the Bandit's Sweetheart,' or 'It Can't Happen in Burro Alley' . . . was adapted by Raymond Otis from an old dime novel, and is said to be one of the most hair-raising, breath-quickening, tear-jerking melerdramas yet to be shown here. . . . The novel from which the masterpiece has been adapted was printed in 1882, a year after Billy's death. It would seem, from perusal of it, that it was written by an Englishman who had never seen Billy nor the Southwest, but who had heard about both. Blood curdles are never sacrificed to accuracy in either novel or play" (*Santa Fe New Mexican*, 27 August 1937, p.

2). In addition, "the 1937 season was highlighted by the St. Francis Players' production of 'The Sheep of San Cristobal,' a miracle play of New Mexico folklore which was adapted by local writer Raymond Otis from the story by Frank Applegate" (Nestor, ibid., pp. 43, 45). Also see Weigle, Introduction to *Miguel*, p. xiii; Ina Sizer Cassidy, "Art and Artists of New Mexico," *New Mexico Magazine*, October 1938, p. 45.

11. For field writer Lorin W. Brown's recollections of both Scher and Fisher, see Brown with Briggs and Weigle, *Hispano Folklife*, pp. 25, 26, 247. Vardis Fisher had edited *Idaho: A Guide in Word and Picture* (Caldwell, Idaho: Caxton Printers, 1937), the first state guidebook to be published. For his experiences on that project, see his autobiographical novel, *Orphans in Gethsemane: A Novel of the Past in the Present* (Denver, Colorado: Alan Swallow, 1960), and, e.g., Ronald W. Taber, "Vardis Fisher and the 'Idaho Guide'," *Pacific Northwest Quarterly* 59 (April 1968): 68-76.

12. NA#69. Fisher to Alsberg, 9 August 1939.

13. In a May 20, 1940, letter to national Writers' Program director John D. Newsom, Minton wrote: "The subtitle 'A guide to the Colorful State' was our own designation. There is no official State Name, and we found at least eight names that have been applied, such as 'Sunshine State,' 'Cactus State,' and so on, each worse than the other; so, because it is the most colorful of all the states in various ways, we decided on that for the subtitle, although we don't think it especially good. At any rate, we prefer it to Sunshine State and Cactus State and others that utterly fail to give a hint as to its quality. If you think of a better one, please make the change" (NA#69). For more on the Coronado Cuarto Centennial, see, e.g., Erna Fergusson, "The Coronado Cuarto Centennial," *New Mexico Quarterly* 10 (1940): 67-71; special issue of *New Mexico Magazine*, June 1940; and Thomas Wood Stevens, *The Entrada of Coronado: A Spectacular Historical Drama* (Albuquerque, New Mexico: Ward Anderson Printing for The Coronado Cuarto Centennial Commission, 1940).

14. See, e.g., Brown with Briggs and Weigle, *Hispano Folklife of New Mexico*; Marta Weigle, "Guadalupe Baca de Gallegos' '*Los tres preciosidas* (The Three Treasures)': Notes on the Tale, Its Narrator and Collector [Bright Lynn]," *New Mexico Folklore Record* 15 (1980-81): 31-35; Lou Sage Batchen, *Las Placitas: Historical Facts and Legends* (Placitas, New Mexico: Tumbleweed Press, 1972); "In Writers' Program Days: Annette Hesch Thorp and 'Some New Mexico Grandmothers'," in Weigle with Powell, "Women and the FWP in New Mexico," in press; note on Reyes N. Martinez, in Cleofas M. Jaramillo, *The Genuine New Mexico Tasty Recipes: With Additional Materials on Traditional Hispano Food* (Santa Fe, New Mexico: Ancient City Press, 1981), p. 28.

15. Cleo Jaramillo, *Romance of a Little Village Girl* (San Antonio, Texas: Naylor, 1955), p. 176.

16. Ibid., p. 173. Also see Marta Weigle, "About Cleofas Martinez de Jaramillo," in Jaramillo, *Genuine New Mexico Tasty Recipes*, pp. 19-20. The article referred to, Elizabeth Willis De Huff, "Intriguing Mexican Dishes," appeared in *Holland's, The Magazine of the South*, March 1935, pp. 34, 47.

17. Designer Marceil Taylor and her husband, printer Maurice Taylor, met the Ernest Thompson Seton's in Cedar Rapids, Iowa, and came to New Mexico at their behest in 1938. The Seton Village Press flourished until 1943 (Clark Kimball, ed., with Maurice and Marceil Taylor, "A History of The Seton Village Press, with Bibliography," ms. in preparation, 1981). Among its publications were: Cleofas M. Jaramillo, *Shadows of the Past (Sombras del pasado)* (1941; reprint, Santa Fe, New Mexico: Ancient City Press, 1972); idem, *The Genuine New Mexico Tasty Recipes (Potajes sabrosos)*, copyright 1939, reprint 1942 (reprint, Ancient City Press, 1981); Aurora Lucero-White, *The Folklore of New Mexico: Volume One* (1941). Lucero-White was the author of New Mexico's only contribution to *American Stuff: An Anthology of Prose & Verse* by Members of the Federal Writers' Project with Sixteen Prints by the Federal Art Project (New York: Viking Press, 1937). Her "Americana No. 7: Romances and Corridos of New Mexico" (pp. 168-75)

was accepted over "unsuitable" poems by Ina Sizer Cassidy, Thomas Files Bledsoe, and Alice Corbin Henderson and short stories by Jack Thorp, Lester Raines and three other workers (NA#69).

18. Phyllis S. Morales, *Fray Angelico Chavez: A Bibliography of His Published Writings (1925-1978)* (Santa Fe, New Mexico: The Lightning Tree-Jene Lyon, Publisher, 1980).

19. Quoted in Marta Weigle, *Brothers of Light, Brothers of Blood: The Penitentes of the Southwest* (Albuquerque: University of New Mexico Press, 1976), p. 107. In her "Los Paisanos" obituary notice, Julia Keleher does not mention the Brotherhood: "Carl Taylor, whose tragic death occurred just at the time this column went to press, would have seen his first book, *Odyssey of the Islands*, published this spring by *Scribner's*. This book deals with the Philippines, where Mr. Taylor spent several years gathering material. . . . Mr. Taylor recently sold a series of articles to the *Wide World* magazine on the 'American Border Patrol,' and was working at the time of his death on a series concerning the 'Texas Rangers' " *(New Mexico Quarterly* 6 [1936]: 52-53).

20. Cited in Weigle, *Brothers*, p. 108.

21. Tingley to Hays, 3 April 1936, Miscellaneous Papers of Governor Clyde Tingley, New Mexico State Records Center and Archives, Santa Fe.

22. For more on this and related matters, see Marta Weigle, "The Penitente Brotherhood in Southwestern Fiction: Notes on Folklife and Literature," in *The American Self: Myth, Ideology, and Popular Culture*, ed. Sam B. Girgus (Albuquerque: University of New Mexico Press, 1981), pp. 221-30.

23. *Santa Fe New Mexican*, 28 June 1938, and 30 September 1938. Spud Johnson reported in *The Horse Fly*, 12 November 1938, that: "Blanche Grant, Victor White and ex-mayor John Sanchez were among Taos writers who motored to Santa Fe Monday, with fresh novels under their arms, to interview Mr. H. A. Latham [general editor and vice-president of Macmillan]."

24. The eighty-eight listed are: Myrtle Andrews, Omar Barker, Ruth Laughlin Barker, Don Blanding, Lansing Bloom, Maud Bloom, Lydia Bradford, Roark Bradford, Dorothy Brett, Myron Brinig, Witter Bynner, Ross Calvin, Arthur L. Campa, Isabel Hayden Campbell, Ina Sizer Cassidy, Kate Chapman, Kenneth M. Chapman, Beatrice Chauvenet, Harold Chidsey, Peggy Pond Church, Anna Nolan Clark, William Davey, Elizabeth DeHuff, Thomas C. Donnelly, Brian Boru Dunne, Dorothy Belle Hughes, Erna Fergusson, Harvey Fergusson, George Fitzpatrick, Maurice Garland Fuller, Marie Garland, Frances Gillmore [sic], Florence Glidden, Fred Glidden, John Glidden, Alice Goodwin, Blanche Grant, George P. Hammond, Alice Corbin Henderson, Edgar L. Hewett, Paul Horgan, Robert Hunt, Spud Johnson, Hester Jones, Roy Keech, Phillips Kloss, Farona Konopak, Tom Kromer, Oliver LaFarge, Margaret Larkin, Freida [sic] Lawrence, Haniel Long, Mabel Dodge Lujan, Cyrus McCormick, Grace Meredith, Lucy Sturgis More, Sylvanus Morley, Elizabeth Needham, Deric Nusbaum, Aileen Otero Nusbaum, Ex-Governor Miguel Otero, Nina Otero (Warren), Raymond Otis, T. M. Pearce, Conrad Richter, Orville [sic] Ricketts, Lynn Riggs, Frank Russell, Prof. George St. Clair, Earl Scott, Marion [sic] Scott, Eliz. Shepley Seargeant [sic], Ernest Thompson Seton, Julie Buttree Seton, Jeannette Spiess, Alice Prescott Smith, Wilfred Stedman, Philip Stevenson, Dorothy Stewart, Dorothy Thomas, N. Howard (Jack) Thorpe [sic], John Curtis Underwood, Ruth M. Underhill, Berta Van Stone, Stanley Vestal, Paul A. F. Walter, Paul Walter, Jr., and Louis H. Warner.

25. Ed Sullivan Advertising, *Handbook of Old Santa Fe* (Santa Fe, New Mexico: Rydal Press, 1939), p. 1. Also see Margaret Lohlker, "The House On The Camino Del Monte Sol," *The Santa Fean*, October 1940, p. 23. According to a newspaper account by L. L. Partlow: "One of the most brilliant and versatile writers in America today is Alfred Morang, head of the short story writing group at Arsuna School of Fine Arts in Santa Fe. He began to write only six years ago. The first story he turned out was accepted, and from that time his rise in the literary heavens has been meteoric. . . . As a teacher,

Morang is vastly stimulating as well as effective. His class in short writing at Arsuna has grown rapidly, and he literally pours energy and inspiration into his pupils. The quality of work done by the class is improving in technique and rapidly approaching the mark of saleability. In fact, one of the pupils had the pleasure this week of receiving acceptance of two of her stories by a magazine in New York. Morang is a member of the League of American Writers and the Midwest Literary league. At one time he was head of the New England branch of the former organization. He came to Santa Fe a little over a year ago for his health and intends to make his home permanently in the Southwest. His presence is a distinct addition to the culture and creative life of Santa Fe" (*Santa Fe New Mexican*, 2 September 1938). Also see Edna Robertson and Sarah Nestor, *Artists of the Canyons and Caminos: Santa Fe, The Early Years* (n.p.: Peregrine Smith, 1976), pp. 147-49.

26. Alice Corbin Henderson, "E. Dana Johnson, June 15, 1879-December 10, 1937," *New Mexico Historical Review* 13 (1938): 122, 123-24. Henderson's obituary is followed by an "Obituary as Written by Mr. Johnson *(Written by E. Dana Johnson when he began editing the Plaza Page in the New Mexico Sentinel.),*" ibid., pp. 125-27.

27. Letters soon began to pour in from disappointed readers both within and outside New Mexico. However, it was not until April 1940 that a brochure soliciting financial support for a monthly four-page "Writers" supplement was sent out from *The New Mexico Sentinel* offices in Santa Fe. The plea included a list of 154 Writers' Page contributors, a page to pledge support, and the notice that: "The Sentinel would hope that the very high standards set by Haniel Long as editor of New Mexico Writers would be maintained. These standards included a willingness not only to publish the work of recognized artists but also to help unknown men and women—and in particular the young—get started in writing as a career or as an avocation. The developing of new talent is the best expression of regional literature. Without a medium, its tongue remains silent. Under Mr. Long's editorship, New Mexico Writers was becoming the vehicle for the forming of new artists and new art. William Pillin, of Santa Fe, poet and editor of literary magazines, has offered to try to organize this project into being in the hope that writers in New Mexico and other interested persons may be willing to work cooperatively to secure the necessary support." This revitalization attempt proved unsuccessful.

28. Oliver La Farge, who was in and out of New Mexico during the 1930s, did not settle in Santa Fe permanently to write until 1941 (D'Arcy McNickle, *Indian Man: A Life of Oliver La Farge* [Bloomington: Indiana University Press, 1971], p. 132). He was a member of the board of trustees of the Museum of Navajo Ceremonial Art founded by Miss Mary C. Wheelwright and incorporated in 1937. Alice Corbin Henderson served as curator and board secretary-treasurer. Her husband, William Penhallow Henderson, was architect for the Camino Lejo building. "Designed as an interpretation in modern form of a Navajo ceremonial *Hoghan,* the building itself is an integral background for the exhibition of sand paintings, as well as a repository for the myths, music, poetry, sacred lore and objects connected with Navajo religion . . . [and] thus to perpetuate for the general public, for research students, and for the Indians themselves, this great example of a primitive people's spiritual culture" (from an early, undated Museum brochure in the vertical files, Museum of New Mexico, History Library, Santa Fe).

29. See Marta Weigle, Introduction to reprint edition of Robert Bright, *The Life and Death of Little Jo* (1944; reprint, Albuquerque: University of New Mexico Press, 1978), p. vi.

30. For Waters's description of the Butler Hotel, where he drafted *People of the Valley* (1941), see *Conversations with Frank Waters,* ed. John R. Milton (Chicago: Swallow Press, 1971), pp. 23-26. In *The Horse Fly* of the 25 March 1939, Johnson announced: "Another New Mexico landmark may 'bite the dust' in the near future, it was learned here this week with news of the possible sale of the old Butler Hotel in Mora to merchants who

plan to demolish it & erect modern store buildings on the site. It is hoped by admirers of the charming old building, that Mrs. Butler will be able to rent it, instead; or at least sell it to someone who will preserve the structure with some feeling for its distinction and beauty. 'Monte' Butler, famous gambler, bought the hotel about 75 years ago & his widow has been running it for the past 20 years."

31. Myron Brinig, "*All of Their Lives* (New York: Farrar & Rinehart, 1941). Also see Mabel Major and T. M. Pearce, *Southwest Heritage: A Literary History with Bibliography*, 3d ed. (Albuquerque: University of New Mexico Press, 1972), p. 133. According to Julia Keleher: "*All of Their Lives*, by Myron Brinig, a spring publication, has for its central character Mabel Dodge Luhan of Taos" *(New Mexico Quarterly* 11 [1941]: 382). Keleher had earlier remarked rather snidely in her "Los Paisanos" feature that: "We understand that . . . Mabel Dodge Lujan has gone to New York to be re-psychoanalyzed . . . four books are the result of the last session. . . " *(New Mexico Quarterly* 7 [1937]: 293). Also see Emily Hahn, *Mabel: A Biography of Mabel Dodge Luhan* (Boston: Houghton Mifflin, 1977).

32. Edwin Corle, *Burro Alley* (New York: Random House, 1938).

33. Phillips Kloss, "Background for Renascence," *Santa Fean Inter-American*, vol. 2, no. 3 (holiday number 1941), p. 23.

34. Ibid., pp. 24-25.

35. May Sarton, *A World of Light: Portraits and Celebrations* (New York: W. W. Norton, 1976), pp. 123-24. This first appeared in a slightly altered version as "The Leopard Land: Haniel and Alice Long's Santa Fe," *Southwest Review* 57 (1972): 1.

CODA

On a crisp October morning in 1942, an unmarked jeep bearing two enlisted men, a United States Army general, and a lanky, blue-eyed scientist drove up New Mexico State Route Four through the Jemez wilderness. It was less than a year after Pearl Harbor, and the United States was at war on both fronts. Following orders from President Franklin D. Roosevelt, the four men were on a mission to locate a secret site where physicists from all over the nation could gather to create an atomic bomb, a weapon which would end the war and stop the killing.

The officer was General Leslie Groves, the scientist, J. Robert Oppenheimer. Groves was a practical man concerned with military matters—the ability to maintain secrecy, the availability of supply routes. Oppenheimer was a dreamer, a genius, a creator, an intellectual with a passion for physics, mythology and philosophy. He had spent many summers riding horseback in the Jemez and Sangre de Cristo Mountains and had developed a deep attachment to New Mexico. For years he dreamed of finding a way to combine what he called his "two great loves," physics and New Mexico.[1]

Now it seemed his dream might come true. For, as the jeep traveled through the mountains, Oppenheimer remembered that once on a horseback trip he and his brother Frank had discovered a rustic boys' school set atop a red and rugged mesa several miles north of Jemez. This Los Alamos Ranch School had been founded in 1917 by Ashley Pond, father of poet Peggy Pond Church, as a place "where city boys from wealthy families . . . could regain their heritage of outdoor wisdom at the same time they were being prepared for college and the responsibilities which their position in life demanded."[2] Located thirty-five miles north of Santa Fe, the pioneer log cabin school might be just the place the group hoped to find.

In seeking to combine his love of physics with his love for New Mexico, Oppenheimer differed little from the artists and writers of Santa Fe and Taos. He too thought that the New Mexican mountains and mesas would provide him and his colleagues with the spiritual solace and inspiration they needed to complete their difficult task. There, in splendid isolation, far from the distractions of urban life, Oppenheimer hoped to establish a Utopian colony for physicists, a society "where people could talk freely with each other, where theoretical ideas and experimental finds could affect each other."[3]

Two and a half years later, the clandestine crucible of Los Alamos yielded up its awesome creations—atomic bombs with the explosive power of more than ten thousand tons of TNT—two bombs which destroyed the cities of Hiroshima and Nagasaki, ended World War II, and catapulted New Mexico and the world into the atomic age. "The world was indeed changed. Men had become as gods, though in the process mankind itself had become mortal."[4]

New Mexico too was altered irrevocably. For Peggy Pond Church, who had grown up at Los Alamos, the mesa became "the mushrooming shadow of violent change in which all of us must now go on living."[5] Returning to Santa Fe after the war, artist Cady Wells found that the deserts and mesas which had once inspired his calm landscapes no longer afforded solace. Bombs appeared in his paintings of trees, explosions broke through his skylines. Finally Wells put his adobe house up for sale "to get away from atomic energy."[6]

In 1920 Vachel Lindsay proclaimed to Londoners "that Santa Fe was the spiritual capital of America."[7] Today, that capital has moved to neighboring Los Alamos, for in many ways New Mexico now epitomizes the spirit of the American atomic age. In less than two hours one can drive from Taos Pueblo or the "Ancient City" of Santa Fe to the scientific citadel of Los Alamos, a still-guarded hub of both atomic weapon design and radiation cancer research. The land of enchantment has become a land of contrasts; the state of "sun, silence, and adobe" is now the state of sun, silence, and science. And yet, according to Oppenheimer, these newcomers are not so different from their art colonist predecessors: "Both the man of science and the man of art live always at the edge of mystery, surrounded by it. Both, as the measure of their creation, have always had to do with the harmonization of what is new with what is familiar, with the balance between novelty and synthesis, with the struggle to make partial order in total chaos."[8]

Notes

1. Robert Jungk, *Brighter than a Thousand Suns: A Personal History of the Atomic Scientists*, trans. James Cleugh (New York: Harcourt, Brace and Company, 1958), p. 129.

2. Peggy Pond Church, *The House at Otowi Bridge: The Story of Edith Warner and Los Alamos* (Albuquerque: University of New Mexico Press, 1960), p. 6.

3. James W. Kunetka, *City of Fire: Los Alamos and the Atomic Age, 1943-1945*, rev. ed. (Albuquerque: University of New Mexico Press, 1979), p. 34.

4. Godfrey Hodgson, *America in Our Time: From World War II to Nixon, What Happened and Why* (New York: Vintage Books, 1976), p. 20.

5. Church, *House at Otowi Bridge*, p. 5.

6. Quoted in Daniel Lang, *From Hiroshima to the Moon: Chronicles of Life in the Atomic Age* (New York: Simon and Schuster, 1959), p. 141.

7. Nicholas Vachel Lindsay to Mary Austin, 9 July 1926. T. M. Pearce, ed., *Literary America 1903-1934: The Mary Austin Letters*, Contributions in Women's Studies, no. 5 (Westport, Connecticut: Greenwood Press, 1979), p. 207.

8. Quoted in Jungk, *Brighter than a Thousand Suns*, p. 333.

PORTRAITS AND SELF-PORTRAITS, CONTEMPORARY AND RETROSPECTIVE

Stuart Davis, "New Mexican Gate."
Oil on linen, 1923, 22"x32".
Permanent Collection, Roswell Museum and Art Center, New Mexico.

At last the wisdom of the ages has opened our eyes to the wonderland beyond our western gates, and made us aware not only of nature's
stark and glorious sublimities, but of immediate and vivid creations of
primitive art—one of the rarest, remotest, and most precious things
on earth.

—Harriet Monroe, "In Texas and
New Mexico," *Poetry*, September
1920, p. 326.

Jozef G. Bakos, "The Springtime Rainbow."
Oil, 1923, 29½"x35½".
Museum of New Mexico, Santa Fe.

The Southwestern landscape, more than any other in North America, reduces vainglory in a man and enforces his exact, or at least his reasonable, importance. It is at once a humbling and an ennobling landscape. While not conducive, for an artist, to facile and officious performance, it breeds in him a sobering and releasing sense of time and space and of his possible dignity therein. And even from declining races, the Indian and Spanish colonial, the influence of two cultures, much older than motor-cars, enriches and seasons an American beyond his ordinary birthright. If he but bring water, the desert will bloom.

—Witter Bynner, "Desert Harvest," *Southwest Review*, 1929, pp. 493-94.

William Penhallow Henderson, wood-cut illustration of Brotherhood *morada* (meeting house) and crosses, for his wife's book, p. 23.

Meanwhile, the sun sinking at our backs had turned the cliffs across the valley into splendid cathedral shapes of rose and saffron beauty—a beauty that is touched here in this country with a sometimes terrible sense of eternity, loneliness, and futility. For all the gay laughter of youth on the hillside, the stark parable of the Crucifixion is close to the country's soul. It eats into the heart, this terror; and it is not difficult to imagine how the early Franciscans felt, as they gazed upon this terrible afternoon light on bare mesa and peak, and felt the thorns of this eternal loneliness pressing into their souls. Actual mortification of the flesh is perhaps less poignant.

—Alice Corbin Henderson, *Brothers of Light: The Penitentes of the Southwest,* 1937, p. 49.

Victor Higgins, "Ranchos de Taos Church."
Watercolor, n.d. [1934].
Photographic Record, Public Works of Art Project, Thirteenth
    Region, New Mexico Division.
New Mexico State Records Center and Archives, Santa Fe.

Willard F. Clark, wood engraving for a greeting card, n.d.
Courtesy of the artist.

As a descendant of the Spanish pioneers, I have watched with regret the passing of the old Spanish customs and the rapid adoption of the modern Anglo customs by the new generation.

In my desire to preserve some of the folklore of New Mexico, and in the interest of the rising generation—so few of whom now read the Spanish language—I started some years ago to write this book in English, although because of my Spanish descent my English is rather limited, for which I crave indulgence from those who could have done better.

With the same desire, five years ago I organized a Spanish Folklore Society, in hope that it will carry on the work of preserving the Spanish language and customs after I am gone. On account of familiarity with the old customs, we had not awakened to the fact that they were worth preserving, until in recent years, and have turned our effort to revive them.

My pioneer forefathers, searching through rugged mountains and hills, over almost impassable trails, found the beautiful hidden little valley of the Rio Hondo, in the northern part of New Mexico. In this isolated nook, rich in verdure and scenery, my ancestors built strong-walled houses, fought the Indians and shed their blood to protect their families, and here they left a most interesting folklore, the history of which fills the pages of this book, dating back to my grandmother's time, as far as I can remember.

—Cleofas M. Jaramillo, *Shadows of the
Past (Sombras del pasado)*, 1941, p. 10.

Frank Waters. Photograph courtesy of Clark Kimball and Charlotte J. Stone, The Great Southwest Books, Santa Fe.

To three races and four generations, through all its many names, it has been known simply as the beautiful blue valley. It is not as beautiful as it is blue. Nor always blue. Yet the tone persists when the vegas turn sere and tawny under drought, and the pine slopes white with frost. And seen from above the haze of Indian summer and the winter mists, from the top of the nine thousand foot pass, the valley appears always what it is—a crescent lake of blue draining the shadows of the steep-walled cañons which hem it on all sides.

—Frank Waters, *People of the Valley*, 1941, p. 3.

Gene Kloss, "Indian Ceremony."
Etching/aquatint, n.d. [1934], 11"x 13¾".
Photographic Record, Public Works of Art Project,
 Thirteenth Region, New Mexico Division.
New Mexico State Records Center and Archives, Santa Fe.

The land of the Indians. Their rituals to earth-fecundity, their heal-
ing ceremonies sung and danced throughout clear winter nights, are
the inspiration of city-drowsy people of the Atlantic Coast.

A land of power; a land from which Americans of today may learn
secrets of power and of silence from Americans of yesterday; a land
warm with the abandon and the lusciousness of old Spain, vibrant
with Fiestas as with Corn-dances; to which your White races from the
North have brought dynamism, efficiency, commercialism, but from
which they may learn the mysteries of high desert spaces. And what
is a man who has not known the magic of high desert spaces? Just
another ant.

> —Dane Rudhyar, "The American Southwest: A Land
> of Power," *The Santa Fean*, September 1940, p. 45.

. . . She was a poet of the New England school who had suffered several unfortunate experiences of the heart. One affair in particular had left her avowedly bereft of the future desire for the companionship of man—at least the white man. Her compensation had been the discovery of the Indian, an entirely fortuitous revelation made to her during a casual visit to the Southwest. The Indian had proved so entirely satisfactory that she had disposed of her old home . . . and removed permanently to Santa Fe where, within a surprisingly short time, she had built up and decorated a new home that seemingly had succeeded in obliterating all memory of her unhappy past. . . .

. . . [She] stood nearly six feet tall and was built proportionately. Her massive ankles were set on pedestal-like feet. Her face, clean-cut beneath piles of coarse red hair, streaked with iron-grey, resembled the face of a horse, her great Roman nose ploughing down between her furrowed cheeks. Rugged was the adjective that would have adequately described this woman of fifty, but from coast to coast in the homes of Representatives and Senators she was known as the Little Mother of the Indian. Usually a profanely abusive epithet preceded the diminutive adjective.

—Carl van Vechten, description of Marna Frost
("Mary Austin") in Spider Boy: A Scenario for a
Moving Picture, 1928, pp. 166-67.

Mary Austin on the portal of her *Casa Querida*, ca. 1928. Photograph courtesy of Ciark Kimball and Charlotte J. Stone, The Great Southwest Books, Santa Fe.

A Santa Fe group, Spud Johnson center, with two Taos Indians, at the Pueblo. Photograph courtesy of Clark Kimball and Charlotte J. Stone, The Great Southwest Books, Santa Fe.

Witter Bynner bought and wore and hung on his friends a famous collection of Indian jewelry. Alice Corbin introduced the velvet Navajo blouse. Stetson hats, cowboy boots, flannel shirts, even blankets were the approved costume. Everybody had a pet pueblo, a pet Indian, a pet craft. Pet Indians with pottery, baskets, and weaving to sell were seated by the corner fireplace (copied from the pueblo), plied with tobacco and coffee, asked to sing and tell tales. Jane Henderson [Baumann] made a record by living in Santa Clara all winter and learning a whole repertoire of Indian songs. Mary Austen [sic] discovered and ordered her life to the beat of the Amerindian rhythm. . . . It was obligatory to go to every pueblo dance. Failure to appear on a sunny roof on every saint's day marked one as soulless and without taste.

—Erna Fergusson, "Crusade from Santa Fé,"
North American Review, 1937, pp. 377-78.

Frieda and D. H. Lawrence at the window of their Chapala, Mexico, house. Photograph courtesy of Clark Kimball and Charlotte J. Stone, The Great Southwest Books, Santa Fe. From a limited edition, *Witter Bynner's Photographs of D. H. Lawrence* (Santa Fe: The Great Southwest Books, 1981).

TAOS

by D. H. Lawrence

The Indians say Taos is the heart of the world. Their world, maybe. Some places seem temporary on the face of the earth: San Francisco for example. Some places seem final. They have a true nodality. I never felt that so powerfully as, years ago, in London. The intense powerful nodality of that great heart of the world. And during the war that heart, for me, broke. So it is. Places can lose their living nodality. Rome, to me, has lost hers. In Venice one feels the magic of the glamorous old node that once united East and West, but it is the beauty of an afterlife.

Taos pueblo still retains its old nodality. Not like a great city. But, in its way, like one of the monasteries of Europe. You cannot come upon the ruins of the old great monasteries of England, beside their waters, in some lovely valley, now remote, without feeling that here is one of the choice spots of the earth, where the spirit dwelt. To me it is so important to remember that when Rome collapsed, when the great Roman Empire fell into smoking ruins, and bears roamed in the streets of Lyons, and wolves howled in the deserted streets of Rome, and Europe really was a dark ruin, then, it was not in castles or manors or cottages that life remained vivid. Then those whose souls were still alive withdrew together and gradually built monasteries, and these monasteries and convents, little communities of quiet labour and courage, isolated, helpless, and yet never overcome in a world flooded with devastation, these alone kept the human spirit from disintegration, from going quite dark, in the Dark Ages. These men made the Church, which again made Europe, inspiring the martial faith of the Middle Ages.

Taos pueblo affects me rather like one of the old monasteries. When you get there you feel something final. There is an arrival. The nodality still holds good.

But this is the pueblo. And from the north side to the south side, from the south side to the north side, the perpetual silent wandering intentness of a full-skirted, black-shawled, long-fringed woman in her wide white deerskin boots, the running of children, the silent sauntering of dark-faced men, bare-headed, the two plaits in front of their thin shoulders, and a white sheet like a sash swathed round their loins. They must have something to swathe themselves in.

And if it were sunset, the men swathing themselves in their sheet-like shrouds, leaving only the black place of the eyes visible. And women, darker than ever, with shawls over their heads, busy at the ovens. And cattle being driven to sheds. And men and boys trotting in from the fields, on ponies. And as the night is dark, on one of the roofs, or more often on the bridge, the inevitable drum-drum-drum of the tom-tom, and young men in the dark lifting their voices to the song, like wolves or coyotes crying in music.

There it is then, the pueblo, as it has been since heaven knows when. And the slow dark weaving of the Indian life going on still, though perhaps more waveringly. And oneself, sitting there on a pony, a far-off stranger with gulfs of time between me and this. And yet, the old nodality of the pueblo still holding, like a dark ganglion spinning invisible threads of consciousness. A sense of dryness, almost of weariness, about the pueblo. And a sense of the inalterable. It brings a sick sort of feeling over me, always, to get into the Indian vibration. Like breathing chlorine.

The next day in the morning we went to help erect the great stripped may-pole. It was the straight, smoothed yellow trunk of a big tree. Of course one of the white boys took the bossing of the show. But the Indians were none too ready to obey, and their own fat dark-faced boss gave counterorders. It was the old, amusing contradiction between the white and the dark races. As for me, I just gave a hand steadying the pole as it went up, outsider at both ends of the game.

An American girl came with a camera, and got a snap of us all struggling in the morning light with the great yellow trunk. One of the Indians went to her abruptly, in his quiet, insidious way.

"You give me that kodak. You ain't allowed take no snaps here. You pay fine—one dollar."

She was frightened, but she clung to her camera.

"You're not going to take my kodak from me," she said.

"I'm going to take that film out. And you pay one dollar fine, see."

The girl relinquished the camera, the Indian took out the film.

"Now you pay me one dollar, or I don't give you back this kodak."

Rather sullenly, she took out her purse and gave the two silver half-dollars. The Indian returned the camera, pocketed the money, and turned aside with a sort of triumph. Done it over one specimen of the white race.

There were not very many Indians helping to put up the pole.

"I never see so few boys helping put up the pole," said Tony Romero to me.

"Where are they all?" I asked. He shrugged his shoulders.

Dr. West, a woman doctor from New York who has settled in one of the villages, was with us. Mass was being said inside the church, and she would have liked to go in. She is well enough known too. But two Indians were at the church-door, and one put his elbow in front of her.

"You Catholic?"

"No, I'm not."

"Then you can't come in."

The same almost jeering triumph in giving the white man—or the white woman—a kick. It is the same the whole world over, between dark-skin and white. Dr. West, of course, thinks everything Indian wonderful. But she wasn't used to being rebuffed, and she didn't like it. But she found excuses.

"Of course," she said, "they're quite right to exclude the white people, if the white people can't behave themselves. It seems there were some Americans, boys and girls, in the church yesterday, insulting the images of the saints, shrieking, laughing, and saying they looked like monkeys. So now *no* white people are allowed inside the church."

I listened and said nothing. I had heard the same story at Buddhist temples in Ceylon. For my own part, I have long since passed the stage when I want to crowd up and stare at anybody's spectacle, white man's or dark man's.

I stood on one of the first roofs of the north pueblo. The iron bell of the church began to bang-bang-bang. The sun was down beyond the far-off, thin clear line of the western mesa, the light had ceased glowing on the piñon-dotted foot-hills beyond the south pueblo. The square beneath was thick with people. And the Indians began to come out of church.

Two Indian women brought a little dressed-up Madonna to her platform in the green starting-bower. Then the men slowly gathered round the drum. The bell clanged. The tom-tom beat. The men slowly uplifted their voices. The wild music resounded strangely against the banging of that iron bell, the silence of the many faces, as the group of Indians in their sheets and their best blankets, and in their ear-rings and brilliant scarlet trousers, or emerald trousers, or purple trousers, trimmed with beads, trod the slow bird-dance sideways, in feet of beaded moccasins, or yellow doeskin moccasins, singing all the time like drumming coyotes, slowly down and across the bridge to the south side, and up the incline to the south kiva. One or two Apaches in their beaded waistcoats and big black hats were among the singers, distinguishable by their thick build also. An old Navajo chief was among the encouragers.

As dusk fell, the singers came back under a certain house by the south kiva, and as they passed under the platform they broke and dispersed, it was over. They seemed as if they were grinning subtly as they went: grinning at being there in all that white crowd of inquisitives. It must have been a sort of ordeal, to sing and tread the slow dance between that solid wall of silent, impassive white faces. But the Indians seemed to take no notice. And the crowd only silently, impassively watched. Watched with that strange, static American quality of *laisser faire* and of indomitable curiosity.

—*Dial*, March 1923, pp. 251-54. Reprinted in *Phoenix: The Posthumous Papers of D. H. Lawrence*, edited by Edward D. McDonald, 1936, pp. 100-104.

Carl van Vechten and Tony Luhan. Photograph courtesy of Clark Kimball and Charlotte J. Stone, The Great Southwest Books, Santa Fe.

Mabel Luhan arrived at the end of the week in her car, with Tony Luhan, the Taos Indian whom she had married, and they drove us to Taos. Willa Cather was very much impressed by Tony Luhan, and felt an instant liking and admiration for him. He was a splendid figure, over six feet tall, with a noble head and dignified carriage; there was great simplicity and kindness in his voice and manner. Although Willa Cather had intended to make a very brief visit, we stayed for more than two weeks. During that time Mabel Luhan, while making her guests extremely comfortable, rarely appeared herself, excepting at meals; but she sent us off on long drives about the country with Tony. Tony would sit in the driver's seat, in his silver bracelets and purple blanket, often singing softly to himself; while we sat behind. He took us to some of the almost inaccessible Mexican villages hidden in the Cimarron mountains, where the Penitentes still followed their old fierce customs; and from Tony, Willa Cather learned many things about the country and the people that she could not have learned otherwise. He talked very little, but what he said was always illuminating and curiously poetic.

Although *Eusabio* in *Death Comes for the Archbishop* is a Navaho Indian, I think his character was essentially drawn from Tony Luhan.

—Edith Lewis, *Willa Cather Living: A Personal Record,*
1953, pp. 142-43.

Spud Johnson at work. Photograph courtesy of Clark Kimball and Charlotte J. Stone, The Great Southwest Books, Santa Fe.

THIS, gentle and tough readers, purports to be a weekly newspaper, in spite of the fact that it is smaller and more inadequate than any ever before published.

But it is frankly an experiment. Even a miniature publication has to have news and advertising gathered, has to have the copy written, has to have the type set up and has to be printed, then distributed . . . and whether one lean fellow can do all of these things in the space of one week and still have time to eat and sleep, has yet to be satisfactorily proved.

Supposing it can be done, there still remain the questions: Does the town want it? Is Taos interested? Will it help support it? Will business men advertise in it? Will you contribute news items of interest, subscribe to it and read it?

One of these questions, for this issue at least, has already been answered by the local merchants. In fact, quite a number of our initial advertisers had to be put off until next week, owing to lack of time and space—a fact which we regret, but which we are delighted with, nevertheless.

The remaining question, then: Is this the verdict of you all?

Hoping we may meet again next week to discuss the situation further. . .

Spud Johnson, Editor.

—THE HORSE FLY: SMALLEST AND MOST
INADEQUATE NEWSPAPER EVER PUBLISHED,
vol. 1, no. 1, Taos, New Mexico,
July 9th, 1938, p. 2.

Frieda Lawrence and Mabel Dodge Luhan, with a descendant of D. H. Lawrence's dog in the background. Photograph courtesy of Clark Kimball and Charlotte J. Stone, The Great Southwest Books, Santa Fe.

MABEL DEMURE, COURTROOM COZY

by Spud Johnson

Although a self-confessed mover and shaker you would never know it to see Mabel Luhan in the District Court here this week—on trial for slander and being sued for $50,000.

There she sits in a trimly tailored sand-colored dress covered with white polka-dots, a large panama hat on her head, complete with the inevitable ribbons. . . Demure—that's the only word that describes her.

Meek as a lamb and quiet as a little mouse, she has sat sedately for a whole day before a heart attack confined the plaintiff to his home Tuesday, beside her counsel (five of them) and listened attentively but apparently with unconcern to all that has gone on about her, for all the world as though she were at a concert with her friend Leopold Stokowsky conducting.

Ominous Jury

A villainous-looking jury of twelve Spanish gentlemen from the mountains sits ominously on two long benches to her left. She is completely surrounded by lawyers of all shapes and sizes; and behind her sits her accuser, Dr. Charles Kantor, getting redder in the face every hour as unsavory details are revealed.

The court-room itself has changed imperceptibly as the trial progresses. It is a great barn of a place (The American Legion Hall) with no ceiling, bare rafters, naked electric light bulbs, and holes in the roof through which you can see the sky. And it has been filled to its capacity with friends and enemies, tourists and artists, storekeepers and witnesses, celebrities and Indians, farmers and millionaires, housewives and poets . . . and lawyers.

Monday the trial was interrupted by a thunder and hail-storm of such tremendous force that the judge couldn't hear the lawyer nearest him and the jury was completely cut off from any communication whatever with the interpreter. The roof leaked on all of Mabel's lawyers' law-books—and on Mabel too. She hurriedly donned a red raincoat and scurried for cover. More leaks developed and the entire court room was in a hubub. All the benches had to be moved and Judge Mabry himself had to desert the bench.

When it was over, the whole scene was changed. The entire court room was cozier and friendlier. Chairs and benches were pulled up closer to the principals in the drama in a broad semi-circle and it looked exactly like an after-dinner program or fire-side chat at a mountain hotel or—well, maybe like Seton Village with the Chief himself telling a bed-time story!

And it was in this changed, cozier and more intimate atmosphere that the actual trial started. All before this had been the long slow process of weeding out and selecting a jury, squabbling over technical points of changing this and that word in the complaint, of asking for no jury, and then of asking for a jury again, ad infinitum.

But now some twenty-five witnesses were called and sworn in at once—a wholesale procedure which somewhat confused the Judge, he didn't know quite what to do with all of them.

While he was debating this matter, the Honourable Dorothy Brett (one of the witnesses who had just sworn to tell the whole truth and nothing but) decided that her huge Stetson hat was too large for a witness-box, and without more ado, she threw it across the room to a friend. The enormous sombrero sailed over all of Mabel's lawyers and

landed on top of Robinson Jeffers, California poet, who had that moment arrived with his family from Carmel. . .
Her hat—and everyone's—was in the ring. The trial had started.

The only evidence submitted the first day was that of the Ex-Baron Teddy Von Maltzahn, now in Austria, whose deposition was read by two lawyers: Attorney Kiker asking the questions, Attorneys Remley and Beutler alternately taking the part of the absent witness and answering the questions as Von Matlzahn did some months ago.

The gist of this testimony concerned the details of the dinner-party at Mabel Luhan's house on the evening when the fateful criticisms of Dr. Kantor were said to have been made; but it also included many sidelights, such as why the Baron was anxious to conceal the fact that he was an American citizen, whether he was an acquaintance or a friend of Dr. Kantor, and how bored he was with Dr. Kantor's regular Sunday visit at his ranch. (And here Dr. Kantor blushed.)

—*The New Mexico Sentinel*, 19 June 1938.

E. Martin Hennings, "Across the Valley."
Oil, n.d. [1934], 36"x40".
Photographic Record, Public Works of Art Project,
  Thirteenth Region, New Mexico Division.
New Mexico State Records Center and Archives, Santa Fe.

So it is that we, of varied tongues, live on together and find it good to
be alive in Taos valley. Yet here we do not have the comforts of city
life. No water supply makes home-keeping hard. Bathrooms are a
luxury only a few have, and then only where small electric plants
draw water from wells, pure and clear. There are, however, good
stores where one may find every necessary thing and most luxuries.
Good meals may be had in the hotels, near the center of town, while
the hotel de luxe, San Geronimo Lodge, two miles out, bids fair to
rival any "lodge" in the Southwest, when it opens its doors probably
next fall. So everybody may be happy in Taos, unless it be the one
who looks for creature comforts only. He may have little interest in
the place beyond a visit to the free camping grounds, the garages or
the curio stores.

—Blanche C. Grant, *Taos Today*, 1925, pp. 40-41.

Ernest L. Blumenschein, "Ourselves and Taos Neighbors."
Oil, n.d., 41"x 50".
Courtesy Stark Museum of Art, Orange, Texas.
At the left Bert Phillips leans over to speak with Mrs. Burt Harwood. Next to
them, Oscar Berninghaus talks with Dr. Light. Walter Ufer stands beside Dr.
Light, with Leon Gaspard's head visible between and behind them. D. H.
Lawrence stands with Mrs. Lucille Couse, with Victor Higgins' head barely
visible between Ufer and Mrs. Couse. Helen Blumenschein is seated next to
Mary Blumenschein in the foreground. Mrs. Ward Lockwood's head is just
visible behind and between D. H. Lawrence and Mary Blumenschein. Tony
Luhan stands wrapped in a blanket behind and to the right of Mary Blumen-
schein. Mabel Dodge Luhan is partially visible behind him with Mary Aus-
tin's head just above hers. Kenneth Adams is partially visible behind the two
women, and Joseph Sharp's head appears over Adams' right shoulder. Ernest
Blumenschein stands in the foreground with one hand in his pocket. The
Taos Trumpeter and three unidentified Indian friends are at the far right.
(Also see the key and discussion in Patricia Janis Broder, *Taos: A Painter's
Dream* [Boston: New York Graphic Society, 1980], pp. 286-89.)

PASO POR AQUI!

by Mabel Dodge Luhan

Like to like, the magnetic ones flew to the magnet. Impelled by a mysterious gravitation, the glowing spirits arrived every month every week, and added their lustre to the lustrous Valley.

"This is one of the magnetic centres of the earth," Lawrence said. "Such places are invisibly afire for a while and then the spirit that informs them may withdraw to another neighborhood," he added maliciously. Was he speaking unwittingly of himself?

Those were the days!

Then the great and the semi-great and the lovers of the great appeared in the plaza. They looked like other people but they were a little different from the horde. They had a deeper awareness, more capacity, a larger dimension. Potentiality. They were greater. Because of their own inner life they were able to breathe upon the latent life in the Valley so that it brimmed and gave them what they had come here for, an enhancement of power and beauty, delicate and pristine. So there was an exchange between people and environment, each contributed to the other.

When they descended to the world they gave a shape and an expression to what had impressed them in the high place. Sometimes the Valley reappeared, in New York, Washington, or San Francisco; it was exhibited in outline and color, or in music, poetry and prose. Sometimes it showed itself in faces and behavior and in being. The great visitors and the magical earth had created together an influence, and the impact of one upon the other set up a chain reaction that still continues when the original combination has been altered and replaced by other values. Such as commerce and competition.

Who were they, these bright birds of passage, and where are they now?

Some forgot, like Stokowski. Yet Stokie should have remembered, for he truly experienced the beauty and the strangeness (" 'tis the beauty not the strangeness turns the traveller's heart to stone!"). With unwearying patience he spent night-long hours listening to the Indian songs and tried in vain to write down phrases, failing for lack of a scale! "They are singing in thirty-seconds!" he whispered despairingly.

He returned the following year with a specially built recording machine, but it was not perfected like the ones of today and after the first tryout he shoved it under the table where it remained until his departure. But what of it? What do we get now from perfect recordings with their full volume and accurate tone? Do we get more than

Teams at hitching posts near Taos plaza, May 1939. Department of Development Collection, New Mexico State Records Center and Archives, Santa Fe.

the bare, dead facts? Do we get the life waves, the imponderable life vibrations that, heart to heart, enable us to know the singers and the players? Do we get the life of them? Not, I think, from any canned music. The germ has been destroyed.

So maybe Stokie did not forget. Maybe he remembered and gave up.

And of the others, some died, like D. H. Lawrence, Willa Cather and Dr. A. A. Brill.

We know what Lawrence did when he went away. He began to die quite soon and maybe he should have stayed, but then we should not have *Lady Chatterley's Lover* with its prophetic foresight of broken class distinctions and its revaluation of real life. Something he got in Taos enabled him to write this, but only outside and away he learned that.

He had a fine time putting a period to the importance of economic situations and in reinstating the flesh, giving it first place before money and what money could buy; demonstrating the extravagant finality of Victoria's materialism. What would *she* do for love?

One remembers her fantastic gesture towards her lover upon his birthday, setting him definitely far down on the list of her importances, empire and the like!

"To John Brown, a pair of silver-plated cuff links—not too much, God knows, for such a faithful friend!"

The book that came out of Willa when she left Taos was better loved than all her other books. Perhaps there is more love in it.

In *Death Comes for the Archbishop* it seems we find the verities she soaked up in Taos and Santa Fe, the little tales Tony told on the long, slow, drives around the Valley in the summer afternoons, and the simple immediacy of the Roman Catholic Church as it is known here where its realities seem stronger than all its grand organization. The realities stayed with her, for upon her return to the frantic world she drew upon them to the end, as we see in *The Shadow and the Rock*, maybe having found here security and certainty in the midst of chaos.

Taos was simply and deeply imbued with the Roman faith in those days, for both the Spanish people and the Indians dwelt in an intimate proximity to God.

For the Indians it was a more recent experience than for the Spaniards (or Mexicans as they were called then before the public schools decided this nomenclature was an insult!).

The Spaniards had espoused Jesus Christ since the early Roman days of crucifixion, but to the Indians He and His Mother were guests of a mere three hundred years, having been introduced by the Catholic priests when they arrived with the King's soldiers.

The Indians always have loved women and children and they steadily offered hospitality and a guest house, called the *Iglesia*, to the newcomers in the Pueblo. They treated them with tenderness and admiration, taking them out for an airing occasionally, taking them to bless the fields, treating them with intimacy and honor.

Possibly because the Pueblo was matriarchal in habit they seemed to revere the Lady Mother more then Her young Son; and there is a story in another Pueblo that hints at this when, during a drought, they carried the image of the little Jesus out to the newly-sown fields and besought Him to bring down the rain. It is told that that night there was cloudburst over the land and it washed out all the seed. The following day the people carried the Virgin Queen through the mud-soaked terrain and, showing it to her, they said:

"Now look at the mess your Son has made!"

In Taos and Santa Fe it was possible to become immersed in this intimate and familiar Catholicism, and in Willa's beautiful book we recognize it.

People used to come to Taos almost as though they had to. Impelled. Like Thornton Wilder, whom I had never met, but who telephoned me from Santa Fe, stammering a little: "I w-w-would like to c-c-come up and see you if I may," then arriving with two heavy bags. (Was it in Taos he learned that all people are just people and so wrote of Caesar and his wife as of the people next door?)

Taos brings out the particularity in people. It is the most individuating place in the world, I think. As Frank Waters says, it is the last outpost of individualism left!

There is no standardization here, no social structure. People do not live according to a single pattern. Every house one enters is different in character from every other, and the occupants resemble no one else.

Side by side, people live their *own* lives and not the community's life. They do as they please, they say what they think, and nobody cares, for everyone is busy doing likewise. There is only one vague imperative seeming to guide them all. If they come and do not fit into the good spirit of Taos, they do not stay. They cannot. Nobody tells them to go away, they just disappear. The "genius loci" of the Valley is benign and tolerant and it maintains a creative direction. Anyone who, in his essential nature, opposes this spirit of the place is forced out by it, for it is very powerful. This spirit does not draw the line at civil crime, it does not object to "moral turpitude," gambling, or even passionate murder. But the mean, the petty, the destructive elements cannot exist here for long. They cannot continue to live and breathe and have their negative being in this place. They go in order to survive in their miserable fashion. The alternative left to them is to change, to overcome their evil star, to be a part of the Taos order and not in opposition to it.

I do not think I am imagining this. Taos does things to people. So many people came! Sometimes they stayed, others went away but came back; some like Georgia O'Keefe never altogether went away; others finally stayed away but now are starkly stripped of half-and-half realities down to bedrock like Jeffers was, as one finds in his play *Medea*. Oh, yes! Taos does things to people.

Some got it through the eye, some through the ear, and others through the pores of the skin.

Robert Edmond Jones was a seer. He saw a life in the old handicrafts and in the ancient hand-built houses, where no spirit level was used, and no plumb line made straight mechanical forms one like another as off an assembly line. He saw the sensitive, refreshing shapes of which the eye would never tire. When he went back to New York he designed the settings for *Til Eulenspiegel*, performed at the Metropolitan Opera House, and they could have come out of Taos handmade.

Nowadays in Taos people try to build crooked so their houses will

"The Big House," home of Mabel Dodge Luhan, Taos. Postcard dated 1931, addressed to Miss Elsie [Elizabeth Shepley] Sergeant, Cosmopolitan Club, East 40th Street, New York, New York. Message: "Love and a happy Christmas from Mabel and Tony." Virginia Johnson Collection, New Mexico State Records Center and Archives, Santa Fe.

look like the old ones. But they do not succeed with them. It is not done like that. In the past there was feeling put into the uneven outlines, for the men were happy building their homes. They were not trying to be artists. Art is a by-product of living; it is not living, in itself.

In bygone days the settlers in Taos Valley had a true sense of proportion, unconscious and valid, springing from the heart. Their building was functional—wooden pillars of right dimension supported portales that were of the proper height and depth for their uses. They were not added for decoration or "interesting shadows."

What there is left of these old places still retains the *gemütlich*, the charming, the *real* look of natural beauty, inimitable, and not to be repeated in our mechanized age.

John Marin was another seer. He saw so essentially that he delivered the landscape in a few bare strokes of his brush, the color and form with all the freshness of high altitude intensity, massive and clean in the morning of the world. Other Taos painters here before he came wondered why they had not seen it like that and straightway adopted his vision, turning it into a formula. But they lacked something he had. What was it?

One night I had the Indian boys come down to dance for Dr. Brill at a little party we gave him. He watched them with his glowing red face, so full of good will, all lighted up.

The boys flashed by him, their golden brown bodies gleaming, the bells ringing on their ankles. How happy! How happy! The big drum and the singers supported them and never let them sag. The longer they danced, the more dance they had in them, so after a while we had to withdraw to the living room and let them go on in their accelerating ecstasy; for since we were not participating we could not endure, without fatigue overlong, just watching! When we closed the door upon them, they afforded a faint delirious background of delight to the little speech Dr. Brill was making to the guests:

". . .Descartes said: '*Je pense donc je suis*,' but I prefer to say: '*J'agis donc je suis*.' I move, therefore I am! This dancing embodies my feeling perfectly. True and complete being is in the movement of the whole body and not only in the movement of the mind. In New York there is an old gentleman who is a patient of mine. In his eighties now, he is vigorous and indomitable. But one day his son and his daughter-in-law came to see me and they were very worried about him.

"What should we do doctor? Father keeps on *going!* He goes out at night dancing with his little sweetheart! Imagine! Dancing for hours at his age! He will not listen to us! What if he should have a *heart attack* and *die?*"

" 'Well, now, wouldn't that be wonderful?' I asked them. 'Wouldn't it be fine for him to die dancing instead of immobilized in his bed? *I* think so,' " and he grinned around at the faces turned up to him.

Everyone clapped at his words except one or two who pulled down their lips and glanced at each other, while the dim pounding of feet and drum in the distance emphasized the wonder of motion.

We persuaded John Collier to come to Taos for his vacation, and he came bringing Lucy and his three little boys.

The world had been too much with him and he had a quick conversion to the mysterious enlightenment of our Taos *ambiente*.

After the months passed, he left to take up his work in San Francisco again but soon he wrote that he could not stay away. Taos had done something to him!

What followed has been a long story, too long to tell here in detail, besides being already known.

Briefly he organized the American Indian Defense Association; he successfully fought the Government in its Bureau of Indian Affairs; and, superseding the antique routine that dated back to the Civil War, he became himself Commissioner of Indian Affairs.

Street leading to Taos Pueblo, May 1939. Department of Development Collection, New Mexico State Records Center and Archives, Santa Fe.

In that role he placed the emphasis upon Indians instead of upon the Indian Bureau employees. Under Roosevelt he established a New Deal for the Indians, who, paying a visit to the President, asked for it themselves and obtained it when Mr. Roosevelt sent them over to see Mr. Ickes who was then Secretary of the Interior.

Those were the days! When they came to an end, under the change of administration Democracy has to endure, Collier organized the Institute of Ethnic Affairs, enlarging his field to include all minority and some majority groups existing in Mexico, and the countries south and east and all islands flying our flag. He has unified these in a measure of solidarity so they have become a "factor." It is still too early to know what this means. Probably more than anthropological and ethnological knowledge, probably political values. Or perhaps cosmic progress of some kind? Probably.

As far as the artists are concerned, something started here long ago, as you will see in the following pages by other writers.

I can touch here very briefly only upon a few other personalities who came to Taos in earlier years.

Mr. and Mrs. Bert Harwood, fresh from Paris during the first World War, recognized its wonder and responded to it with generosity and creativeness. But it was harder then than now to get the inhabitants

Harwood Foundation, Taos. John Gaw Meem Collection, New Mexico State Records Center and Archives, Santa Fe.

to cooperate. Bert was grieved because he could not organize a branch of the Red Cross association. There was not enough interest among the people of the community. But now, with Time's unfailing justice, the Red Cross conducts its meetings and business in Bert Harwood's house.

When Mrs. Harwood died, she bequeathed her beautiful place and everything in it to the University of New Mexico for a social center, where it now provides art classes, conducts a lending library that includes a bookmobile supplying reading to all the Taos County people, and where all kinds of meetings are held and exhibitions of all types are shown. She has contributed enormously to the socialization of the whole community.

Another fabulous contributor to Taos, Dr. Victor Thorne, became an active influence of the same kind. Inheriting Mr. Manby's large property, he reconstructed the house and provided maintenance for the beautiful garden surrounded by its fertile fields. More than this, he contributed freely to many community efforts by doubling the earnings of many bazaars, money-making community sales, and hospital group efforts, although he was unable himself to be in Taos.

He delegated our socially conscious Helen Williams to manage his property in a helpful and benevolent spirit, so that numberless people have been aided by her administration of it. "Thorne House" is another active and positive influence in Taos Valley.

One of the results of Dr. Thorne's contribution will presently result in the Kit Carson Memorial Park, which will include the old cemetery where the latter is buried; and the former Manby land will provide a beautiful park for the townspeople.

When one looks back one finds in retrospect how many people have enlarged the Taos spirit! Dasburg, one of the foremost painters of the century, came and has stayed for decades. His stimulating, penetrating instruction has inoculated countless students who have carried it to the outer world.

Emil Bisstram built up his large art school in Taos, and now overflows with it during the winter season into the larger environment of Los Angeles, where he indubitably permeates his groups with the mysterious Taos influence.

What happened to Marsden Hartley in our town? He wrote me years later that after his months here in the Valley his painting seemed to have gained a larger dimension that appeared in it involuntarily, unbidden but welcome!

And Brett! Coming to Taos she developed her unique talent in a touching appreciation of the simple beauty and truth of Indian life that the English Slade School certainly did not arouse! . . . "and knowing this is truth and truth is beauty . . . what further shall be sought for or declared?" Browning said.

What I have set down here are but a few hints about the exchange of influence between Taos and those who passed through, and but a few names of the greater number of those, for a list without the stories attached is only sterile and tiresome, and I have not the space for more. But as I tell even this little, I discover for myself that the balance between these two, the environment and the people, is not even.

Environment is the stronger for as long as it does something more for the people than the people do for it, and that is still true today. *Taos continues to do something to people.* But we do not know how long this will last, for there are new and powerful elements at work all over the world and not only in this little Valley.

Some call it Progress and some call it Commerce and some call it merely Change.

" 'Tis a heartbreak to the wise that things are in the same place for a short time only!"

The irrational and irresponsible universe, we think sometimes, we all unknowing . . . and without faith.

—*New Mexico Quarterly* 21 (1951): 137-46.

Lynn Riggs. Photograph courtesy of Clark Kimball and Charlotte J. Stone, The Great Southwest Books, Santa Fe.

MORNING WALK—SANTA FE

by Lynn Riggs

In Burro Alley I saw no one,
(This was hours before the sun)
Only the gray adobe walls
Leaning down like waterfalls,
Only the weedy patios
No longer gay with strumming beaux.
Don Gaspar Street, processional,
Dipped and bowed; its shoulders tall
Were red with brick, gigantic words
Rose and soared thereon like birds.

The Alameda was a way
As tranquil as a field in May.
Under the cottonwoods it ran,
And under them I met a man
With frosty beard and cherry eyes.
He looked at me without surprise
Although I carried no pail of food
Nor drove a burro lashed with wood.

I met four burros on Cañon Road,
Every burro with his load;
I looked at them as anyone should
Seeing a burro winged with wood.
Exactly as a river moves
Flowed the placid burro hooves.
I walked away from Cañon Road:
Mine had become a winged load.
The dawn was nearer than I knew;
The icy air came up like dew.
De Vargas Street was like a lane;
On Monte Sol I met the rain,
Dripping he brought me home again.

—Alice Corbin Henderson, compiler,
*The Turquoise Trail: An Anthology of
New Mexico Poetry*, 1928, pp. 115-16.
(Copyrighted in *The Iron Dish*,
Doubleday Doran, 1930, pp. 29-30.)

Alice Corbin Henderson writing a poem. Frame from the 1931 film, "A Day in Santa Fe," produced by Lynn Riggs and James Hughes. New Mexico State Records Center and Archives, Santa Fe.

"Alice Corbin, where art thou?" runs a query often in the minds and memories of the Old Guard who witnessed the launching of *Poetry: A Magazine of Verse* in 1912. She had a gallant heart and a gay smile and the great expectations required for the sailing of that dauntless little ship. A poet, a creative critic and editor, she has a definite and highlighted place in the story of American literature of that period. When some of us arrive at where we can with ease look backward and record with care and deliberation certain adventures we have seen and shared, Alice Corbin will stand forth in elements of both the angelic and the demoniac. Only one having both those elements could have the range of affectionate understanding, compassion through identity, necessary to ride herd on Vachel and Carl, Edgar Lee and Ezra, Robinson and Hal Bynner, H. D. and Amy, John Gould Fletcher and Edwin Arlington Robinson, those two lawyers Archie MacLeish and Wally Stevens—and God knows who all, by the way of clowns, acrobats, trapeze artists, sword swallowers and fire eaters. "Alice Corbin, where art thou?" Withersoever thou art, if you ain't got sweet reminiscences, who has?

—Carl Sandburg, "Alice," *New Mexico Quarterly Review* 19 (1949): 56.

Paul Lantz, "Landscape."
Oil, n.d. [1934].
Photographic Record, Public Works of Art Project,
  Thirteenth Region, New Mexico Division.
New Mexico State Records Center and Archives, Santa Fe.

SANTA FE IN THE TWENTIES

by Ruth Laughlin

I always think of the William Penhallow Hendersons as smiling; of
Whippie stalking along in high-heeled boots, eyes twinkling under
his big sombrero, small moustache widened in a grin and a merry
quip for me as we passed; of the smile that lifted Alice Corbin's
round, red cheeks and shone deeply in her brown eyes. Through a
friendship of more than thirty years it is good to recall those smiling
faces. The smiles were never fatuous or merely polite. They expressed

deep humor and courage and the inner resources of creative artists who faced life with high challenge and a gay curiosity as to what would happen next.

One day last fall, when the cottonwoods on the Tesuque hillside below her house were shining gold, Alice Corbin and I laughed over the memories of Santa Fe in the 1920's.

"Years ago you told me that only the newcomer should write of the Southwest," I reminded Alice. "You said that first impressions were clear, vivid and exciting but that after six months the scene became too familiar and lost its sharp focus."

"I've changed my time limit on that," she laughed, "though the memory of my first Christmas in Santa Fe is so vivid that I can almost feel the crisp cold air now. We came here in 1916 and I have written about the impact of New Mexico ever since. There is still much that I want to say. . . ."

"Your poems in the *Turquoise Trail* and *Red Earth* express what all of us would like to say about this country," I said.

"We loved this Red Earth country from the beginning, even though we came here for my health," Alice explained. "We wanted to see all of it . . . every pueblo, every Indian dance, every Spanish village. We rode horseback to Chimayo and stayed all night with Mr. Chavez whose family built the Sanctuario long ago as their private chapel. That was during the First World War and the little statue of Santiago wore a tin lemon sieve on his head, bent to look like a war helmet. His arm was broken and Willie mended it with tissue paper and glue."

That act of helping to save a prized relic was typical of the Hendersons. They valued the historic traditions of Santa Fe and worked to preserve them. They took a vital interest in the town and supported every worthy civic project whether it was concerned with art, architecture, writing, the Fiesta, or a water trough for thirsty horses hitched near the plaza.

Alice Corbin spent her first year at Sunmount Sanitarium, and Whippie and the small daughter Alice lived in a near-by adobe house on the loma south of town. When Alice moved down to join them she discovered that the rutted dirt road in front of their home was called Telephone Road in honor of the proud new telephone poles marching up the hill. She changed that to the original Spanish name, El Camino del Monte Sol, the Road to the Sun Mountain. Other artists and writers soon built their studios near the Hendersons and the Camino became famous, but I always think of the name as a monument to the poetic sensitiveness of Alice Corbin.

In our busy lives the years pass rapidly and mostly without specific dates or events. It was my visit with Alice Corbin and my realization of what she had meant to Santa Fe that brought me a fresh evaluation

Spectators gathering at amphitheatre for "Pageant of Old Santa Fe," directed
by Thomas Wood Stevens, Santa Fe Fiesta, August 5, 1926. John Gaw Meem
Collection, New Mexico State Records Center and Archives, Santa Fe.

of the last three decades. At the close of the 1940's I realize that many
members of the original art colony have passed on, others have reached
distinguished maturity in spite of the devastating years of World War
II, and a new group is now adding vitality to the old town. I think of
the 1930's as the depression years when many plans were thwarted
but also as a period when the art colony settled in and became an
integral part of Santa Fe. I look back to the 1920's as an astonishing
decade that flourished with initial impetus, creative urge and significant civic development.

Early in the twentieth century the fame of the Taos Art Colony
encouraged many young artists to come to the Southwest instead of
Paris. Santa Fe's pioneer artists were Kenneth Chapman and Carlos
Vierra, followed in 1912 by Gerald and Ina Sizer Cassidy. During the
next eighteen years probably no art colony in the United States had a
more active roster than Santa Fe. The artists in permanent residence
included W. P. Henderson, Warren Rollins, Albert Schmidt, Sheldon
Parsons, Gustave Baumann, Olive Rush, Raymond Jonson, B. J. O.
Norfeldt [sic], Dorothy Stewart, Henry Balink, Preston McCrossen,
Datus Myers, Andrew Dasburg, Vernon Hunter, Theodore Van Soelen,
John Sloan, Randall Davey, Julius Rohlshoven [sic], McHarg Daven-

port, William Lumpkins, Frank Applegate, Josef [sic] Bakos, Freemont [sic] Ellis, Willard Nash, Will Shuster, Walter Mruck [sic] and three sculptors, Eugenie Shonnard, Allan Clark and George Blodgett. Among the writers were Alice Corbin, Mary Austin, Witter Bynner, Willard Johnson, Haniel Long, Ida Raugh [sic], Glenway Westcott [sic], Lynn Riggs, Isabel Campbell, Elizabeth De Huff, Ruth Laughlin, Omar Barker, Roark Bradford, Earl and Marion Scott, Dorothy Hughes, John Curtis Underwood, Peggy Pond Church, Ray Otis, Phillip [sic] E. Stevenson, Thomas Wood Stevens and Helen Stevens.

In the 1920's Santa Fe was a small, friendly town where everyone knew everyone else and each individual's work was a valuable asset to the community. Whippie Henderson painted the murals for the Country Club where we danced, and Gerald Cassidy painted the murals for the movie theatre. The Little Theatre had enthusiastic members including Jane Baumann, Anna V. Huey, Hazel Pond, Norman Magee, Edwin Brooks, John Evans, Jim Macmillan and Robert Brown. Ashley Pond slid down a pole from his bedroom to his garage to jump in his car, race to a burning building and lead the Volunteer Fire Department whose staff numbered several artists and professional men.

During those years Lynn Riggs wrote his first one-act play called *Knives From Syria* with the encouragement of Ida Raugh. Glenway Westcott and Ted Stevenson struggled with their first novels, Mary Austin wrote books and articles, exhorted audiences and presided in Buddha-like majesty over a young crop of writers jokingly called the Genius Club. Marsden Hartley found inspiration in New Mexico's primitive religious art and wrote sensitive interpretations of Indian ceremonies. Poets gathered around Alice Corbin and Witter Bynner, and Spud Johnson published their poems in his temperamentally gaited literary magazine, *The Laughing Horse.*

Frank Applegate stopped over on a cross-country trek and stayed the rest of his life. His versatile gifts included ceramics, painting, writing, and collecting primitive art in bultos and santos. He bought land on the Camino opposite the Hendersons and encouraged a group of young artists to mix adobes and build their homes on that hillside. They called themselves the Cinco Pintores, the five painters being Will Shuster, Josef Bakos, Willard Nash, Freemont Ellis and Walter Mruck [all sic]. These artists delighted in the plastic lines of adobe architecture but the sloping lintels of Mruck's house even went beyond the local vagaries. For years his place was known as the "Adam and Eve House" on account of the colossal nude figures moulded on the street side of his fireplace. Across the road Mary Austin began to build her "Beloved House" and below her Alice and Datus Myers completed a spacious home with tiled walls, patios and fountains, studios and

B.J.O. Nordfeldt, "Canyon Road."
Lithograph, n.d. [1934], 10"x 13".
Photographic Record, Public Works of Art Project,
    Thirteenth Region, New Mexico Division.
New Mexico State Records Center and Archives, Santa Fe.

library. By this time the Hendersons had added rooms and studios to their vanguard adobe home.

Outside these simple mud houses conformed to traditional Spanish-Indian lines, but inside the artists expressed their individual tastes. Witter Bynner installed his fine Chinese carvings, paintings and jade in his adobe home. John Sloan painted the geometric lines of Indian design on his floors and ceilings. Gus Baumann carved lintels and doorways with the skill he had long used for wood-block prints. The etcher in B. J. O. Nordfelt [sic] found expression in the carved and gilded panels set into his ceiling. Randall Davey restored a Spanish balcony on his house at the end of Canyon Road, and Theodore Van

Soelen and Albert Schmidt built homes at Tesuque. Olive Rush, Sheldon Parsons, and Gerald and Ina Cassidy bought historic houses on Canyon Road and added carved beams, church panels and patio gardens.

No one took as intense an interest in Spanish-Indian architecture as Carlos Vierra. He studied and photographed every old building he could find and preached his gospel of the long heritage of native architecture so vehemently that it became known as the "Santa Fe Style," although buildings at the State University in Albuquerque had been designed along Indian lines some years before.

The archaeologist, Sylvanus Griswold Morley, was the first to restore an old adobe for his home and show that native construction and carving was more attractive than the new-fangled red brick bungalows. Fired by the enthusiasm of Sylvanus Morley and Carlos Vierra that generous patron of the arts, the Honorable Frank Springer, gave the first large contribution toward a State Art Museum, to be built along the lines of New Mexico's venerable mission churches. Later Mr. Springer commissioned Carlos Vierra to build a new house along the old lines which remains to this day one of the best examples of its kind.

A young architect, who was then a patient at Sunmount, spent days with Carlos Vierra studying old photographs and plans. His name was John Gaw Meem and by 1923 he had designed his first "Santa Fe Style" homes. A few years later the Santa Fe railroad chose him to remodel and enlarge La Fonda Hotel. Since then his name has become synonymous with the best designs of southwestern architecture.

This was the era of the world-wide renaissance of native crafts. It was a revolt against the mechanized destruction of World War I, a nostalgic longing for peace and a hunger for beauty produced by a man's own hands. New Mexico's Indian and Spanish handicrafts assumed new importance in this revival. The art colony led movements to sustain and preserve such indigenous crafts as pottery, silver and tin smithing, embroidery and weaving.

The Hendersons, Mary Austin, Frank Applegate, the Senior and Junior Leonora Curtins, Mary Wheelwright, Frank and Harry Mera, John Gaw Meem and Carlos Vierra, were leaders in organizing the Spanish Colonial Arts Society and the Indian Arts Fund. Through the latter ancient Indian pottery was saved and the best examples of new pottery were added to form a collection that has become an inspiration to international designers and to the modern Indian craftsmen.

The Indian Arts Fund collection of pottery, blankets, baskets and silver was the inspiration for building the Laboratory of Anthropology with financial aid from the Rockefeller Foundation and on land south of town donated by Amelia Elizabeth White and Francis Wilson.

Near the Laboratory Mary Wheelwright planned a unique museum for Navajo Ceremonial Arts. William Penhallow Henderson designed this museum on the lines of Navajo hogan, and Alice Corbin wrote the text for the Navajo legends explaining the Navajo sand paintings.

The art colony did not closet itself in an adobe tower to paint and write but became articulate and intensely interested citizens. These people had discovered an Old World charm and tranquility in Santa Fe and were determined to preserve it. They fought against tearing down old houses and replacing them with filling stations, against reducing Santa Fe to that ugly American sameness that is labeled Progress, against Texas Club Women who innocently planned a Culture Center. They were individualists who argued violently with each other but united against too much change in their adopted home. Whippie Henderson felt this so strongly that he began to design buildings and planned the restoration of Sena Plaza for Amelia Elizabeth White. Alice Corbin always spoke up at any meeting where the original character of Santa Fe was imperiled.

Human rights as well as civic problems gained a champion in Alice Corbin. She was an original member of an organization formed to defeat the Bursum bill and its threat to pueblo lands. For twenty-five years she has worked with the New Mexico Association on Indian Affairs to help the Indians and encourage their arts and crafts.

As a writer her influence was also widespread and vital. Although she had resigned as associate editor of *Poetry* when she left Chicago, she continued to serve as long-distance adviser and was in touch with numerous poets who submitted their work to that important magazine. When Harriet Monroe, editor of *Poetry*, visited Alice in Santa Fe the local group gathered around the Henderson fireplace and talked far into the night about old and new forms of literature.

Other friends of Alice Corbin came to find out why she was so enthusiastic about an off-the-railroad western town. Witter Bynner planned a three-day stop to see Alice and give a lecture, and became a permanent resident. Bynner took over the adobe house of Paul Berlin [sic], the painter, and his wife Natalie Curtis, who wrote of Indian music. Among others who lived here for part of the year were Arthur Davison Ficke, Edna St. Vincent Millay, Robert Henri, George Bellows and Nicolas Roerick [sic]. Willa Cather came here to check material for her classic *Death Comes for the Archbishop*. Alma Gluck sang at informal evenings at the Hendersons, Ernest Block composed his American Symphony, and Adolf Bohlm interpreted Russian dances. Sinclair Lewis wandered in and out of studios, Carl Sandburg chanted ballads to his guitar, and Vachel Lindsay gave his inimitable "Chinese Nightingale" as a special treat for his friend Alice Corbin.

Although automobiles did not have modern high-speed motors,

other New Mexico writers and artists traveled the dirt roads to join the Santa Fe parties. Mabel Dodge Luhan and Tony, D. H. Lawrence and Frieda, Ernest Blumenschein, Victor Higgins, Howard Cook, Barbara Latham and Kenneth Adams came down from Taos; Erna and Harvey Fergusson came up from Albuquerque, Paul Horgan from Roswell, and Oliver La Farge from field work in the Indian country.

Everyone looked forward to John and Dolly Sloan's annual celebration August 4. One year the Bohemian crowd was startled to see a white horse join the party in the studio. Every year the audience demanded that Hal Bynner repeat his sermon by the Negro preacher, Randall Davey give his hilarious interpretations, and John Sloan go through his act of finding the hair in the soup.

Visiting, talking, partying are essential recreations for artists. Evenings at the Sloans', Hendersons', Hal Bynner's, or Mary Austin's offered exchange of thoughts and often heated arguments. They served as cross-pollenization to fertilize the artist's half-formed plans. I remember one evening when we were all sitting on the floor in front of the fireplace and Dolly whispered, "Don't disturb Sloan. I can see that he is getting an idea for a picture." Between celebrations the art colony did serious work and gained national recognition.

Alice Corbin's appreciation of New Mexico grew deeper each year. She collected a fine library of southwestern books and studied New Mexican history, Indian myths, Penitente rituals and the folk legends and customs of her Spanish-American and Indian neighbors. She was always eager to get first hand information from such authorities as Edgar L. Hewett, Paul A. F. Walter, E. Dana Johnson, Charles F. Lummis, Nina Otero-Warren, Kenneth Chapman and Harry Mera. She delighted in Howard Thorpe's [sic] early reminiscences and encouraged him to write his collections of cowboy stories and ballads. She was an enthusiastic friend and admirer of Eugene Manlove Rhodes and, in later years, took the lead in an effort to bring out a memorial edition of all his books and make his grave a literary shrine.

Her generous help for young writers as well as those who have attained distinction has been a fine and lasting influence. Her interest has deepened with thirty years' residence and today she is still eager to add her smiling wisdom and encouragement to any constructive development in the arts or community life. In Santa Fe we value Alice Corbin as a good citizen, a distinguished poet and a beloved neighbor.

—*New Mexico Quarterly Review* 19 (1949): 58-66.

"Pageant of Old Santa Fe," Santa Fe Fiesta, August 5, 1926. John Gaw Meem Collection, New Mexico State Records Center and Archives, Santa Fe.

A CHRISTMAS BALLAD OF
THE FIRE FIGHTER'S FAMILY

by Ruth and Will Barker

'Twas the night before Christmas and all through the town
Not a creature was stirring from grown children down.
The Barkers were sleeping all snug in their beds
While visions of Christmas danced through their heads,
When out of the night there arose a long wail,
As though hell had pulled the devil's black tail.
It shrieked and fluttered, it wavered and moaned,
And lifting our heads we listened and groaned.
'Twas the fire-fighter's siren calling so wild,
"Come, you brave firemen, come save my child!"
Will dashed to his closet, and Jean, half asleep,
Pulled out papa's pants and coat lined with sheep.
La Ru grabbed his helmet, and Laughlin his boots
To save frantic moments while the siren still toots.
Ruth rushed to the 'phone for number and street,
"Oh, hurry, my darling, 'tis the bootlegger's suite."
One buckle, one heave, all helping of course
We harnessed up Will like a fire-engine horse.
He whinnied and nickered and tore through the door,
And started his car with a terrible roar.
Red engines were racing with firemen aboard
To save Bootlegger Joe and his Christmas cheer hoard.
O'er barrels and bottles the blue flames were leaping,
Close to the still the red fire was creeping.
The Chemical started, but the Chief with a crash,
Yelled, "Stop, laddies, stop, or you'll spoil all the mash."
Will sprang to his place, second nozzle he spattered
And put out the flames from all barrels that mattered.
Bootlegger Joe called the brave firemen in,
And locked all the doors with a wink and a grin.
Pale wife and children watched at their door,
Never had fires lasted so long before.
'Twas bright Christmas morn when William came home;
Singed were his eyebrows, blackened his dome.
But he shouted right merrily as he hove in sight,
"Merry Christmas to all and to all a goodnight."

Christmas,
Santa Fe, 1930

—Raymond Otis, "The Santa Fe Volunteer
Fire Department: A History of Its Life
and Reputation," n.d., p. 3.

The Santa Fe Volunteer Fire Department, March 25, 1933: (front row) Ray Otis, Ashley Pond, Alex Barnes, Herb Greer, Bill Martin, Juan Sedillo, Bill Roberts, and Reese Fullerton; (middle row) John Stump, George Mignardot, Ellis Bauer, Felix Wheeler (driver), Fred Thompson and Joe McCabe; (back row) John Wheeler (Felix's son), Eddie Brooks, "Leather" Gans, Herb Mendenhall, Norman McGee and Dr. Bob Brown. *The [Santa Fe] New Mexican,* 5 June 1966. D. Margolis Collection, New Mexico State Records Center and Archives, Santa Fe.

John Collier hung in effigy at the corner of Lincoln and Palace Avenues, Santa Fe, February 1931. The photograph is taken from beneath the portal of the Palace of the Governors and shows both the Fine Arts Museum and the New Mexican Publishing Corporation building beyond. John Gaw Meem Collection, New Mexico State Records Center and Archives, Santa Fe.

The large sign, visible in other photographs, contains a message composed by Witter Bynner:

COLLIERS FOXOLOGY

Praise *God* from whom all
Blessings flow—Praise *God*
for Indians here below—
No matter who may pay the
cost, without the Indians
I'd be lost—Whoever really
helps the tribes receives my
curses and my jibes; and there
for Mr. Hagerman I try to hurt you
all I can—If there were many more
like you I should have nothing left to
do—Love for the Indians is my boast
yet I love John Collier most—
    Amen—

Artists and writers, who agreed with ex-governor of New Mexico Herbert J. Hagerman's handling of Navajo affairs as special commissioner to the Navajos in the early twenties and who felt that Commissioner Collier had alienated the Pueblos following the Pueblo Lands Act in 1924, met Hagerman's train at Lamy after Senate investigations of him in 1931. They escorted him back to Santa Fe and ended their demonstration by hanging the effigy on the corner of the Plaza. (See Kenneth R. Philp, *John Collier's Crusade for Indian Reform, 1920-1954* [Tucson: University of Arizona Press, 1977], pp, 109-11.)

Artists of the Modern School, with poets and writers, decided about 1926 that the historical parade was not typically Santa Fe, since it might be staged anywhere, so they instituted their own fiesta and named it El Pasatiempo. Immediately it proved a "howling success," producing rhythms of laughter as it proceeded among the crowded lines of spectators. Since then it has been substituted for the historical procession as an "hysterical pageant" in the Fiesta program and is always led by Dolly Sloan (Mrs. John Sloan, of New York and Santa Fe) in flowing white skirt, high Spanish comb and white lace mantilla, with Witter Bynner, the poet, who impersonates Indians and Mexican peons so skillfully that one day on the plaza, as he stood in costume talking to a group of appreciative real Indians, a tourist selected him as the "most typical" Indian, asked the privilege of taking his photograph in broken English (which tourists often use in addressing the Native American) and then smilingly handed him a dime in compensation. John Sloan doesn't parade, but furnishes many ideas. One year he deserted his painting for weeks, carving and decorating Indian hobby horses, such as are used in Indian ceremonies in the Pueblos, which cavorted on their human legs with most "outlandish" riders.

* * *

There is [also] street dancing, where once I danced for hours opposite Witter Bynner and Dolly Sloan with a Mexican sheepherder from the mountains, who chatted to me continuously, with perfumed breath, on how *muy bonita* I was with all of the charms of the universe, assuring me that he would immediately build a new adobe house to which to take me as his bride; and then I was to discover that he was almost totally blind, but oh, how he could dance, improvising as he stepped!

—Elizabeth Willis De Huff, "The Santa Fe Fiesta," *The Santa Fean*, Fiesta Edition 1941, pp. 30, 33.

Dolly Sloan and Witter Bynner leading an early Santa Fe Fiesta Pasatiempo parade. Photograph courtesy of Clark Kimball and Charlotte J. Stone, The Great Southwest Books, Santa Fe.

The Federal Writers' Project float for the September 5, 1938, Santa Fe Fiesta Pasatiempo ("Hysterical") parade. Ina Sizer Cassidy sits on the side underneath the sign proclaiming the still unfinished "American Guide-Book." Museum of New Mexico, Santa Fe.

I wish we lived in Kansas,
Where everything is flat—
No peak to make the tourists point,
And say *"What's that?"*

But here in dear New Mexico,
A million humps an' hollers
Keep us sweating all the week
And spoil our clean White Collars!

And every mountain wears the name
Of Spanish Don or Lady,
Of outlaw, Saint, or Indian tribe—
All sanctified, or shady!

I think it would be simpler far
To call the CCCs,
And have them roll the country flat,
So we could take our ease!

—Alice Corbin Henderson,
"Lines Mumbled in Sleep,"
30 July 1936, in *Over the
Turquoise Trail*, vol. 1,
no. 1, 1937, p. 3.

Unidentified Santa Fe writer at his typewriter. Virginia Johnson Collection, New Mexico State Records Center and Archives, Santa Fe.

THE SANTA FE GROUP

by Elizabeth Shepley Sergeant

Ever since my first visit to New Mexico in 1920, I have felt sure that Santa Fe is not just another part of the United States, but in some sense a separate land, with a being and laws of its own. The blend of cultures—Indian-Spanish-Mexican, Pioneer-Southwestern and Colonist Southwestern (New York, Chicago and what-not)—is unique and creates a ferment, a sense of growth, and a divine discontent. A writer, however small his income, may here wake every day, in a setting esthetically pleasing and somewhat exotic, historical and timeless, with perhaps too keen a sense of stimulus.

The quasi-regional school of arts and letters which is here in process of formation is nevertheless leisurely in pace as it is extended in space— stretching in one direction towards Albuquerque, a bourgeois business town (in the eyes of Santa Fe anyhow) containing certain cases like the University of New Mexico and the homestead of the Fergusson family; and in the other direction to Tesuque Valley to Pojoaque, and beyond that to Taos. In Tesuque Valley (formerly entirely rustic, native, and dirt-farmer) I found on returning to my own Mud House, not only a group of resident painters but the shining Rydal Press owned and run—hand run—by a tall, dark, young man locally known as "Wally" Goodwin, late of Lippincott, and his pretty and efficient Philadelphia wife, who very curly headed and in blue jeans, with a couple of little boys running about in the offing, attends to the end-papers and the binding. When I arrived the Rydal Press was printing the first four books of the new and intriguing self-publishing authors' group known as Writers' Editions: "The Sun Turns West," by Alice Corbin; "Atlantides," by Haniel Long; "Foretaste," by Peggy Pond Church; and a reprint of Eugene Manlove Rhodes's "Penalosa." When I left, a year later, it was completing the last copies of Frieda Lawrence's "Not I But the Wind"—in the very beautiful private edition.

Passing swiftly from Tesuque to Pojoaque, the literary colony perhaps halts at the Rio Grande home of Cyrus McCormick, for a drink, and then stops at Maria Garland's for another. Mr. McCormick is a genial worldly giant, Mrs. Garland is a much-married lady, statuesque and generous, whom some compare with Rose O'Neill—perhaps because she writes a little poetry, preserves a siren youth, and offers Delphic hospitality to artists, writers, and mystics. Alcalde, where she lives, is probably the last stop before Taos, where, once you have emerged from the canyon of the Rio Grande, you will soon find yourself at Mabel Luhan's having tea with your sybilline hostess and whatever guests may just then be living in the Pink House or the Log Cabin or the Florentine guest room—say Thornton Wilder, Myron Brinig, or Muriel Draper. Besides Mabel (the most talked of New Mexico writer bar none), you might find Spud Johnson, darkling, slender, and a bit plaintive, either in the office of the *Taos Valley News*—the local paper which he now edits—or in his Mexican house in Placita, where *Laughing Horse*, a delightful little magazine—the only one to date printed in this region—is waiting for the depression to lift. From Spud's you would rush on to those high ranches where Frieda Lawrence and Brett abide, and the ghost of D. H. L. still walks. Taos must admit that Lawrence wrote the most clairvoyant pictures of Indian ceremonies ever written in English, as Santa Fe must admit "Death Comes for the Archbishop" as the best novel ever written out of its setting and material.

But I am not concerned here with the outlying provinces, rather with Santa Fe itself as literary capital. You, gentle reader, must understand how it is that even in these days of electric ice boxes, bathrooms, and oil furnaces, when copy for the pulps and the slicks is shot into the friendly slots at the Spanish-style post-office which now faces the old cathedral—when the sound of the electric typewriter may be heard in the Sena Plaza itself, within hearing of those who are browsing in the Villagra Bookshop—turning over, perhaps, Mrs. Van Stone's illustrated translation of "Los Pastores," the Mexican mystery play still given up Canyon Road at Christmas, or Chapman's magnificently illustrated Pueblo pottery books—how it is that Santa Fe is so little spoiled by its present self-consciousness about its background that writers long established never leave, and others come. Why it is that Witter Bynner, who with his roaring, rowdy laugh that contrasts so oddly with his Harvard accents, is still inviting you to cocktail parties, in a Mexican patio adjacent to Chinese treasures—why it is that Lynn Riggs is building here—that John Gould Fletcher, that rather grouchy but truly conversable man and poet, comes for the summers— that Oliver La Farge has leased a house for two years and made Santa Fe his headquarters, why it is that a creative writer like Long, who does not study the market but produces from his own inner laws, and who does not depend on regional material at all—at least so far— finds this a satisfying environment.

No doubt La Farge, whom you might meet any day in the frescoed Fonda café eating a savory sixty-cent lunch (wine included), doffing his broad-brimmed hat with the chin-band to the zooming of the Mexican orchestra in the patio, displaying his cerise tie with the conch shell, exchanging views of Cutting's election or the latest wrinkle in Indian affairs, with the communists or the elite, may be thinking of writing a Pueblo novel to follow the Navajo—on this point I am not informed, but I can tell you that La Farge is loved by his Indian friends, and that his rather lanky, bony structure, like his well-browned skin and his air of reserving judgment, thinking things over, fits well into the local scene. But there are other poets and story tellers: who take to Santa Fe for its outskirts because they can dig in a garden, lie in the sun, jaunt into the mountains, talk with primitive neighbors on human terms, buy their wood from the back of a burro, and contribute manually to their own wants and comforts. In this unindustrialized New Mexico, even science is largely the science of archaeologist, ethnologist, anthropologist—the sort of science that unconsciously feeds the novelist, the poet.

Science produced the first Southwest classics: Bandelier, Cushing, Lummis were scientists in whom the story telling instinct ran strong. Eugene Manlove Rhodes, now unfortunately dead, like Frank Apple-

Santa Fe Plaza looking toward La Fonda Hotel, ca. 1940. Museum of New Mexico, Santa Fe.

gate and Mary Austin, perhaps owed something to science—as certainly the latter two were anxious to make clear that they did. As the Southwest discoveries and research have grown in bulk and complexity, the scientist-recorders have largely ceased to be literary, and the greater part of the material has become too technical for the layman. Even the commercially printed and nobly illustrated books on blankets, or pottery, are primarily for specialists and collectors. The average reader must turn to more popular works. In fact there are many.

Between "pure science" which in this region still produces the lion's share of printed words, actually written out of the Southwest by somebody, and "pure creation" which provides still but little in bulk, there lies a field rich in material for the objective writer, the authentic collector of local data, the reteller of local folk tales, out of the Indian or Spanish, the "popularizer" who may here be more than journalist, exploiter, or tourist—I mean the real "creative" lover or interpreter of his material.

To understand how this "regional" school came into being, I would glance back to the halcyon days of the nineteen-twenties, when one could rent two or three rooms in Santa Fe for ten dollars a month. The artists and writers of those days kept their horses in the dooryard, their butter in the well (if there was a well), and heated their small adobe rooms, hung with dusky saints (bought for nothing on their riding trips through the little native villages along the Sangre de Cristo Mountains), with pinon and cedar burned in small oval adobe fireplaces and air tight stoves.

Indeed the first fragrant, intoxicating breath of the land, as you descended from the single-track, slow-going train of cars that brought you from the junction at Lamy, was the pungent incense that arose from the mud chimneys of the flat-roofed town. Like an offering in which the spirits of home and wilds, the geniuses of several primitive races united, the smoky incense floated off again—over the Plaza, where sat the gaunt Mexican men and the black shawled women, over the Governor's Palace, to the pink sandy lomas, with the little Palestinian-looking Mexican houses set on their sides, to the cedar-grown reaches of the Pueblo grants, with their sky-terraced Indian buildings, and beyond them, to the dark, snowcapped mountains which surround the ancient city.

Alice Corbin, one of Santa Fe's most familiar literary personalities—now known to many summer visitors as the plump and jocund leader of the Poets' Round Up, an August garden festival whose spontaneity leads many into their first understanding of what this literary colony is about—came here from Chicago as early as 1916. It seemed in those days as if writers for some reason slightly removed from the competitive struggle tended to migrate here. Alice Corbin had been an editor of a still popular and often revised twentieth century poets' anthology with Harriet Monroe. She had been an editor of the *Poetry Magazine*. She was restless and fertile minded and it was hard to settle down into an invalid's bed. But her vivid talk delivered from that platform was my first literary adventure in New Mexico. Her first book of poems, "Red Earth," poignant and restrained, seems to stand for the first fruits, delicious fruits of this soil from the pen of a sensitive colonist. Alice Corbin became, to the regret of many, more grand-

Sheldon Parsons, "December in Santa Fe."
Oil, n.d. [1934], 24"x36".
Photographic Record, Public Works of Art Project,
   Thirteenth Region, New Mexico Division.
New Mexico State Records Center and Archives, Santa Fe.

mother than author as the years rolled by,—"The Sun Turns West" is but her second volume in a dozen years.

Mary Austin with her high Spanish comb followed Alice Corbin in 1918 but did not settle in Santa Fe or build her substantial house, which so generously helped to foster local arts and talents, until considerably later. When I first knew her here, she seemed scarcely more of a resident than Willa Cather or Lawrence. Visiting writers of this magnitude brought real nourishment to colonist writers who had decided to take the plunge and become regular taxpayers and readers of that watched-for local paper, *The Santa Fe New Mexican*, owned by Senator Cutting and humorously and affectionately edited by a tall man—who on occasion can be a bitter adversary—Dana Johnson. And the publication of "Blood of the Conquerors" in 1921, the first novel of New Mexico by a native son, though not adding the author himself to the growing Santa Fe group—for Harvey Fergusson lived

East or in Albuquerque—undoubtedly gave a proud enhancement to New Mexico as a fertile and untouched field for the novelist.

Not long after Bynner, came his friend Arthur Davison Ficke (but not to stay forever as he did), and still a little later Haniel Long, another sensitive poet, settled down on the Acequia with his wife and son. Long is now no less beloved in Santa Fe than Bynner. All that Santa Fe lacks of conversation and bookish and literary tradition from other than southwest sources is to be found cherished in this quiet house and garden. Long, like Bynner, is a tall man though a slender one, and a very expressive personality. Despite his love of books and gardens and music, he belongs to the outland regions.

With earlier years—years before Santa Fe grew so definitely literary—I associate also a group of gifted (then) youngsters not now identified with the town but still bearing some Southwest imprint, and in the minds of older literary citizens like Alice Corbin, associated with the rising tide of letters. For several years one met them in the byways: Yvor Winters, the noblest of spirits, now a Stanford professor, and a late Pacific editor of *Hound and Horn*, then a young poet, seeking his way; Janet Lewis, the exquisite author of "The Invasion," now Mrs. Winters, also then chiefly a poet; Glenway Wescott, a glowing and precocious youth, already definitely headed for Literature with a large L, Maurice Leisermann of Chicago, another poet of the same generation.

To the same years belong the first appearances of *Laughing Horse*, which might be considered a steed useful in the formation of a regional tradition. Another contributor to the tradition was Jack Thorp—ex-New Englander, ex-cowpuncher, broad and bulky as Applegate was spare. Thorp provided that pleasant volume, "Songs of the Cowboys," probably the offering of a one-book author (though if he would, he might have a great deal more to tell us of his early days on the range). Still another creative agent in rendering the folk tradition in readable English was Elizabeth Willis De Huff, who out of unusual opportunities as wife of the then principal of the Indian Boarding School began to write down for white children the legends and stories related by Indian children. "Taytay's Tales" and its successors still hold their place, and Mrs. De Huff is now known to many visitors as an intelligent lecturer on the "background" which even natives can never get to the bottom of.

The difficulty of getting to the bottom of New Mexico is, I suspect, why even a novelist like Harvey Fergusson ends by turning to chronicle—or interpretation. "Rio Grande" does not quite bear out the early forecast that local novelists of "Anglo" or even Spanish or Indian stock might swiftly arise out of old roots. When Arthur (Yvor) Winters was teaching in Los Cerrillos high school he used to prophesy great things of the Spanish inheritors, but so far, we must grant, most of the forty Santa Fe authors are colonists, and of the native sons or daughters most, like Erna Fergusson or Ruth Barker, have so far worked in the objective realm rather than the creative. "Dancing Gods" is a good book which has helped many intelligent people into the Pueblo mysteries. "Caballeros" is very much the reward of a pioneer family's picturesque inheritance. Peggy Pond Church, a pristine young poetess of "Anglo" blood, is probably the first real New Mexican to produce a book of undeniable poetic promise out of her region and her life, her still young life.

Writers' Editions, while seeking a business czar, intends publishing soon at least three more books: "Land of Horizontal Yellow," by Spud Johnson; a long poem of John Gould Fletcher's about America today, tomorrow, and yesterday; and Long's "Sonatas," prose poems published in part in *Space*, a new and excellent "little magazine," edited in Oklahoma, but drawing heavily on Santa Fe talent. Beyond this small and rather esoteric group, we have the novelists, the other poets,—for instance Axel Clark—the writers of mystery, adventure, and detective stories. I think of Raymond Otis, a young author once of Chicago, who has already published "Fire in the Night," the first story to deal with the Santa Fe social potpourri. Otis promises to do more and better with a forthcoming Penitente novel. He has some of the characteristics of the woodland creature, even to faun ears, and eyes set a little crooked in his head,—he will bear watching. So will Phil Stevenson, the communist and correspondent of the *New Masses*. Then there is Marion Winnick, the author of "Juniper Hill" who rides horseback and lunches at the Fonda every day, plans the rest of her trilogy, and talks with a very New England or Bostonese accent. And there is Ina Sizer Cassidy, the Western breezy widow of a well-known Santa Fe artist, who has done much journalism and is now collecting Navajo poems—she of course not reckoned among the novelists.

Such are the writers of Santa Fe whom many dangers seem to confront: the danger of provincialism or homesickness for Eastern roots—for though the planes bring East and West together, writers are rarely fliers, and newspapers come late and slow—of becoming a prey to the near-writer and appreciative, uncritical circle that steadily grows in a place so charming to live in as this; of falling victim to the summer visitor, disrespectful of working hours; and finally of succumbing to the monumental, indifferent abundance of the land itself, with its recurrent festivals native or fabricated, its round of balls and doings, a prey to the sun, magical, restorative and indolent.

—*The Saturday Review of Literature*, 8 December
1934, pp. 352, 354.

Fremont Ellis, "Landscape Santa Fe."
Oil, n.d. [1934], 26"x 39".
Photographic Record, Public Works of Art Project,
   Thirteenth Region, New Mexico Division.
New Mexico State Records Center and Archives, Santa Fe.

PLIGHT IN SANTA FE

Santa Fe, October 16, 1937

Dear Mr. Editor:

The lure of sociability in Santa Fe is a dangerous thing. One's friends are close at hand; associations are frequent and intimate, for there are relatively few distractions. This is a threat to the creative life.

Everybody has more or less genius for sociability. A person attempting serious work in Santa Fe must guard against his genius for friendship. His attempts to coddle his talent for sociability into submission to his wish to create, too often take the form of telling his friends what he is doing, or plans to do. "Now I am writing a novel. Now I am going to write a play." From there his loose talking proceeds to a telling of the muddled contents of his brain about the novel or the play, and the ultimate dissipation in thin air of all the idea contained—which with some discipline and work might have been shaped and evolved into something worth while.

This is the thing which stigmatizes and nullifies most of the work done in Santa Fe. The creating of anything here tends to become a community effort. Individual genius is hardly ever given a chance to express itself. Community expression is well and good in its place, but it has no place in art, for if art is anything at all it is the reflection of the scene and the time in the brain of one individual capable of transmuting it. When more than one person enters the arena of creation, all of its issue loses its significance as art, and it becomes a tour de force—mere entertainment. Even in a collaboration, which is not the ideal form of creation, if anything that is art emerges from it, that part is the product of one of the workers, and not both.

One sees so much of this—oneself is guilty of it so often that the heart grows sick. For it is hard to work alone in a place where one's friends are solicitous and criticism is non-existent. That is the great disadvantage of attempting to make Santa Fe one's work-place. It is a play-place, and any place like it is more or less the same.

Yours sincerely,
RAYMOND OTIS.

—*The New Mexico Sentinel*, 17 November 1937.

Ray and Bina Otis, Santa Fe.   Courtesy of   Emily Otis Barnes, Santa Fe.

Painter Gladys Brown and her husband, poet Arthur Davison Ficke. Photograph courtesy of Clark Kimball and Charlotte J. Stone, The Great Southwest Books, Santa Fe.

And if a day comes when the whole problem of the artists is being too self consciously reviewed, there are pinons and cedars and golden miles of chamisa, and the gorgeous inferno of the desert, red palisades, blue fogged buttes, and ranges on which the snow lingers, in lightening flashes of white even after the aspens have made the lower mountains green and young as walls of moss.

—Evelyn Scott, "The Santa Fe Art Colony,"
Wings, October 1930, p. 13.

During my earlier New Mexico period—that of late boyhood—it had been an appropriately intoxicating experience to go to Santa Fe from Albuquerque (where we lived) and encounter writers and painters in the flesh. The artistic aspirant attaches an extra, rather touching, value to mingling with his elders in the world of the arts, not always to learn anything technical—that is a different and quite strict process—but often to breathe a climate and absorb justification for his own often socially unorthodox values. I then uncritically accepted the idea of a "colony" of artists and writers at Santa Fe and Taos, but it was not long until some of the individuals who were locally called "sensitives" began to seem somewhat grotesque, self-advertising, and responsive to opportunities for envy and competition. Viewing the Paris phenomenon of the expatriates, I thought that it too could be seen in effect as a "colony," though it was set down far away in the midst of a great capital of culture and style; and I suppose, apart from the notoriety of some of the names, French, English, Irish, American, of various participants, its essential character was not remarkably different from what I had observed in northern New Mexico, where certain temperaments and habits of non-conformity were pretty much like what prevailed in the Parisian circles of American revolt against the tone of the victory-proud, Babbitt-governed United States. I could hold my view of all that in New Mexico as well as in Paris.

—Paul Horgan, *Approaches to Writing*, 1968, 1973, pp. 220-221.

Paul Horgan. Photograph courtesy of Clark Kimball and Charlotte J. Stone, The Great Southwest Books, Santa Fe.

Haniel and Alice Long. Photograph courtesy of Clark Kimball and Charlotte J. Stone, The Great Southwest Books, Santa Fe.

I saw it first in December, 1940, the high plateau among the red and purple mountains, where Santa Fe lies in a wide open bowl, a city built of adobe, traversed by mountain streams lined with cottonwoods, a city that, though a capital, had at that time kept the air of a village, spread out onto foothills covered with piñons, tawny earth dotted with these small dark pines so it looked like a leopard skin—the leopard land. Then, in December, the earth looked blood-red among the patches of snow, and the mountains, luminous and bare, looked like mountains on the moon. I was unprepared in every way, unprepared for the air itself, seven thousand feet up, thin and dry so there is a bubble of physical excitement in one's chest; unprepared for the huge bare landscape that reminded me of Chinese paintings, and of northern Spain—for my target had been a friend rather than a city, a friend I had never seen, but who had written me a letter when my first novel came out, Haniel Long, the poet.

—May Sarton, "The Leopard Land: Haniel and Alice Long's Santa Fe," *Southwest Review*, 1972, p. 1 (reprinted with slight alterations in May Sarton, *A World of Light: Portraits and Celebrations*, 1976, pp. 123-24).

The first time I visited Santa Fe, the obvious things impressed me. The colorful vistas, striking personalities, sophisticated lavish hospitality and cosmopolitan conversations merged into a pictorial whole that exhilarated at every turn. The mind and all the senses seemed to be supplied delightfully.

"Where in America can such another spot be found?" I cried with a childish delight of discovery. Remembering the exquisite Diwan-i-Khas palace in Dehli, I transposed its ancient Persian inscription to the sun-baked walls of Santa Fe: "Be there a Paradise on earth; it is this, oh, it is this, oh, it is this!"

When my visit ended, I went away reluctantly. But I was already planning a return—and another—and another. With steady repetition, I tasted the atmosphere of Santa Fe.

Yet each succeeding time, part of my delight vanished. The colorful vistas swirled away in dust storms. The striking personalities turned out to be a too literal interpretation of that adjective. The sophisticated lavish hospitality proved fraught with feuds and cross-currents (as one grew more aware of the local scene) and the cosmopolitan conversations gradually changed, as all cosmopolitan conversations do, into the provincial and parochial. The mind and all the senses became confused distressingly.

These revelations could be true of other places, if not in such proportions; and today I can blithely remark (along with Sir William Gilbert) that "things are seldom what they seem; skimmed milk often masquerades as cream." Now I enjoy Santa Fe for what it is, not as a Paradise.

—Carolyn Bancroft, "Calcutta Feels Like Santa Fe,"
New Mexico Sentinel, 22 December 1937.

Harvey Fergusson and Witter Bynner. Photograph courtesy of Clark Kimball and Charlotte J. Stone, The Great Southwest Books, Santa Fe.

To me, home is less a town or a house or a society than a region—
this piece of the earth. I am sure I would still want to return to it if
some unimaginable catastrophe swept it clean of every human trace. I
must begin with this emotion because it is a primary fact of my experience and seems to have determined the pattern of my life. All through
my youth I dreamed of owning a ranch or of being a forest ranger—of
reposing peacefully in the bosom of my native earth—but this was
not to be. I developed an urge to write and a need to learn, and both
of them carried me to cities. I needed libraries and people but I also
needed to get away from my own origins, perhaps in order to see
them with some detachment. The need to go was in part mysterious
but it was irresistible. So was the need to come back. Whenever I was
away from the West I had an acute longing for it. The result was that I
spent much of my life leaving this country and returning, traveling a
hundred thousand miles, having always the spirit of an itinerant or a
camper. This going and coming was long the rhythm of my existence.

During the years I lived in the East nostalgia was the most constant
emotion of my life. Since I moved to California I feel much more at
home. The Sierra Nevadas are much like the mountains I knew in my
youth, the Mojave Desert is wide enough and desolate enough to
appall any truly domesticated man and to satisfy anyone who has the
West in his blood. The West is all of a piece but I still think of New
Mexico as its vital center.

—Harvey Fergusson, *Home in the West: An Inquiry into
My Origins*, 1944, pp. 4-5.

Cady Wells, "Mesas."
Watercolor, n.d. [1934], 23"x29".
Photographic Record, Public Works of Art Project,
  Thirteenth Region, New Mexico Division.
New Mexico State Records Center and Archives, Santa Fe.

PUBLICATIONS
EPHEMERAL AND
EXEMPLARY

AN APPRECIATION OF NEW MEXICO

By Zane Grey

(Author of "Riders of the Purple Sage," "The Lone Star
Ranger," etc.)

New Mexico is to me magic words of enchantment.
I have written half a dozen novels trying to tell of its
beauty and romance, and health for body and soul. But
I still have to write the most convincing one; and this
is because ten years of travel over the deserts, plateaus,
mountains and forests of this wonderland have only
served to make me see more, and grow more, and love
more.

The secret of the fascination of the Southwest is ex-
ceedingly hard to define in words. But the secret of
health and renewed life to be found there seems to be
a matter of the senses. That is to say, you must see,
smell, feel, hear, and taste this wonderful country, and
once having done so, you will never be the same again.
It must be done to be believed. Never a one of the
many people whom I have bidden ride over this region
has failed to bless me for the suggestion.

To see any part of New Mexico, even from the train
window, is to realize something of immensity, their tremendous range from desert floor to mountain peak, her
vivid color and beauty. To see two hundred miles of
wild and rugged country as clear beneath your eyes as
if you were seeing Central Park from the top of the Plaza, is an experience never to be forgotten. To see the
Grand Canyon full of purple smoke at dawn or sublimely
fired at sunset is to be elevated in soul. To see the red
rocks; the alkali flats like snow; the sand dunes so
graceful and curved; the long cedar slopes, speckled
green and gray, leading up to the bold peaks; the vast
black belts of timber; the Navajo facing the sunrise with
his silent prayer, the Hopi in his lonely cliff dwellings
with their monuments of a vanished race; the endless
slopes of sage, green and gray, and purple on the
heights; the natural stones bridges and the petrified forests—and a thousand more beautiful sights—that is to
see New Mexico and the Southwest.

The smell of cedar smoke, like burning leaves in autumn; the smell of the desert, dry and clean and somehow new; the smell of the sand and dust, especially
after a rain; the tangy odor of the great plateaus of
cedar and juniper when your nostrils seem glued as
with pitch; and the sweet fragrance of the pine forests,
and the indescribable and exhilarating perfume of the
purple sage; to know these is to learn the purity of atmosphere never breathed in populous places. To feel the
wind in your face, to ride in the teeth of sand storm
and flying dust and furious squall; to feel the cold of
dawn nip your ears and the heat of noon burn your back,
to hear the thunder of the Rio Grande and the roar of
mountain streams, and the rustle of sand through the
sage, and the moan of the night breeze in the spruce,
the mourn of the wolf and the whistle of the stag, to
feel the silence and loneliness of the desert,—all this is
to grow young again. And to taste the air, water, and
meat of the open is to go back hundreds of years when
man was savage and free.

The saddle horse, the pack-train, the wagon are
the happiest and most profitable modes of travel; but
alas! that I must write it—the automobile has at last
claimed the Great Southwest, and good roads lead every-
where. I would preserve these wild lands for the horse
and mule, but this is sentiment, and selfish perhaps.
But after all it does not matter how one travels. Only
go! There never should have been the thousands of tourists going to Europe before the war when they were ig-
norant of this land of enchantment. I have a feeling of
pity for those with means and leisure who do not know
our own, our native land.

ZANE GREY.

SANTA FE
THE OLDEST CITY IN THE UNITED STATES

OLDEST CHURCH IN AMERICA

"The City Unique"
"The Home of Contentment and Enjoyment"

SANTA FE
THE GATEWAY OF THE "GREATEST FIFTY MILE SQUARE IN AMERICA"

=== *America's Oldest Playground* ===

The Vacation Land Which Always Enchants

ISSUED BY
THE SANTA FE NEW MEXICAN
SANTA FE, NEW MEXICO

FEBRUARY

New Mexico Description 35 CENTS

9.7.89

MOTOR CAMPER & TOURIST

With which is combined

The NEW YORK MOTORIST

Edited by D. W. DE MOTT

Camping With the Original Americans

EXPERIMENTER PUBLISHING COMPANY, NEW YORK, PUBLISHERS OF

RADIO NEWS - SCIENCE & INVENTION - THE EXPERIMENTER - MOTOR CAMPER & TOURIST

One of the Fleet of Harveycars

Foreword

THE many drives possible out from Old Santa Fe' penetrate a region as rich in archaeological and ethnological interest as it is in scenic beauty and grandeur. American history, vivid and fascinating, was being written here long before the Founding of Jamestown, the Voyage of Hendrik Hudson or the Coming of the Pilgrims.

In threading these roads to Yesterday you may come to know well the mountains, canyons and valleys that girdle the old city—and still miss half the feast. On every side you will find the visible records of the Forgotten People, the enduring impress of the Spanish padres and conquistadores, the life of the Indian, the Spanish-American and the frontier Southwest demanding interpretation. The country about you is saturated with history, legend and human interest—for those who know it.

The Courier Service

A trained Courier Service will provide visitors with interesting and authentic information about all these trips and in other ways add to your pleasure and comfort. The couriers are young women with intimate personal knowledge of the region, supplemented by special training under the following Advisory Board:

DR. EDGAR L. HEWETT, Director, School of American Research.

DR. A. V. KIDDER, Department of American Archaeology. Phillips Andover Academy, Andover, Mass.

DR. S. G. MORLEY, Associate of Carnegie Institute. In charge expeditions, Central American Archaeology.

MR. F. W. HODGE, Director, Museum of the American Indian, New York.

DR. CHARLES F. LUMMIS, author of "Land of Poco Tiempo," "Mesa, Canyon and Pueblo," etc.

MR. PAUL F. WALTER, President, The Historical Society of New Mexico.

Members of the Courier Service accompany all cars over the Indian-detour without additional charge. Special courier service, too, is included in the charges quoted for all of the longer optional drives covered in the following pages and for the Afternoon Tour of Old Santa Fé.

2

3

—Eugene Manlove Rhodes

Neglecting Fractions

Americans have reluctantly discovered part of New Mexico's wonderland; thanks to art and automobiles. Santa Fé, Taos, Acoma, and Zuñi are known in the land; but Southern New Mexico is still unpainted and unknown.

Reasons are not far to seek. Trunk lines run from Albuquerque to the Coast, from El Paso to the Coast. The country between has been mastered by a vigorous people on horseback, whose energies, a century back, turned to experience rather than to chronicle. Painters, historians, and archaeologists crowded in the north to study the historic and prehistoric pueblos, and the brave footsteps of old Spain. An unexpected result of their labors has been to add a new mistake to an old one. It has long been held that New York is America; it is now taught that Santa Fé is New Mexico.

Santa Fé, herself so long neglected, is firmly incredulous of beauty, interest, or charm to south-

28

29

ward; deports herself stepsisterly, as toward another Cinderella. Yet some of us have never understood why longitude is not counted from the Meridian of Mesilla.

Through the Cinderella country you can find old men, mild and frail, who tell of days when they were first-men in an untrodden land. Time was when they were less mild and frail, when two of them made a crowd. You will hear of Apache raiders, Victorio, Nané and Geronimo, of Kinney the outlaw, the Lincoln County War, the Tonto Basin. But these are old unhappy far-off things, gladly forgotten. Neglecting fractions, their tale is of work and not of war; of trail herds and roundups, roads, wells and ditches; of friendship and pleasant campfires, of hunger and thirst and weariness hardly to be borne. But not once do they voice regret for money lost, chances missed, herds that are no more. Their talk is of essential things; joy and laughter and all delight.

Bueno, pues! These people are my people, their ways are mine. With your permission, we will pass lightly by cotton, coal and copper; alfalfa, fruit, cattle and sheep; turquoise, silver, potash and oil; the rich valley of the Pecos, the great reclamation projects headed by the Elephant Butte Dam; even the Mesilla Valley, said to be the most fertile land in the world; and by cheerful cities, Roswell, Alamogordo, Las Cruces, Silver City and a dozen others, brisk, bold and flourishing. The homeseeker who does not see this country has wronged himself. That is true; but you will find your delight in other things; mystery and the magic of distance, the mountains and the long leagues and the sun.

The Pecos, the Rio Grande, the Gila; the little mountain rivers, tributaries swift and elfin, dancing in the sun; rolling plain and sea-broad desert; fifty mountain ranges, pine-black or granite-golden, gray, brown and rose-red, blue, purple, lavender, lilac or opal, changing with every hour and mile, no day the same, fantastic, a kaleidoscope of the gods; and we, too, are of the Enchanted Empire.

When Oliver Loving died, the Tall Men (Emerson Hough gave the name) followed in the trail he made with John Chisum. They brought here the body of an old tradition, by way of Texas, Kentucky and Virginia; before that, from Drake's England, and Elizabeth's. We of the Puritan stock, when we met the Tall Men here, learned two things of value: the art of Neglecting Fractions and the use of the Positive Degree. For the best man their word was "He'll do to take along." Any place, any purpose. Even so, when we say that the Ruidoso is beautiful, Organ Peaks or Black Range, it really makes no difference what Er or Est places may be elsewhere. Ruidoso, Organ, or Black Range, with a hundred others, less known but not less loved, would still be beautiful in Italy, California or Algiers. Our great "show places" are Carlsbad Caverns, Ruidoso, Cloudcroft, the White Sands, Elephant Butte Dam and Palomas Hot Springs. As Philip said to Nathaniel, "Come and see."

It is true that little happened in South New Mexico three hundred years ago. But something has chanced here since 1865; the meeting of North, South, East and West; Latin and Saxon, Puritan and Cavalier. Three hundred years from now, Oliver Loving and his friends will be as far in the past as Oñate is from today. But the inquirer of 2227 can not say, "Oblige me by referring to the files." There are no files. All that will ever be known of those stirring years is locked in a few gray heads. Old timers lived hard, rode hard, worked hard and drank easily. Worse than all, they breathed alkali dust around the herds. So they suffer from bronchitis, and upon slight provocation they die of pneumonia. Future historians will be grateful to any man with a gift of listening, who will listen now—not long—through Southern New Mexico.

"Nay, crowd not; haste not; we are going, Gentlemen!"

YE FIRST APPEARANCE OF

Yᵉ Communitye Theatre

of ye Anciente La Villa de Real de Santa Fe de San Francisco de Assisi

Under
Ye Direction
of

Marye Austin

Assisted by
ye

Community
Artists
Players
Strollers
Musicians

and

Commone
Folkes

In Ye Halle of Sainte Francis
of ye
Museum of New Mexico

On ye Day of St. Valentine, in ye Month of
Sprout-Kale, the Fourteenth Day in
the Year of Our Lord

One Thousand Nine Hundred and Nineteen

THE SANTA FE PLAYERS

PRESENT

"SURE FIRE"

Episodes in the Life of Billy the Kid

By PHILIP STEVENSON

Directed by Margery Wilson

CHARACTERS
In the order of their appearance

BOB OLLINGER, an ex-deputy sheriff .... John K. C. Andrews
PAT GARRETT, a storekeeper of Fort Sumner .... Dave Steele
SAM MILLER, a sheep and cattle man of Fort Sumner .... Dan T. Kelly
NITA, his daughter .... Olinda Rodrigues
SENORA MILLER, his mother .... Jane Baumann
APOLONIO, a servant .... Wesley Connor, Jr.
GENERAL LEW WALLACE, Governor of New Mexico .... G. C. Moore
ORDERLY .... Charles Davis
MRS. WALLACE .... Virginia Catron
BILLY THE KID .... George Gormly
JACK GAMBRELL, Sheriff of Lincoln County .... John W. Brown
CELSA) .... Evaline Myers
JIM) .... Guests at the baile .... Deric Nusbaum
NELL) .... Betty Applegate
JOHN W. POE) .... Charles Bowen
KIP McKINNEY) .... Members of Pat Garrett's possee .... J. L. Breese, Jr.
BELL) .... Joseph Stevenson
OLD MAN GEISS, Jailer of Lincoln .... Robert O. Brown
Other GUESTS, NEIGHBORS, etc. Rosina Brown, Margaret Kelly, Maria Gutierrez, Mrs. Paul
Gonzalez, Mrs. Abran Sena, Ramona Montoya, Robert O. Brown ,Luna Leopold, Frank
Montoya, Paul Gonzalez, Manuel Abeyta, Patricio Sanchez.

MUSICIANS: Tony F. Cruz, Julio Gonzalez, Pablo F. Griego, Pablo Sanchez.

SCENES

ACT ONE

·The Sala of the Miller home in Fort Sumner, N. M. on a summer afternoon in 1880.

ACT TWO

The same. 10:30 p. m. on a night in Christmas Week, 1880.

ACT THREE

The Loft of the Court House in Lincoln, N. M. on the afternoon of April 28th, 1881.

ACT FOUR

The Patio of the Miller home, about 11 p. m. on the night of July 14th, 1881.

PRODUCTION STAFF
Business Manager—Edwin Brooks

SETS: John Meem, John Windsor, Eugene Van Cleave, Paul Lantz, Hubert Jeffus, Warren Triggs, John
Carroll, H. K. Greer.

LIGHTS: Raymond Jonson, Eugene Griffin.

COSTUMES: Rosina Brown, Richie March, Florence Gardesky, Ruth Laughlin Barker, Lola Delgado.

PROPERTIES: (Hand) Calla F. Hay, Dorothy Belle Flanagan, John Hay, Howard Coluzzi.
(Furniture) Louise Wright, Virginia Morley.

MAKE-UP: Gladys Stevenson, Jeanette Lord, Dorothy Belle Flanagan.

PUBLICITY: McHarg Davenport, E. Dana Johnson, Glenn Brill, Ruth Laughlin Barker, Langdon Mitchell,
Witter Bynner, Alice Corbin Henderson, Haniel Long, Anna V. Huey.

MUSIC: Catherine Ware Nielsen.

The Santa Fe Players wish to express their appreciation to all those who have lent furniture, costumes, guns and services.

SANTA FE WORLD PREMIERE

WARNER BROTHERS' MOTION PICTURE

"SANTA FE TRAIL"

FRIDAY, DECEMBER 13

2:30 P. M. Band parades from Santa Fe railway station.

3:15 P. M. Mass welcome at Santa Fe Station here followed by a parade to the Palace of the Governors.

3:45 P. M. Introduction of Guests at the Plaza.

4:30 to 5:00 P. M. Indian Ceremonial Dances at St. Francis Auditorium. Auspices New Mexico Association for Indian Affairs.

5:30 P. M. Dramatic Reception of the Pioneers (the Stars) by the Gran Cabildo of Santa Fe, circa 1860, followed by burning of a gigantic Tio Coco, or Bogey Man (Friday the 13th).

8:00 to 9:00 P. M. Band concert in the Plaza.

8:15 to 8:45 P. M. Indian Ceremonial Dances at St. Francis Auditorium.

9:00 P. M. Second introduction of Our Guests from terrace of La Fonda. Presentation of corsage to Miss

De Havilland by Santa Fe Trail Chapter, Children of the American Revolution.

10:30 P. M. Grand Costume Baile at La Fonda, a galaxy of Stars, and unique entertainment.

SATURDAY, DECEMBER 14

11:30 A. M. Ski-ball Tea, ski and snow party at the Hyde Park Ski Lodge. Santa Fe Winter Sports Club hosts.

4:00 P. M. Colorful costume parade, presenting Stars and Indians.

5:00 to 5:30 and 7:00 to 7:30 P. M. Indian Ceremonial Dances at St. Francis Auditorium.

8:15 P. M. Premiere "Santa Fe Trail," Paris Theatre.

8:45 P. M. Premiere "Santa Fe Trail," Lensic Theatre.

9:30 P. M. Premiere "Santa Fe Trail," Burro Alley Theatre.

9:30 P. M. Grand costume "Hollywood-Santa Fe Baile."

Both Days · · All Day · · All Pueblo Indian Market in Portal of Old Palace of the Governors

---

•LA CANTINA DEL PARIAN•
WINE LIST

WINES
CHAMPAGNE

Gordon Rouge - Lansows per bottle 7.50 — Vintners per bottle 3.50

SPARKLING BURGUNDY

Vintners per bottle 3.50 — Ambassador per bottle 2.50
Sherry-Imported 35 — Domestic 15 — Port-Domestic 15
Burgundy-Domestic 15 — Claret-Domestic 15

LIQUEURS AND CORDIALS

Benedictine 35 — Cointreau 35 — Chartreuse, Green or Yellow 35
Cream de Menthe 25 — Cream de Cacao 25 — Absinthe 35

MIXED DRINKS
COCKTAILS

Martini 25 — Manhattan 30 — Bronx 30 — Tequila 35 —
Bacardi 35—Old Fashioned 30—Tequila Daisy 35—Daiquiri 35

FIZZES

Gin 25 — Sloe Gin 25 — Silver 30 — Golden 30 — Royal 35
Tom Collins 30

WHISKIES
BOURBON

Sunny Brook (17 yrs.) 50 — Old Grand Dad 35 — Old Taylor 35
Black Hawk 30

RYE

Seagrams 7 cr. 30 — Seagrams 5 cr. 25 — Canadian Club 30 —
Rock and Rye 25

SCOTCH

Vat 64 30 — King William IV 30 — Black and White 30 —
Johnie Walker Red 30 — Haig and Haig 5 Star 30 — Johnie
Walker Black 40 — Haig and Haig Pinch Bottle 40

BRANDY

Hennessey 40 — Monnet 40 — 6 Marnier 40

BEER

Carta Blanca 35 — Budweiser 20 — Pabst 20 — Harry Mitchel 15

LA
FONDA

IN OLD SANTA FE

Dinner

THE HARVEY COMPANY

THE SANTA FE PLAZA

Saturday July 31, 1937

A Weekly or Seminario Devoted to La Villa Antigua, or Old Santa Fe; Printed at the Clark Studio and The Rydal Press in This Venerable Town Under Direction of E. Dana Johnson Box 96 in the Postoffice. Tel. 1758 The Price is 10 Cents a Copy, Six Months for Two and a Half Dollars, One Year for Five Dollars.

Copyright, 1937, by E. Dana Johnson
Saturday July 31, 1937

And always the Home-Town Folks, without whom there would be no Old Santa Fe; the cow-puncher, genuine or synthetic, the dude and the Archbishop the Franciscan and the dusky chauffeur from Dallas, the Laissez Faire Club on the corner, Indian Detour buses weaving to and fro and automobiles bearing the placard of every state in the union.

The life and atmosphere of Old Santa Fe is a large order for a small publication. Perhaps the SANTA FE PLAZA may help point the way to survival of the Village under the press of the Cosmopolis, and help keep the old things as the transcontinental traffic crowds the narrow streets.

May they be always narrow, and may people always come who like narrow old streets and quiet gardens behind adobe walls.

- EDITORIAL -

CAN WE REFLECT IT?

The old Plaza of Santa Fe, the Plaza de Constitution under Mexico, trodden by many races since Onate or Peralta laid it out in 1605-09 is the crossroads of the world and has been for three and a third centuries.

Around it and through it ebbs and flows the life of the Ancient City.

Today it is compound of Santiago of Santa Clara and Tony of Taos; of Juan and Jesus and Jose and Manuel, descendants of Coronado's hardy desert excursionists; of Alderman Gonzales, and the Joneses in their trailer from Bucksport, Me.; of savants from Vienna and hill-folk from Cordova and Truchas; Artist Hullenkremer from Buda-Pest; turismo from Texas, painters from Paris, bone-diggers and a fringe of Greenwich village, resident artists in adobe haciendas; writers for the pulps and slicks, politicos from Rio Arriba and the Carlsbad Caverns, Mahjeed Fattah from Jerusalem, G. Park our eminent restaurateur and laundryman from Canton, dark captains from Martinique, Vilayevitch from the steppes, Beloli from Milan and Stokowski from Manhattan, Clarkson from Scotland and Bakos from Poland, Dubasches from Bombay, Mme. Sedillo from Copenhagen, governors from Toluca, Navajos from Two Gray Hills, Jicarilla Apaches in high hat from Dulce, Mr. Justice Kisch from Allahabad, the Gaekwar of Baroda and the Peshwa of Poona, Katharine Mayo with her Face of Mother India,(no double entendre); and shouldering his way through the Plaza is possibly Pat Hurley or William Allen White of Emporia or bulky Harvester Cy McCormick of Nambe.

Crossing the Plaza may be Director Hewett of the School of American Research, and his staff and that of the Historical society, Director Chapman of the Laboratory of Anthropology and his trusty men, or

even Grand Sachem Ernest Thomson-Seton of Seton Village, of all of whom and their activities more anon in these columns.

THE BALLAD OF
SANTA FEE SAL

Illustrated With Engravings on Wood

Being a Sad Song Without Any
Music, But With Much Rhyme, Reason
AND TRUTH; also A MORAL

Written, Illustrated & Printed
at Taos, New Mexico, in the Studio of

THE LAUGHING HORSE

Which is situated near one of the Curves of the
Acequia Madre about a Mile from the Village itself

by SPUD JOHNSON, a
PAMPHLETEER

of no Mean experience and Originality, believe
it or not. AND NOW OFFERED to the PUBLIC

at TEN CENTS per copy

oh, boy! only 10 cents!

SANTA FEE SAL
A BALLAD

I always said, "It's a quaint little town."
And I always thought it was;
But listen, my boy, while I write down
My story and its cause.

It's a long time now since I left the city,
Though it's longer than it seems:
The reason is — oh, what a pity ! —
That I've lost all my dreams.

I came to the town called Santa Fee
With all my youth and beauty;
I came with equanimity
And bringing all my booty.

I came to forget the smoke and grime
And all my misdeeds, too;
I came to forget the city's crime
And start my life anew.

A little house on the brow of a hill,
  A quaint little house of mud —
(The dear old place is standing still
  With a sign on it: "Help Wanted.")

That quaint little house with a door of blue,
  A serape on the bed,
Some ears of corn of colored hue
  And chile scarlet red —

Oh, dear little house of my abode:
  No basement and no attic:
You stood aloof from the dusty road
  —So simple, yet erratic.

'Twas there I lived for a span of years —
  (What happiness that covers!)
I lived with no regrets or tears,
  Without bathrooms or lovers.

But listen, my boy, and I will show
  How everything that mattered
Was taken from me, leaving woe,
  And all my life was shattered.

Santa Fee Sal, a Memory in Basswood

Which, it must be admitted, is almost an exact
copy of a Portrait by Maria M. de Orozco, who
is a schoolgirl in Guadalajara, Mexico ---- but
she'll never know the difference, I'll bet.

They took the earth beneath my feet,
  My dusty, winding trail
And made of it a hard paved street,
  Despite my anguished wail.

They brought electric lights to take
  The place of my sweet oil,
And telephones which simply make
  My very blood to boil.

They brought out artists—oh, my soul!
  And writers from the East.
My cup ran over—AND my bowl:
  God, what a bitter feast!

They made a beastly city-thing;
  A city council taxed us:
And now the city people fling
  A golf-club in the cactus.

Contract bridge is now the rage;
  Simplicity is dampened;
Orchids grow instead of sage —
  Society is rampant!

And so, my boy, I came to live
  Up in this big hotel,
And I've nothing now that I can give,
  Except the key to hell !

Try to forget your Santa Fee Sal,
  Go back to old New York
And find yourself a rural gal
  In the wilds of Central Park.

This is the Cartoon
Which Was Censored
By The Mayor of Santa Fe

Who prevented its inclusion in
LAUGHING HORSE NO. 17

Chronic Appendicitis, of course!   *By Will Shuster*

SHE IS A FRIEND of the Indians and the Spanish-Americans, writes about the Olympians of American Arts and Letters, and is the undisputed intellectual high priestess of Taos.

What Witter Bynner is to the Southwest along poetic lines, Mabel Dodge Lujan is to Taos along creative prose.

Mabel Dodge Lujan has been described as absorbing, witty, sensational, frank and gay. She is all of that and something more. She is Mabel Dodge Lujan, a Southwestern institution, by many looked upon and envied, she is a character that Oscar Berninghaus's series of kindly caricatures will be incomplete without.

She is the gayest entertainer on record in present days. She has acted as hostess to fabulously titled persons. Great and near great who at some time or another have visited Taos have absorbed a particle or two of that artistic atmosphere that Taos is nationally famous for.

Undoubtedly, she is the wealthiest resident of the Southwest. Her income comes from power. The dew drops of Niagra Falls have been kind to her economic stability. Being the grand hostess that she is, Mabel Dodge Lujan, has made the whole world her backyard playground.

At Villa Curonia, in romantic Florence, Italy, she showed all Europeans that when an American entertains, she entertains. Nothing was too good for her guests. Leading world citizens came and went. There was Eleanor Duse; Lady Paget; Gertrude Stein who writes like Gertrude Stein, because nobody else will write like her, due to the fact that nobody else likes to write like Gertrude Stein; Gordon Craig, the liberator of the theater; Jacques Emile Blanche and countless others. All have received Mabel Dodge Lujan's hospitality. Her "European Experiences" speak about them.

An author of the first rank, her books are characterized for their candid exposé of the workings of the human psychic machinery. The aesthetic Lorenzo -- better known as D. H. Lawrence -- was her friend in Taos . . . have you read "Lorenzo in Taos?"

In spite of her leading position in the literary and social world of America, Mabel Dodge Lujan takes time to think about matters that pertain to little Taos.

As a resident of Taos she has formed definite economic theories regarding the economic salvation of the native Spanish-Americans. She opines that true relief will come by the establishment of community barter markets where the public congregates, exhibits its goods and exchanges the same for other goods from their friend neighbors. She also believes that eating Chile is detrimental to racial imagination.

The Taos Indians, she cherishes their friendship. She has them nearest to her heart. She married the most picturesque of all Taos Indians, Tony Lujan.

EVEN if he had the name of John Pappapatheodorokoumoundroyianokopoulos —and this happens to be a real name— Long John, "The Hermes' of Taos will still be known as Long John for he really is long.

Oscar Berninghaus who drew this kindly cariacature of Long John, must have felt that it should resemble Long John.

He is picturesque to look at. Most interesting to talk to. Berninghaus claims that Walter Ufer is the most interesting story teller in Taos, while Ufer counter claims that Long John with his Irish yarns, far surpasses him.

With the Olympians of artistic Taos, Long John seems to get along most amiably. He is their messenger . . . their Hermes . . .who carries their tidings, their thoughts in writing to other parts, just like ancient Hermes on wings of swiftness carried the messages of one god to another and thus kept Mount Olympus well informed on what was what in classic Greece.

The Taonites in their daily doings, in their daily arguments and maybe in their daily Bacchanalean feasts, consider Long John as one of the members of this Olympian family.

THE HORSE FLY

Smallest and Most Inadequate Newspaper Ever Published

Vol. I, No. 25., Five Cents a Copy.   *Taos, New Mexico, December 24, 1938*

FIRES SWEEP TAOS!

Christmas Conflagrations All The Rage This Year

"A little fire is a friendly fire," they say; and so Taos, having had quite enough unfriendly fires, has adopted the lowly bonfire, pitch torches, & candle-lit luminarios of humble origin as its holiday symbols of happy celebration. ⏎ In the villages as well as out in the hills beacons burn and roof-tops are lined with the paper lanterns which the earliest Spanish colonists bequeathed as a charming method of saying to friend and to stranger alike —

Christmas Eve at the Taos Indian Pueblo

(by Ila McAfee)

A Merry Christmas!

 from   *The Entire Staff of*
THE HORSE FLY

From
The
Pueblo

Bigger Jump Than Everybody

An Indian Story by An Indian — Joe Sun-Hawk

*Woodlock by
Manville
Chapman*

It happen long time ago, when three Indian boys come to big river.

"We jump this big river," say one boy. "We see who good jumper."

"Sure. Sure." the other boys say.

The first boy jump. Big jump. But only fall in middle this big river.

The second boy jump. Big, big jump. But only so far; maybe this far from other boy. He land in river, too.

Then the last boy, she take off his moccasins. Bigger jump than everybody. Past the middle this big river. Past the second boy in river, too. But not 'cross this big river. And then he see in the water a big black snake with his mouth open. So this boy he turn around in middle of air—and jump back !

This very good story. It make Indian laugh. But most peoples don't see nothing. Not even that Indian boy's face, when he look down and see that big black snake.

Other Stories by Joe Sun-Hawk will be printed in The Horse Fly from time to time during 1939.

THE HORSE FLY

Smallest and Most Inadequate Newspaper Ever Published

Vol. I, No. 38. Five Cents a Copy.   *Taos, New Mexico, April 1, 1939*

PENITENTE CRUCIFIXION
Woodblock by Manville Chapman

Once Upon A Time Good Friday Was Celebrated Like This In Good Old Taos!

Mystery Canyon Suggests Weird & Horrid Rites To Lone Rider

Early Thursday morning, Westcott Burgess was riding alone in a blind canyon off Pot Creek, when he suddenly came upon five oddly disposed corpses which gave him a turn from which he has not yet recovered. ☞ And yet the cadavers were nothing more startling than: 1. A white hen with its feet tied securely together and wedged into the crotch of a tree. 2, 3. & 4. A magpie, a turkey, and a black crow, all intact and laid out carefully on the ground, not crumpled in a normal death-position. 5. The decapitated head of a white horse, also intact, the body nowhere to be found in the vicinity. All of these mysterious corpses within a twenty foot circle, and the strange death-canyon itself many miles from the nearest human habitation. . . .

Witchcraft?? Black magic?? Horrid, perverted sacrificial rites? Mere chance? Or what?

These are some of the questions Burgess is asking. Can you answer?

THE PENITENTES PROTEST

We are glad to print the following letter, but we must protest, in our turn, that no criticism of the Penitentes was intended by our publication of Mr Chapman's engraving. It was no more than an historical note and we are sorry if it offended.

Taos, N.M., April 5, 1939

Dear Sir: We note your reproduction of a penitente crucifixion as you so term it; & the expression that, 'once upon a time Good Friday was celebrated like this in good old Taos.' ⟨ Perhaps it would be well to add that the cut or photographic scene is also a true reproduction of Chapman's work; actually taken from true life some 300 years ago, and in which Manville, came in with the first advent of the Anglo-Saxon race. No doubt Chapman, found himself in a promised land; flowing with milk & honey and he choose to use for his debut the penitentes upon the American Continent. It appears that his research works have servived through all ages down to the moment. ⟨ It might be well for Chapman to also include in his digests of the penitentes the imaginatory mental indigestions which Burgess, is having in this lonely & dark undiscovered cannon, which from prehistoric conclussions is located some where in the Southeast pole of Taos County. ⟨ Com-

ing down to brass tacks, Mr Johnson, we know that there are a few world unknown writers in Taos & what would be friends of the native people or the penitentes that have made great efforts to enrich their bins with gold, writing great falsifications and exaggeraticns about the penitentes. ⟨ We believe that our doings are in accord with the Christian religion of which we are members and we resent criticism on the part of would be friends like yourself, Chapman, and others now living in Taos. ⟨ We could cite, many religions & their practices, but feel it uncalled for. Let us keep in mind the greatest charter ever written by civilized man in this continent, The Constitution of America. Do also unto others as you would have them do unto you. Let us work together in the right way which is the only way.

Yours truly,

Juan J. Tenorio
Levi Martinez
Alfonzo T. Martinez
Commission: of the organization
of Jesus Christ of Nazareth

"Far better than statistics of aridity, altitude or racial distribution, these poems bring out the distinctive charm and individuality of that sun-baked anachronism, with its Indians and its Spanish great-grand-children, which is New Mexico."—The Scarsdale Inquirer.

"She has not been content to give us merely the material of poetry or English translations of Mexican poetry. She has accomplished the transmutation of what in lesser hands would have been transmitted only as the picturesque and the exotic into real poetry in English."—Chicago Evening Post.

"There is a continuous musical play of drums and thunders, lightning play of turquoise and corn-color and brilliant red rags. There is a quiet sense of hovering death, and of time going on forever in the dusty desert, never arriving: the going and coming and going of generations. Alice Corbin is a good listener; she has felt the pulse of pueblo life. And her book offers a breath of a different, more pungent air."—New York Evening Post

" . . . . Clean and aloof as the high deliberate table lands where it was written; elusive as the grave, questioning faces of the dying nations of copper-skinned people whose last homes are there. . . . .

Attractions of a house swept and garnished, ready for a hurdy-gurdy or the undertaker; an open door for tambourines and bells, or crape and a coffin—there is a hospitality that widely varied in Red Earth."—Carl Sandburg.

Published by
Ralph Fletcher Seymour, Chicago
Price $1.50
For Sale in Santa Fe

Our shop is equipped to do personal and bus-
ess printing including copper plate engraving and
eel embossing.

For the month of August we are offering 100
nnouncements of not more than five lines with env-
opes and the choice of any of our woodcut designs
r $ 3.00.

CLARK'S STUDIO

Santa Fe, New Mexico

7o East Garcia St.   Phone 380

ompiled by Roberta Robey   Printed by Clark's Studio

'he cover design and the design shown
bove are two of our new designs for this
eason's greeting cards.

CLARK'S STUDIO

Santa Fe, New Mexico

7o East Garcia St.   Phone 380

ompiled by Roberta Robey   Printed by Clark's Studio

"With the buffalo went the Indian and with the cattle came the cowboy. Created by that northward sweep of the long-horned herds he was briefly the dominant figure in the whole Southwest as the mountain man had been before him and the Mexican rico before that. He was a figure as distinctive as either of these but the period of his importance was hardly more than a generation. It came to an end when money and fences laid hold of the grasslands. But he survives in the imaginations of men - - - he is an immortal stereotype."

Rio Grande - Harvey Fergusson

A SECRET ? YES ? ? ? ? ?

The Harper Prize Novel
1933-34
has been written by
Paul Horgan
of
Roswell, N. M.
Price-$2:50

The judges of the contest
were
Dorothy Canfield   Harry Hansen
Sinclair Lewis

-Previous winners of the Harper Prize-
Margaret Wilson   Anne Parrish
Glenway Wescott   Julian Green
Robert Raynolds

THE IDEAL GIFT FROM SANTA FE IS A SOUTHWESTERN BOOK

Autumn: Golden fountain.
And the winds neighing
Amid the monotonous hills:
Desolation of the old gods,
Rain that lifts and rain that
          moves away;
In the green-black torrent
Scarlet leaves.

Preludes and Symphonies
by- John Gould Fletcher

At the End of the Santa Fe Trail Sister Blandina	2.00
Caballeros - Barker	3.00
Earth Horizon - Austin	4.00
Indian Earth - Bynner	2.50
Native Tales of New Mexico Applegate	2.50
Our Native Cacti - Higgins	2.50
Mammals of New Mexico	1.00
Rainmakers - Coolidge	4.00
Tay Tay's Tales - DeHuff	2.00
Death Comes to the Archbishop Cather - .95, 2.50, 5.00	
Birds of New Mexico - Bailey	5.00
Spanish Folk Songs - Van Stone	1.50
Singing Cowboy - Larkin	3.50
Dancing Gods - Fergusson	3.00
Odyssey of Cabeza de Vaca- Bishop	3.00
Rio Grande-Fergusson	3.00
Mexican Houses	15.00
Old Santa Fe-Twitchell	5.00

Album	M. R. Rinehart
All Passion Spent	V. Sackville-West
Alien Corn	Sidney Howard
Ann Vickers	Sinclair Lewis
As the Earth Turns	Gladys Carroll
Caballeros	Ruth L. Barker
Design for Living	Noel Coward
Earth Horizon	Mary Austin
Eva Gay	Evelyn Scott
God's Little Acre	Erskine Caldwell
Helene	Vicki Baum
House of Exile	Nora Waln
Intimate Memories	Mabel Luhan
Last Adam	John Gould Cozzens
Lawrence and Brett	Dorothy Brett
Letters of D. H. Lawrence	Huxley
Life Begins at Forty	Pitkin
Magnificent Obsession	Lloyd Douglas
One More Spring	Robert Nathan
No Nice Girl Swears	A. L. Moats
Pageant	G. B. Lancaster
Saint and Mr. Teal	Charteris
Shanghai Bund Murders	Van W. Mason
Second Common Reader	Virginia Woolf

Anthony Adverse	Hervey Allen
Emerald Clasp	Francis Beeding
Evelyn Prentice	W. E. Woodward
Golden Book of Crime	Crime Club
Grand Canary	A. J. Cronin
Great Circle	Conrad Aiken
Little Man, What Now ?	Fallada
Looking Backward	Norman Douglas
Obelists of the Sea	C. D. King
Man Wants but Little	Wilson Wright
Murder of the Only Witness	Fletcher
Marie Antoinette	Zweig
Miss Lonelyhearts	Nathaniel West
Men of Good Will	Jules Romain
P. C. Richardson's First Case	Thomson
No Time Like the Present	Storm Jameson
Shoes that Walked Twice	Toussaint-Samat
Sleepers East	F. Nebel
Stranger's Return	Phil Stong
Rio Grande	Harvey Fergusson
Travail of Gold	E. F. Benson

Our rental charges are three and five cents per day. There is a minimum charge of ten cents.

Album	Rinehart
Alien Corn	Howard
Ann Vickers	Lewis
As the Earth Turns	Carroll
Eva Gay	Scott
House of Exile	Waln
Intimate Memories	Luhan
Lawrence and Brett	Brett
Letters of D. H. Lawrence	Huxley
Life Begins at Forty	Pitkin
Magnificent Obsession	Douglas
One More Spring	Nathan
No Nice Girl Swears	Moats
South Moon Under	Rawlings
Stranger's Return	Stong
Sleepers East	Nebel
Rio Grande	Fergusson
Marie Antoinette	Zweig
Men of Good Will	Romain
No Time Like the Present	Jameson
Grand Canary	Cronin
Little Man, What Now?	Fallada
Looking Backward	Douglas
Anthony Adverse	Allen

You may make a reservation on any book in the Rental Library-Telephone 666.

All Men are Enemies	Aldington
Andrew's Harvest	Evans
Autobiography of Alice Tobias	Stein
Dark Hazard	Burnett
Dona Celastis	Dell
Farm	Bromfield
Fault of the Angels	Horgan
Golden Ripple	Waugh
Heavy Weather	Wodehouse
First World War	Stallings
Jeremiah and the Princess	Oppenheim
Lion of Petra	Mundy
Mad Hatter Mystery	Carr
Mummy Case Mystery	Morran
Marriage in Gotham	Ross
Mellon's Millions	O'Conner
Miss Bishop	Aldrich
Montana Rides	Evans
Murder on Tour	Downing
Philosophy of Solitude	Powys
Pure and Impure	Colette
Solal	Cohen
Those Disturbing Miracles	Douglas
Werewolf	Endore
Wonder Hero	Priestly

Our rental charges are three and five cents per day. There is a minimum charge of ten cents.

OF

At the End of the Santa Fe Trail	
Sister Blandina	2.00
Caballeros - Barker	3.00
Earth Horizon - Austin	4.00
Indian Earth - Bynner	2.50
Native Tales of New Mexico	
Applegate	2.50
Our Native Cacti - Higgins	2.50
Mammals of New Mexico	1.00
Rainmakers - Coolidge	4.00
Tay Tay's Tales - DeHuff	2.00
Death Comes to the Archbishop	
Cather - .95, 2.50, 5.00	
Birds of New Mexico - Bailey	5.00
Spanish Folk Songs - Van Stone	1.50
Singing Cowboy - Larkin	3.50
Dancing Gods - Fergusson	3.00
Odyssey of Cabeza de Vaca- Bishop	3.00
Rio Grande-Fergusson	3.00
Mexican Houses	15.00
Old Santa Fe-Twitchell	5.00

Turquoise Trail- A. C. Henderson	$2.25
Flowering Stone- George Dillon	1.75
Conquistador (Pulitzer Prize 1933)	
Archibald McLeish	2.50
Fatal Interview- Edna S. Millay	2.00
Draft of xxx Cantos- Ezra Pound	2.50
Collected Poems of Elinor Wylie	3.50
The Single Glow - Axton Clark	1.50
April Twilights- Willa Cather	2.00
Indian Earth- Witter Bynner	2.50
Selected Poems of Francis Thompson	2.00
New Poetry-Monroe and Henderson	3.00
Collected Poems of E.A. Robinson	5.00
Oxford Book of English Verse	3.75
Dark Certainty- Dorothy Flanagan	1.50
Name and Nature of Poetry-	
Housman	1.00

And, don't forget that the Poet's Round-
up comes about the middle of August.

The test of time entitles these to be sold
at **one dollar** each.

Adams Family
Animals Looking at You
Cheiro's Book of Numbers
Elizabeth and Essex
Education of a Princess
Favorite Novels of Rider-Haggard
Human Body
Human Mind
Fountain
Kit Carson
Lives of a Bengal Lancer
Meaning of a Liberal Education
O' Pioneers
Plumed Serpent
Queen Victoria
Rasputin
Riata and Spurs
Story of Mankind
Washington Merry-Go-Round
War and Peace
Plutarch's Lives
Complete Novels of Jane Austen
The Medici
Les Miserables
Twelve Famous Plays of the Restoration
and Eighteenth Century

Don't Forget these Outstanding Juveniles

The Christ Child - Petersham	2.00
Bob, Son of Battle - Ollivant	1.00
Deric with the Indians - Nusbaum	1.75
Painted Pig - Morrow	2.00
Pop-Up Pinocchio - Collodi	2.00
Waterless Mountain - Armer	2.50
Smoky - James	1.00
One Little Indian Boy - Brock	1.50
Little Women - Alcott	1.00
Millions of Cats - Wanda Gag	1.50
Famous Animal Stories -Seton	3.50
Cambridge Book of Poetry	
for Children	2.50
Mickey Mouse	.50
Hitty - Field	2.50
Picture Book of Animals	2.50

THE RYDAL PRESS
of Santa Fe New Mexico
A BRIEF ACCOUNT OF
ITS HISTORY AND
ITS PURPOSE

T HE ROYAL CITY OF THE HO-
LY FAITH OF SAINT FRANCIS OF ASSISI WAS THE FULL TITLE
GIVEN TO THE LITTLE TOWN OF SANTA FE, NEW MEXICO,
by the Spanish. Today it is merely called Santa Fe, which means "Holy
Faith," and the rest of the ponderous appellation has gone the way of so
many of the more laborious and lengthy methods and practices in this
streamlined era. However, the country in which it lies has not changed
so much in spite of the three cultural influences to which it has been
subjected; Indian first, then Spanish, and finally the American pioneer.
For all this, Santa Fe still remains a town of mud houses (with some of
hollow tile), the prevailing spoken language is over fifty per cent Spanish, voting ballots are printed in the two languages, and politically and
physically the town is more like a foreign country than almost any other
part of the United States.

It may have seemed out of the ordinary to some to have picked this
particular locality for the establishment of a press of any kind, especially
one primarily for the printing of books, so often associated with the
large commercial publishing of the East, and particularly one which has
as one of its aims the development of the mechanized side of bookmaking.

From its original inception The Rydal Press has been partly experimental. Its birth is not recorded in any registry, but it grew from a small

room in a private house in Rydal, Pennsylvania, where a few fonts of type were kept to "play with." This seems to be a habit with many typographers all over the country, who may or may not have other interests but who will have their little press in their own house and will take their leisure time to play with their hobby. They often involve every available member of their family and anybody else, who is willing, in setting type and eventually printing some small and sometimes

some large pieces for themselves first, and later as they grow, for the world. In this way The Rydal Press began, as so many presses of this nature have begun.

In 1933 a number of Southwestern writers were considering the possibility of publishing their books under a group program, establishing their own editorial board, and financing their own books. The only deterring element was the lack of proper manufacturing facilities and someone with a good working knowledge of publishing practices. Later in this article the details of this plan are gone into more fully, by one of the founders. The owner of The Rydal Press was asked to do this work and the press moved to Santa Fe with as much alacrity as a press can muster in moving.

The new home of the press was on a small ranch outside of Santa Fe. All overhead was necessarily reduced to a minimum and on the ranch there was a large frame building which provided the necessary floor space for the composition and press rooms in one section and the bindery in another. Later a stock room and office were added. Perhaps the most serious problem at the start was the procuring of adequate labor, because this talent had to come from some distance, and then, with imported labor, there was always the question as to whether the press would have enough work to support it.

The first six months' operation of the press established a number of facts upon which the later policies were largely based. It was definitely proven that handset books were out of the question for us when it came to any book of more than a few pages. The original intention was to make books which were not to fall in the de luxe price class yet had sufficient care taken in their making to give them a pleasing and permanent dress. From the very beginning we have endeavored to use materials which are better than in the average trade book and yet make these to sell for a price which, although perhaps in some cases slightly higher than similar trade publications, still would come into fair competition with them. With this in mind, the press installed a Monotype and a small cylinder  press. The Monotype furnished a machine on which we could compose with as close spacing as we chose, provided sorts for our cases for handsetting and correcting, and with the possibility of the use of the English Monotype as well as the American company's type faces, there was an almost unlimited field from which to choose. This particular medium of composition seems to be the ideal one for books and other work of the nature of that which the press is doing. It always has the possibility of handsetting, if it is desired to use it as such, and the Monotype face makes a particularly good surface from which to print from type.

The press has imported the English face designed by Eric Gill, Perpetua, in which this particular article is set, and as far as it is known, it is the only press which has this face for machine composition in the United States. This face offers excellent printing qualities on both smooth and rough finished papers and is well adapted to both cylinder press and the Colts Armory press type of printing. The face was imported through the Lanston Monotype Corporation of Philadelphia and run with no difficulty whatsoever.

During the last six months the press has moved into a larger place in Santa Fe proper. This time it is in its own mud house and incidentally, although mud houses don't stand up under the seaboard climates, here in this very dry climate the mud walls and roof offer one of the best mediums to maintain uniform temperatures in a pressroom.

The Rydal Press has always wanted to publish a few books under its own imprint each year. The Southwest offers a large variety of material which can be drawn from the old cultures in this country. This includes Spanish, Indian, and American Colonial periods and, although much has been written and published already, almost every week something new comes up indigenous to the Southwest which has merit. Some of these books we hope to be able to do in a fine way, others of a more general nature can be handled in more of a commercial manner, but we would rather establish a style of our own than to return to strictly period

work in the typo-
shop and controlled by
sible to develop this
laid out in one office
followed in some dis-
chanical operations
by the person doing
cally under his super-
us the method by
sults may be most
be our policy to make
as possible from the
point and still keep
priced field. It will

graphy. Being a small
one person, it is pos-
style as the work isn't
and the instructions
tant press .The me-
are carried out either
the layout or practi-
vision. This seems to
which the desired re-
easily obtained. It will
any book as attractive
bookmaking stand-
them in a moderately
always be our endeav-

or to keep books from appearing over-stuffed, either in price or paper, bulking books and *very precious* books being our two pet abominations and things to be avoided.

The development of The Rydal Press has been so closely associated with the idea of Writers' Editions and their regional publication program that Haniel Long, one of the Writers' Editions' founders has been kind enough to write the following description of their aims and purposes. This article was published in a slightly different form some time ago in "Higher Education and Society" by the University of Oklahoma Press but Mr. Long has made some revisions for its present use.

Publishing is an elastic occupation. The hard-pressed writer of today can return to the methods of his Greek and Roman predecessors, who sold their work through scribes, and not for a penny. Plato, who had a good library, paid three hundred minae (a large sum) for three small treatises of Philolaus the Pythagorean. Martial informs us that his epigrams can be purchased for five denarii (no doubt at one of the booksellers in the Vicus Sandalarius); he confides this information to us in the midst of the epigrams themselves, so that it is not the least pointed or the least surprising of his thrusts. The system of the ancients can return whenever a commercial system gags a writer because he is not a good risk. Among the many poor risks during the last eighty years, and the list is really rather an impressive one, were Walt Whitman, Samuel Butler, and Edward Carpenter among others.

Four years ago last Mexico, three poets, tor concerned to help from native American cident, and formed lishing enterprise. without a dramatic automatic fashion that cape from jail if they Of course we were mans, or Carpenters, turn the minute it no- In this venture, the on a handful of gagged

May, in Santa Fe, New a novelist, and an edi- good writing grow soil, met half by ac- a co-operative pub- This event took place gesture, in the same prisoners would es- found a window open. not Butlers, Whit- but any worm will tices what to turn to. effect of a simple idea writers, I see the first

robin after a long, hard winter. Next week there may be another robin, and the week after still another; who knows? For behind the private press is the stored-up energy of writers incapable in some or all of their aspects of being good commercial risks. Decentralization in publishing, from the angle of the belles-lettres, does not mean a haughty rejection of the commercial standard (which is bound up with mass distribution and serves many useful ends). It means simply that there can be other tests for a book than, *will it pay to publish it?* For the belles-lettres the private press can serve the same function as the senate filibuster: it can allow a minority to go on expressing itself as long as the minority cares to. So informal a method of producing and distributing books will encourage the growth of critical centers outside of New York. In the past we have always had formidable critics scattered through the land, and as soon as the sod is broken and the seed planted, we shall have them again in all their glory.

Our Santa Fe enterprise has much of the makeshift in it. Such is apt to be the path of the pioneer; and the writers to whom I have referred, who in their individual practice attempted to decentralize publishing, have found it so. Edward Carpenter sold only seven hundred copies of "Towards Democracy," in seven years. When the Labor Press of Birmingham went bankrupt, he had to smuggle his property off the premises, in a pouring rain, and in a hired truck, with a good part of a ton of "Towards Democracy" on board, he tells us. Carpenter lived to see his books make money, but Samuel Butler did not. Butler estimated that it cost him seven hundred and seventy-nine pounds sterling to talk as long as he pleased on subjects that pleased him. None the less, when his publishers started a new magazine with-out including him as a contributor to it, he made the remark, "Perhaps it is better I should not have a chance of becoming a hack writer, for I should grasp it at once if it were of-fered to me." Writers' Editions is not endowed, and has no other patrons than its customers. We each of us assume the risk of our own

books, as best we can. In one instance one of us underwrote the book of another. With our associate members we have now grown from five to seventeen, and we include a few writers who are published in the East and are well known. We include them only because they believe in our venture and wish to help it. Membership is elective, but not exclusive, and could spread rapidly if there were good reason for having many members. There is better reason for encouraging the increase of private presses.

No one need belong to our group to publish his book under our imprint. Manuscripts submitted to us are passed upon sometimes by almost the whole group. In this endorsement of a writer by a group of his fellows, we may possess, if we are able to make use of it, a guarantee of disinterestedness and quality out of the scope of the ordinary publisher.

Writers' Editions is co-operative, because we each surrender a share of our profits to an endowment fund, the purpose of which is to publish good books that otherwise might not see the light of day. This fund is growing satisfactorily, considering the impromptu manner in which we do business. Another principle of ours is to pool our lists of prospective buyers of books. These lists are our greatest money asset. We like to defray the total cost of a book at once, through mail order subscriptions which come in upon announcement of publication; and we are generally successful in doing so.

Whether our books should be beautifully printed and expensive, or the reverse, is a question of policy we are not as yet agreed upon. Whether we wish to surrender a book to a commercial publisher if he wishes to print a second edition of it, is another such question; and so is the extent to which we should work with our old friends the retail booksellers. The passage of time will doubtless ripen our judgment in such matters. It may be we shall never agree however; but what of it? These are all questions for each writer to settle for himself, as he wishes.

But we are already sure that the fate of the private press in general depends up-

on the cultivated nuclei of the universities over the country. Our group has published thirteen books up to the present, and we are now bringing out two more. The literary critics have been friendly and fair to us, a number of the regular publishers have helped in various ways, including advice. Though we follow Samuel Butler in talking about what we care to talk about, we have not thus far found it so expensive as he did. On some of our books for which the figures are complete, we are making a good profit. As we become better known, our friends increase, but whether we turn out to be a premature robin, and winter will set in again and leave the landscape bleak and robinless, depends on the suffrage we can win, by intrinsic merit, from the cultivated élite of the country, most of whom have their roots in one university campus or another. The new publishing will stand or fall with the new education. Both are born of a critical but wonderful moment in the nation's history.

Up to the present time The Rydal Press has printed some thirty books and published three. This year, 1938, the first of a series of books on early days in the Southwest will be issued. The titles in this series are chosen from narratives, mostly personal ones, of the early days of this country. They are edited by men or women authorities on these subjects and are chosen for their present interest as well as their historical significance. Another series which the Press is issuing is a group of shorter books by modern authors on Southwestern subjects. We hope that this latter group will be of truly literary significance in national as well as regional importance.

In its few years of operation in the Southwest, The Rydal Press has endeavored to make this section of the country conscious of the development in better made books as well as to help in making the country as a whole interested in the Southwest, its past and present cultures, and its history. The Press itself is neither a large printing factory nor a small private press but falls between the two, attempting to avoid the disadvantages and partake of the advantages of both.

Printed for The Annual of Bookmaking, 1938, at The Rydal Press, Santa Fe, New Mexico. The illustrations used are from wood blocks by Willard Clark, except for the printer's mark of "the little saint" which was designed by Warren Chappell.

WRITERS' EDITIONS, INC. ANNOUNCES

A BOOK FOR THOSE INTERESTED
IN THE ART OF THE PRIMITIVE SOUTHWEST

FRIJOLES CANYON PICTOGRAPHS
BY GUSTAVE BAUMANN

FOREWORD BY
ALFRED VINCENT KIDDER

THE ARTIST TO HIS FRIENDS —

The book printed on a hand press is, we know, an anomaly in these days of multiple power presses capable of converting quantities of roll paper into printed pages. Yet there are books of special interest that can be better done by hand, notably when the producer, rebelling against the impersonal and complicated machine, is willing to see it through almost single handed.

Problems have arisen peculiar to this book of mine that at times have no precedent in my years of print-making experience. To draw, cut and print a book is a sort of endurance test. The ink that flows well today may not do so tomorrow. On the other hand, slight variations in handmade paper that would be disastrous on a power press can be turned to advantage and made to yield an interesting quality not otherwise attainable.

While at work I had to redesign the book as I originally visualized it to conform to the typographical limitations of the page. The question of what kind of text should supplement the illustrations also had to be considered; was it to be diverting or enlightening? Which would better hold the reader unfamiliar with the subject matter? And last but not least, I renewed my acquaintance with the thousand and one other problems that like mischievous sprites scamper over the work table, hide under the bed of the press, and reverse signatures!

The idea of presenting these pictographs in book form has intrigued me for a long time. Now that the book is completed, they may perhaps add a small link in the continuity of American cultural experiences.

HANIEL LONG COMMENTS —

When Gustave Baumann first came to the Southwest many years ago, he was so delighted by the cave drawings at Rito de los Frijoles, then in good condition but now more or less obliterated, that he made drawings of them for himself; and he has now put together a book of that first excitement and delight of his, with a running text and two-color cuts of the drawings. There are twenty-six woodcuts, and Baumann has printed them himself, and written an introduction and commentaries. The result is an unusual book: here an artist has saved for those who value such things, and has saved with care and thought, the art of a people as it was in the dawn of their history, and with something of the surprise of dawn in his appreciation of it.

Gustave Baumann spent his early years in Chicago, where he developed an interest in typography and wood engraving. He then studied in Munich, in the days when Munich meant artistic adventure. Upon returning home he established his studio in Nashville, Brown County, Indiana. We next find him in Taos, New Mexico, and then in Santa Fe, where he appears to be permanently located. As one of the foremost color-print makers he has received numerous awards and is widely represented in art museums and private collections.

FRIJOLES CANYON PICTOGRAPHS

The book is bound in cloth
Printed in two colors on hand made paper
The number of pages is 48, size of announcement
The number of woodcuts 26
One of these extending over 4 pages
and signed by the artist
The hand press edition is 480
Of which 300 are offered for sale at $6.00
You will find order blank enclosed

**ADDRESS GUSTAVE BAUMANN 409 CAMINO DE LAS ANIMAS
SANTA FE, NEW MEXICO**

JULY 1940　　　　　　　　　　　　　　　　**10 Cents**

THE · SANTA · FEAN

A NATIONAL MONTHLY

WOODBLOCK—WILLARD F. CLARK

LAWRENCE RAND BYNON—OBSERVATIONS NATIONAL AND INTERNATIONAL
Alfred Morang — P. H. Wistrand — John L. Sinclair — Jacob Scher
Harold Butcher — Alfred Hazen Stoddard — Helen E. Cunningham
Roy A. Keech — Elizabeth B. Fierlein — Lorin W. Brown
Jean Cady — Alva Woodward — Margaret Lohlker

Woodcarvers of Cordova

By MARGARET LOHLKER

IGHT spots of blue and green paint seemed from a distance to be splashed on the screen door. But coming closer, the visitor who had driven up the twisted road from Chimayo saw that the door was ornamented with borders and bars of little trees, flowers, birds and scrolls, carved in thick wood and gaily colored. The door and window frames were carved too, so that the little adobe house looked like the pictures in old storybooks of the witch's gingerbread house.

Here, however, lived no witch, but a smiling Spanish family. In the center of the decorated screen door were ornate carved letters spelling "J. D.—Cordova—N. M." Jose Dolores Lopez, who had thus signed his work, was no longer among the living. But his work was being carried on by the whole family, and many of the products of the elder carver's knife still remained in the house.

Courteously invited to enter, the visitor looked around the cedar and pine scented room. On one of the tables was a "Tree of Life," some eighteen inches high. Each leaf was carefully carved in an elaborate oakleaf pattern. Apples abounded among the leaves, and through the foliage peered the face of Satan, leering out at the Adam and Eve who stood frozen beside the tree, Eve with an apple in her stiffly outstretched hand.

Appropriately near by stood a grisly figure of "El Muerto," made more terrifying somehow by the fact that the skull was inhumanly small in proportion to the body. He was crowded by San Miguel stepping firmly on an expressive white pine demon, and San Pedro with his key. Near by, on a table of its own, stood the loveliest piece of carving in the room—a Nativity scene in which every tiny detail was worked out with exquisite care, from the carved corbels supporting the small ceiling beams to the calmly royal expressions of the three Kings bringing their gifts to the Holy Child.

Among the smaller carvings were a number of lively pigs. After the religious subjects that occupy the minds of the devout artists of New Mexico mountain villages like Cordova, it is natural that the things they see around them should appeal as models for their work. These wooden pigs had the same look as the live ones that grunted in their cedar pole pen behind the house.

Examining carved crosses and animals and boxes, the visitor found it easy to imagine himself in a Swiss woodcarver's home in an Alpine village. Outside, the illusion remained. The compact little town clung to the edge of its narrow valley, with neat checkered fields and laden apple trees just below, and the mountains rising sharply on the other side. Even the burro rolling happily on his back in the dust nearby added to the picture, the sight of a donkey's long ears being common in all mountainous lands where his strength and sureness are needed on steep trails. And the log-built sheds and pig pens at the edge of the town looked like nothing one would expect to see in America. The brown adobe houses and the soft Spanish words of the laughing clusters of children were the only threads holding the scene to New Mexico.

The air was full of the soft sound of running water from the acequias, the irrigation ditches running above and below the village and branching across it, the arteries that brought life to the gardens and fields. One little roadway had a cascade down its hollowed center.

This was the season of the preparation of food for winter. Meat was drying on lines in front of the houses, apples were shriveling to durable sweetness on the roofs, and beans were piled in the yards to dry and be threshed. The visitor's last impression, as he finally turned to the road up the hillside, was of a little town close to the earth, confident, welcoming the change of seasons, and picturing the beauty of Heaven and earth in wood from the trees of its own sheltering mountains.

—FRITZ BROESKE

Not All the Fingers of One's Hand

BY LORIN W. BROWN

HE canvas-covered wagon slowly made its way up the last grade, on one side of which stood the first house of the little mountain village. As the team of diminutive, shaggy-maned horses pulled it along the road that led into the village square, its passage brought many an inquiring face to door and window and left speculation in its wake. —What did the trader have to sell?—

The village had just begun to rouse itself for the day's activities; smoke columns rose straight, their light blue transparent before the rays of the newly risen sun. A long line of water carriers dotted the path to the river, that flowed below the ridge on which the village nestled. These, for the most part, boys and girls, moved up the hill with quick short steps, arms stretched tautly downward by the weight of the pails of water.

Curiosity urged them to accelerate their pace; to finish this daily morning chore so that they might investigate this strange wagon, and see what of interest it might portend.

Two boys who had just turned their nimble, quick-footed flock out of one of the many pole corrals in the rear of the village, permitted the goats to scatter over the rocky hillside, in care of their faithful dogs. They, too, must steal furtively back to the center of the village and inform themselves fully about the new arrival. He promised to furnish them a subject of conversation with which to while away the long day before them on the foothills sloping to the river where their motley charges grazed.

A burro dozed in the shade of the high, thick adobe walls of the village church, ax and rope knotted to rude, wooden saddle; philosophically he accepted this break in the day's routine of wood gathering while his master investigated the why and the wherefore of the advent of this stranger in their midst.

When the trader brought his horses to a welcome stop, in the open space before the church, he was immediately surrounded by a noisy, inquiring group of children. "*Que vende?*"—they asked, and sped back home to acquaint their mothers,—the stranger was selling beans, new *pinto* beans.

The village *inocente* shuffled up on mis-shapen feet, bowing and grimacing, one hand upholding overalls precariously hung on hunch-backed shape,—the other extended in greeting, his leer of welcome, one he always assumed when discharging his duties as self-appointed, official greeter of the community.

The sound of wood chopping ceased throughout the village almost with one accord; and soon the villagers converged from the encircling houses of the square toward the spot whereon the trader's wagon stood.

The trader rolled the canvas cover of his wagon on to the rearmost hoop, and standing atop a sack of beans, took his belt up a notch, as if girding himself for a fray.

"*Si, frijol nuevo de l' Estancia*, good beans and very clean." This statement by the trader was met with an immediate and characteristic, — "*Como lo vende?*" — from many of the upturned faces in the group gathered round the wagon.

"*Doce reales l' almud*,"—ejaculations of dismay and exaggerated incredulity met his reply. "*Ay!*, a dollar and a half an *almud!*—*Muy caro!*"

Yet the supply of beans was running low in most of the humble households and the women dissembled the necessity

they had of buying by critically inspecting the beans within an opened sack poised near the edge of the wagon box.— Their own bean fields would not be ripe for another month or so and their men could not work with this indispensable food lacking on the table. "*No hay remedio*, we must have beans."

Soon dish pans and snow-white flour sacks were brought, into which heaping *almuds* of beans were poured. Money and ground chili were accepted in exchange. The astute trader joked and flirted and cautiously met protests of short measure with banter and bare-faced flattery.

A tall man, one of the villagers, stood looking on as he leaned a negligent shoulder on a rear wagon wheel.

His intelligent eyes, outlined by the fine wrinkles of one whose discernment is keen yet tempered with toleration, seemed to be absorbed and fix themselves on the wooden box, the *almud* in which the trader measured each successive purchase. His expression indicated that he questioned the size and capacity of the trader's measure.

Finally he broke into speech,—"*Amigo!*, I will buy an *almud* of beans if you will measure them in my own *almud*. See! here is the money and I can soon fetch my measure. *Que dice?*—I do not believe your *almud* is an honest one—"

The trader paused briefly, glanced toward the questioning one and with a good-natured smile, shrugged his shoulders as he raised his hand above his head, fingers outspread against the sky. "*Mire amigo!*" he called out and nodded toward the hand he held aloft.

The crowd stopped to gaze and wonder at the gesture, and wondering, never understood. The fault-finder however, was quick to grasp the significance of the outspread hand. Highly amused and admiring the ingenuity and audacity of the trader, he smiled despite himself. The proverb so artfully symbolized was true,—*No todos los dedos de la mano son igual*—not all the fingers of one's hand are of the same length—.

He accepted the rebuke and decided to mind his own business. Was he not a trader also, and had not this sly one in the wagon recognized in him a kindred soul?—He stepped up to the wagon, purchased his *almud* of beans, exchanging a knowing smile with the trader as he handed over his dollar and a half.

HAROLD E WEST

The Coronado Cuarto Centennial Commission

of

New Mexico

invites you to be present at the

Opening Ceremonies of the Coronado Cuarto Centennial

and the Dedication of the Coronado Monument

consisting of

The Coronado Museum

and the

Ruins and Kiva of the Ancient Pueblo of Kuaua

near Bernalillo, New Mexico

on the afternoon of May 29, 1940

You are requested to be present at the junction of Highways No. 85 and No. 44 by two o'clock in order
that your car may be properly placed in
the approach procession.

SOURCES FOR THE
"PUBLICATIONS EPHEMERAL AND EXEMPLARY"

I. *Santa Fe: The Gateway of the "Greatest Fifty Mile Square in America"* pamphlet, with "An Appreciation of New Mexico," by Zane Grey. History Library, Museum of New Mexico, Santa Fe.

II. *Motor Camper & Tourist*, vol. 2, no. 9, February 1926. This issue contains ten articles with New Mexico in the title, including "The Romance of New Mexico" by Gilean Douglas, "Motor Adventuring in New Mexico" by Waldo Lockwood, and "Why New Mexico Interests the Tourist" by Manuel Carleton. History Library, Museum of New Mexico, Santa Fe.

III. "Roads to Yesterday" and "The Courier Service," pp. 2-3 of *Roads to Yesterday: Motor Drives out from Old Santa Fé*, Harveycars, n.d. History Library, Museum of New Mexico, Santa Fe.

IV. Eugene Manlove Rhodes, "Neglecting Fractions," *They Know New Mexico: Intimate Sketches by Western Writers*, issued by The Passenger Department, Atchison, Topeka & Santa Fe Railway, 1928, pp. 28-31. Private collection, Santa Fe.

V. "Sunmount Santa Fe: The Sanitorium Different," *Official Program*, Santa Fé Fiesta, September 4-6, 1922. History Library, Museum of New Mexico, Santa Fe.

VI. "Ye First Appearance of Ye Communitye Theatre" program, p. 1. New Mexico State Records Center and Archives, Santa Fe.

VII. Philip Stevenson's "Sure Fire" playbill. History Library, Museum of New Mexico, Santa Fe.

VIII. Program for the Santa Fe World Premiere of Warner Brothers' "The Santa Fe Trail," December 13-14, 1940. The program notes proclaim: "The gaiety of a thousand fiestas that for 300 years warmly signalized the arrival of caravans at the 'End of the Trail', echoes sharply again off the sheer slopes of the Sangre de Cristo (Blood of Christ) Mountains. Never such a fabulous party of visitors to welcome as the group today, wherein the oldest political capitol in North America is made the entertainment capital of the world through your gracious presence." Designed and printed at Clark's Studio, Santa Fe. Collection of Willard F. Clark.

IX. "Where the artists and writers go to dine and talk," *Santa Fe Visitor's Guide*, 1931, p. 6. History Library, Museum of New Mexico, Santa Fe.

X. Wine list for La Cantina del Parian. Designed and printed at Clark's Studio, Santa Fe. Collection of Willard F. Clark.

XI. Dinner menu for La Fonda Hotel. Designed and printed at Clark's Studio, Santa Fe. Collection of Willard F. Clark.

XII. *The Santa Fe Plaza*, vol. 1, no. 1, p. 4. History Library, Museum of New Mexico, Santa Fe.

XIII. *The Ballad of Santa Fee Sal*. History Library, Museum of New Mexico, Santa Fe.

XIV. Will Shuster cartoon censored from *Laughing Horse* No. 17, February 1930. J. C. McConvery was the mayor of Santa Fe from 1928 to 1931. History Library, Museum of New Mexico, Santa Fe.

XV. Mabel Dodge Lujan [sic] and "Long John," pp. 28-29 of the Souvenir Program for the International Satiric Ball, sponsored by The Art League of New Mexico in Carlisle Gymnasium, University of New Mexico, Albuquerque, Wednesday, February 5, 1936. T. M. Pearce Collection, Zimmerman Library, University of New Mexico, Albuquerque.

XVI. "Fire Sweeps Taos" and "Bigger Jump Than Everybody," *The Horse Fly*, 24 December 1938, pp. 1, 4. History Library, Museum of New Mexico, Santa Fe.

XVII. "Once Upon A Time Good Friday Was Celebrated Like This In Good Old

Taos!," *The Horse Fly*, 1 April 1939, p. 1. History Library, Museum of New Mexico, Santa Fe.

XVIII. "The Penitentes Protest," *The Horse Fly*, 8 April 1939, p. 3. History Library, Museum of New Mexico, Santa Fe.

XIX. *Red Earth* announcement, *Official Program*, Santa Fé Fiesta, September 5-8, 1921. History Library, Museum of New Mexico, Santa Fe.

XX. *The Villagra Book Shop*, August 1933 and September 1933. Collection of Nancy Applegate, The Villagrá Book Shop, Santa Fe.

XXI. "The Rydal Press of Santa Fe New Mexico: A Brief Account of Its History and Its Purpose," *Colophon: The Annual of Bookmaking*, Vol. I (New York: The Colophon, 1938), n.p. Special Collections, Zimmerman Library, University of New Mexico, Albuquerque.

XXII. "Writers' Editions, Inc. Announces." History Library, Museum of New Mexico, Santa Fe.

XXIII. *The Santa Fean*, July 1940. Margaret Lohlker, "Woodcarvers of Cordova," and Lorin W. Brown, "Not All the Fingers of One's Hand," appear on pages 13 and 16, respectively, of that inaugural issue. Brown's was originally written as "The Proverb" (16 November 1938), part of his work for the New Mexico Federal Writers' Project (see Brown with Charles L. Briggs and Marta Weigle, *Hispano Folklife of New Mexico* [Albuquerque: University of New Mexico Press, 1978], pp. 93-95, 263). For more about José Dolores López see Charles L. Briggs, *The Woodcarvers of Córdova, New Mexico* (Knoxville: University of Tennessee Press, 1980).

XXIV. Invitation from The Coronado Cuarto Centennial Commission, designed and printed at Clark's Studio, Santa Fe. Collection of Willard F. Clark.

A DIRECTORY OF
NEW MEXICO WRITERS

COMPILED FROM 1930s SOURCES

The four New Mexico Round Tables on Southwest Literature held at New Mexico Normal University, Las Vegas, 1933-36, spurred academic interest in "an attempted literary dictionary of the Writers and Writings of New Mexico." Students in a senior seminar on Southwestern literature queried librarians and writers, many of them during personal interviews at the Second Round Table in July 1934. According to English and Speech Department Chair Lester Raines's foreword to the "preliminary volume" in 1934:

The problem of which authors to include soon presented itself. Many writers were residents of the state but had written nothing of southwestern interest, while others outside the state had written in excellent fashion of the New Mexican locale or have become New Mexicans by adoption, hence the title of the book to enable us to include all varieties.

The list, admittedly, is not complete but does mark a beginning at collecting information concerning the literary resources of the state. It also proves that New Mexico has cause to be proud of its literary folk.

Both *Writers and Writings of New Mexico* (1934) and *More New Mexico Writers and Writings* (1935)—indicated as W&W and MW&W, respectively—form the basis for the following directory. We have included most of the persons the NMNU students researched and excluded most of those whose single titles were listed in the 1935 edition without biographical particulars under Musicians, Writers on Flora and Fauna, Writers on Missions, Writers of Travels, and Writers of Histories, although many of the latter are given full treatment as "Authors" and are thus incorporated below.

William Felter of Tucumcari spoke about "Collecting Verse of New Mexico" at the Fourth Round Table on July 11, 1936. Some of the poets whose poems he and John L. McCarty collected in their 1935 volume, *New Mexico in Verse* (Dalhart [Texas] Publishing Company), were amateurs whose work does not appear elsewhere. Their names are followed by the designation "poem NMV" in the directory.

Names, and occasionally residences and biographical notes, about "New Mexicans at home or abroad" whose literary efforts Haniel Long chose for his weekly Writers' Page in the *New Mexico Sentinel*, 1937-38, also have been added to the NMNU lists. In many instances these contributors are virtually anonymous amateurs whose verse or prose—indicated as "poetry/sketch NMS"—are one-time attempts. Writers' page contributions by well-known writers or those about whom biographical and bibliographical data is available are *not* indicated.

Several of Spud Johnson's notes on contributors to *Laughing Horse* have also been included.

Finally, we have incorporated autobiographical and biographical materials assembled by Alison Dana and Margaret Lohlker in the special edition of *The Santa Fe New Mexican*, 26 June 1940: "Artists and Writers: A List of Prominent Artists and Writers of New Mexico" (indicated as "A&W" below). In subsequent issues of the newspaper, the editors divulged the names of those queried who had not had time or inclination to reply. Such writers are designated as "Also deserving"—the editors' term—in the directory which follows.

Newspapers and typewritten mimeographs are notoriously inaccurate documents. Thus we have consulted several additional references, four of them from the 1940s. These include:

Anderson, John Q., Edwin W. Gaston, Jr., and James W. Lee, eds., *Southwestern American Literature: A Biliography* (Chicago: The Swallow Press, 1980).

Major, Mabel, and T.M. Pearce, eds., *Signature of the Sun: Southwest Verse, 1900-1950* (Albuquerque: University of New Mexico Press, 1950).

Major, Mabel, and T. M. Pearce, *Southwest Heritage: A Literary History with Bibliography*, 2d ed. (Albuquerque: University of New Mexico Press, 1948).

Saunders, Lyle, comp., *A Guide to Materials Bearing on Cultural Relations in New Mexico* (Albuquerque: University of New Mexico Press, 1944).

Tully, Marjorie F., and Juan B. Rael, *An Annotated Bibliography of Spanish Folklore in New Mexico and Southern Colorado* (Albuquerque: University of New Mexico Press, 1950).

Other books, book jackets and pamphlets were consulted ad hoc.

A complete entry gives the author's name or names, birth place and date, education, visitor or resident status in New Mexico, profession, genres of work, and death place and date *only when deceased before 1942*. If the person had been employed at one time on the New Mexico Federal Writers' Project (NMFWP) between 1936 and 1941, this is indicated, but the full complement of several hundred people so employed has not been incorporated below. A *selected* list of the author's relevant works, primarily books or plays, concludes the entry. Sometimes this list is more inclusive for lesser known individuals. In any case, it is meant to be indicative, not definitive.

ABEITA, LOUISE (E-Yeh-Shure', Blue Corn): b. Laguna, NM, 1926; ed. U of NM; res. Isleta Pueblo; teacher; poetry, juveniles. *I Am a Pueblo Indian Girl* (1939).

ADAMS, HILDA B.: res. Ranchos de Taos. Poem, sketches NMS.

AGNEW, EDITH: b. Denver, Colo., 1898; ed. Park Coll, Mo.; moved to Holman, NM; librarian, teacher, poet.

ALSBERG, CORA: res. Santa Fe and NY. Poem NMS.

AMBERG, GEORGE: res. Albuquerque and Los Angeles. Sketches NMS.

AMSDEN, CHARLES AVERY: b. Iowa, 1899; raised Farmington, NM; ed. U of NM, Harvard, U of Toulouse, France; museum curator; monographs. *Navaho Weaving* (1934).

ANDERSON, LILLIE GERHART: res. Tucumcari; NMFWP. Sketch NMS.

ANDERSON, MAXWELL: b. Atlantic, Pa., 1888; ed. U of N.D., Stanford; journalist, playwright; essays, drama. *Night Over Taos* (1932).

APPLEGATE, FRANK: b. Atlanta, Ill., 1882; ed. U of Ill., Pa. Academy of Fine Arts, Philadelphia, Julian Academy, Paris; to Santa Fe, 1921; artist and writer; essays, short stories; d. 1931. *Indian Stories from the Pueblos* (1929), *Native Tales of New Mexico* (1932).

ARMER, LAURA ADAMS: b. Sacramento, Calif., 1874; ed. Calif. School of Design; res. Navajo reservation 1920s; artist, film maker, writer; juveniles. *Waterless Mountain* (1931), *Dark Circle of Branches* (1933), *Trader's Children* (1937).

ARNIM, DOROTHY: Sketch NMS.

ARTHUR, ESTHER: Book review NMS.

AUSTIN, MARY: b. Carlinville, Ill., 1868; ed. Blackburn Coll; res. Santa Fe from 1924; writer; fiction, nonfiction, poetry; d. 1934. *The American Rhythm* (1923, 1930), *Land of Journeys' Ending* (1924), *The Children Sing in the Far West* (1928), *Starry Adventure* (1931), *Earth Horizon: An Autobiography* (1932), *Indian Pottery of the Rio Grande* (1934), *One Smoke Stories* (1934).

BAKOS, TERESA: b. Nervi, Italy; ed. Italy; res. Santa Fe; artist, writer; art history and criticism.

BANCROFT, CAROLYN: Sketch NMS.

BANDELIER, ADOLPH FRANCIS ALPHONSE: b. Berne, Switzerland, 1840; to NM 1880; archeologist, historian, ethnologist; monographs, fiction, d. 1914. *Final Report of Investigations Among the Indians of the Southwestern United States, Carried on Mainly in the Years from 1880-1885* (1890-92), *The Delight Makers* (1890), *The Gilded Man* (1893), *The Journey of Alvar Nuñez Cabeza de Vaca and His Companions from Florida to the Pacific, 1528-1536* (1905).

BARKER, ELSA McCORMICK (sister of Wilfred McCormick, Mrs. S. Omar Barker): b. Ill.; raised Hagerman, NM; ed. NM Normal U; res. Tecolotenos, NM; teacher, writer; western fiction.

BARKER, RUTH LAUGHLIN: see Laughlin, Ruth.

BARKER, S. OMAR: b. Beulah, NM, 1894; ed. NM Normal U; teacher, journalist, cowboy, writer; poetry, nonfiction, fiction. *Vientos de las Sierras* (1924), *Buckaroo Ballads* (1928).

BARNES, NELLIE: her *American Indian Love Lyrics* (1925) written in Santa Fe.

BECHDOLDT, FRED(ERICK) R.: b. 1874; western fiction, legend, history. *When the West Was Young* (1922), *Tales of the Old Timers* (1924), *Giants of the Old West* (1930).

BELLOLI, GIORGIO (Georgio): b. Venice, Italy, 1907; ed. Royal Naval Academy, Accademia di Belle Arti and Ca'Foscari, Venice; res. Santa Fe from 1930; sculptor, architect, writer; nonfiction, translations. Essays NMS, A&W.

BENTON, ALICE GILL: b. Mayville, Mich., 1890; ed. U of S. Calif., Mich. State Coll, Kan. State Teachers Coll, U of NM; poetry.

BISHOP, MORRIS: b. Willard, NY; ed. Cornell; language prof.; monographs. *Odyssey of Cabeza de Vaca* (1933).

BLAKE, FORRESTER AVERY: b. Detroit, Mich., 1912; ed. of U of Mich.; frequent NM visitor; novels, history. *Riding the Mustang Trail* (1935).

BLEDSOE, THOMAS FILES: res. Santa Fe; journalist, poet; NMFWP. Sketches NMS.

BLOOM, LANSING BARTLETT: res. Albuquerque; UNM prof., historian, editor; monographs. *New Mexico in the Great War* (1927), *New Mexico History and Civics* (with Thomas C. Donnelly, 1933).

BLOOM, MAUDE McFIE: res. Albuquerque; folklorist, poet, playwright. *Tonita of the Holy Faith* (1924).

BLYTHING, HOPE: Sketch NMS.

BOGGS, TOM: Poem NMS.

BOLT, ETHEL M.: res. Hot Springs, NM. Sketch NMS.

BOTKIN, BENJAMIN A.: b. Boston, Mass., 1901; ed. Harvard, Columbia, U of Neb.; frequent NM visitor; English prof., editor; with FWP; nonfiction, folklore. Edited *Folk-Say: A Regional Miscellany* (1929-32), *The Southwest Scene: An Anthology of Regional Verse* (1931), *Space* (1934-35).

BOWRA, GEORGE B.: Poem NMV.

BOYD, MARY LEOLA: Poem NMV.

BRADFIELD, WESLEY: b. 1876; archeologist; d. 1924. Posthumous *Cameron Creek Village* (1931).

BRADFORD, ROARK: b. Lauderdale Co., Tenn., 1896; Santa Fe visitor; writer; fiction. *John Henry* (1931).

BRAMLETT, WILLLIAM: Sketch NMS.

BRANDEIS, MADELINE: Juveniles. *The Little Indian Weaver* (1928), *Little Rose of the Mesa* (1935).

BRETT, Hon. DOROTHY EUGENIE: b. England, 1883; ed. Slade School, London; to Taos 1924; artist; autobiography. *Lawrence and Brett: A Friendship* (1933).

BRIGHT, ROBERT: b. Sandwich, Mass., 1902; ed. Princeton; to Taos area 1938; journalist, writer; juveniles, fiction.

BRINIG, MYRON: b. Butte, Mont., 1900; ed. Columbia; res. Taos; writer; fiction. *Singermann* (1929), *The Sun Sets in the West* (1935), *All of Their Lives* (1941).

BROCK, EMMA L: b. Fort Shaw, Mont.; ed. U of Minn., Minneapolis School of Art; librarian; juveniles. *One Little Indian Boy* (1932).

BROWN, BELDING: res. Stanley, NM. Sketches NMS.

BROWN, LORIN W.: b. Elizabethtown, NM, 1900; ed. Sterling Coll, Kan.; res. Cordova and Santa Fe; NMFWP; nonfiction, folklore.

BROWNE, CLARA LI: res. Piedmont, Calif.; "fourth generation of a New Mexico family." Poem NMS.

BURNS, WALTER NOBLE: b. 1872; writer; history, fiction; d. 1932. *The Saga of Billy the Kid* (1926), *Tombstone, An Iliad of the Southwest* (1927), *Billy the Kid* (1930), *The One-Way Ride* (1931), *The Robin Hood of El Dorado* (1932).

BUSHBY, DON MAITLAND: b. Pueblo, Colo., 1900; ed. State Teachers Coll, Flagstaff, Ariz., Columbia; teacher, writer; poetry. *Mesquite Smoke, and other Poems* (1926), *Ocatilla Blossoms* (1927), *Don Felipe* (1929), *Tusayan* (1930), edited *The Golden Stallion: An Anthology of Poems Concerning the Southwest* (1930), *Winds of the Desert* (1931), *Purple Sage* (1932), *April Will Return* (1937).

BUTTREE, JULIA M.: see Seton, Julia M.

BYNNER, WITTER: b. Brooklyn, NY, 1881; ed. Harvard; to Santa Fe 1922; writer, lecturer; poetry, drama, translations, nonfiction. *Cake* (1926), *Indian Earth* (1929), *The Persistence of Poetry* (1929), *Roots* (1929), *Eden Tree* (1931), *Selected Poems* (1936), *Against the Cold* (1940).

BYRNE, NELL: Res. Santa Fe. Poems NMS.

CALKINS, THOMAS Y.: Poems NMS.

CALVIN, ROSS: b. Ill.; ed. Harvard, General Theological Seminary, NYC; to Silver City 1927; clergyman, lecturer, writer; nonfiction. *Sky Determines* (1934).

CAMPA, ARTHUR LEON: b. Guaymas, Sonora, Mexico, 1905; ed. U of NM, Columbia; UNM prof., folklorist; monographs. *The Spanish Folksong in the Southwest* (1933), *Spanish Religious Folk Theatre in the Southwest* (1934), *Sayings and Riddles in New Mexico* (1937).

CAMPBELL, ISABEL JONES (Mrs. Walter S. Campbell): b. Rochester, NY, 1895; ed. U of Okla.; summer visitor, then res. Santa Fe; writer, by 1940 on staff of Museum of Navajo Ceremonial Art; fiction, poetry, essays, drama. *Jack Sprat* (novel), *Bacon to the Wolves* (play produced 1934).

CAMPBELL, WALTER STANLEY: see Vestal, Stanley.

CANNON, CORNELIA JAMES: b. St. Paul, Minn., 1876; ed. Radcliffe, Wheaton Coll; writer; fiction, juveniles, nonfiction. *Pueblo Boy* (1926), *Pueblo Girl* (1929), *Lazaro in the Pueblos* (1931), *Fight for the Pueblo* (1934).

CAREY, FRANCES: res. Santa Fe; elementary school teacher; juvenile history.

CARR, HARRY: b. Tipton, Iowa, 1877; journalist. *The West Is Still Wild* (1932).

CASSIDY, INA SIZER: b. Bent Co., Colo., 1869; ed. Columbia; writer; NMFWP; poetry, nonfiction.

CATHER, WILLA: b. Back Creek Valley near Gore, Va., 1873; ed. U of

Neb.; NM visitor; writer; fiction, poetry, nonfiction. *The Song of the Lark* (1915, 1932), *The Professor's House* (1925), *Death Comes for the Archbishop* (1927).

CHAPMAN, KATE (Katherine A. Muller, Mrs. Kenneth M. Chapman): res. Santa Fe; architect. *Adobe Notes* (Laughing Horse Press, 1930), poems NMS.

CHAPMAN, KENNETH MILTON: b. Ligonier, Ind., 1875; ed. NY and Chicago; to Las Vegas, NM, 1899, to Santa Fe 1903; artist, archeologist; monographs. *Pueblo Indian Pottery* (1933, 1938).

CHAVEZ, FRAY ANGELICO: b. Manuel Chavez in Wagon Mound, NM, 1910; ed. Franciscan colleges in Cincinnati, Detroit, Oldenberg, Ind.; res. Peña Blanca; priest, writer, painter; poetry, fiction, nonfiction. *Clothed with the Sun* (1939), *New Mexico Triptych* (1940).

CHENEY, ETHEL B. (Mrs. Morton M. Cheney): b. Warner, N.H., 1882; ed. Warner H. S.; res. Albuquerque; poetry; d. 1941. *Voices from the Fields* (1938), *New Language* (1941).

CHENEY, SUSANNE W.: res. Santa Fe. Poems NMS.

CHURCH, PEGGY POND (Margaret Pond; Mrs. Fermor S. Church): b. Watrous, NM, 1903; ed. Smith Coll; res. Santa Fe, Los Alamos Ranch School; poet. *Foretaste* (1933), *The Burro of Angelitos* (1936), *Familiar Journey* (1936).

CLAFLIN, MAJEL: Sketch NMS.

CLARK, ANN(A) NOLAN: b. Las Vegas, NM, 1896; ed. NM Normal U; res. Tesuque; teacher; NMFWP; juveniles. *Handmade Tales* (1932), *In My Mother's House* (1941).

CLARK, AXTON: college professor retired to Santa Fe; poetry. *The Single Glow* (Villagra Press, 1933).

COAN, CHARLES FLORUS: b. Dayton, Ohio, 1886; ed. Whitman Coll, U of Wash. U of Calif.; to NM 1920; history prof.; monographs; d. 1928. *A Short History of New Mexico* (1925, 1928).

COBURN, WALT: b. Mont., 1889; cowboy, writer; fiction. *The Ring-tailed Rannyhaus* (1927), *Mavericks* (1929), *Barb Wire* (1931), *Law Rides the Range* (1935), *Sky-Pilot Cowboy* (1937).

CODMAN, FLORENCE: res. Santa Fe and NY. Review NMS.

COE, GEORGE W.: b. Brighton, Ky.; fought and rode with Billy the Kid; related autobiography, *Frontier Fighter* (1934), to Nan Hillary Harrison (below).

COMFORT, WILL LEVINGTON: b. Kalamazoo, Mich., 1878; ed. Detroit schools; journalist; fiction, nonfiction; d. 1932. *Apache* (1931, pub. England as *Mangas Colorado*, 1931).

COOLIDGE, DANE: b. Natick, Mass., 1873; ed. Stanford; zoologist; fiction, nonfiction; d. 1940. Numerous western novels, 1910-41; *The Navajo Indians* (with M. Coolidge, 1930), *Navajo Rugs* (with M. Coolidge, 1933), *Texas Cowboys* (1937), *Arizona Cowboys* (1938), *The Last of the Series* (with M. Coolidge, 1939).

COOLIDGE, MARY ROBERTS (Mrs. Dane Coolidge): b. Kingsbury, Ind., 1860; ed. Cornell, Stanford; sociologist; monographs. *The Rainmakers: Indians of Arizona and New Mexico* (1929), *The Navajo Indians* (with D. Coolidge, 1930), *Navajo Rugs* (with D. Coolidge, 1933), *The Last of the Series* (with D. Coolidge, 1939).

CORBIN, ALICE (Mrs. William Penhallow Henderson): b. St. Louis, Mo., 1881; ed. U of Chicago; to Santa Fe 1916; poet, editor; NMFWP; poetry, nonfiction. *Red Earth* (1920), compiled *The Turquoise Trail* (1928), *The Sun Turns West* (1933), *Brothers of Light: The Penitentes of the Southwest* (1937).

COWLES, ERIKA A.: Sketch NMS.

CRABTREE, E. MICHAEL: res. Santa Fe. Poems NMS.

CRAMP, HELEN (Helen C. McCrossen): res. Santa Fe. Poems NMS.

CRANE, LEO: b. Baltimore, Md., 1881; ed. public schools; journalist, Indian agent in NM, 1919-22; fiction, nonfiction. *Indians of the Enchanted Desert* (1925), *Desert Drums: The Pueblo Indians of New Mexico, 1540-1928* (1928).

CRANS, ELINOR: res. Albuquerque; NMFWP. Poem NMV.

CRICHTON, KYLE SAMUEL (pseud. Robert Forsythe): b. Beale, Pa., 1896 or 1898; ed. Lehigh U; res. Albuquerque 1920s, at Methodist Sanatorium, returned to NYC, 1929, frequent visitor thereafter; journalist, editor; fiction, nonfiction. *Law & Order, Ltd., The Rousing Life of Elfego Baca of New Mexico* (1928); as Forsythe: *Redder than the Rose* (1935), *Reading from Left to Right* (1938).

CUNNINGHAM, EUGENE (pseud. Leigh Carder): b. Helena, Ark., 1896; ed. Dallas-Fort Worth public schools; journalist; fiction, nonfiction. *Famous in the West* (1926), *Riders of the Night: A Novel of Cattle-Land* (1932), *Diamond River Man* (1934), *Triggernometry* (1934).

CURTIN, LEONORA F.: b. Colorado Springs, Colo., 1908; ed. private schools in U.S., Switzerland, France; res. Santa Fe; poetry.

CURTIN, LEONORA S. MUSE (Mrs. Thomas E. Curtin): b. NY; ed. privately; first visited NM 1889 and 1896; res. Santa Fe; researcher on native herbs and folk cures.

CURTIS, NATALIE (Mrs. Paul Burlin): b. NYC; ed. in music, France and Germany; ethnomusicologist; d. Paris, 1921, in an accident. *Songs of Ancient America* (1905), *The Indians' Book* (1907, rev. by Paul Burlin, 1923), *Negro Folk-Songs* (1918).

CUSHING, FRANK HAMILTON: b. Northeast, Pa., 1857; ed. Cornell; ethnologist; monographs; d. Florida, 1900. *My Adventures in Zuñi* (1882), *Zuñi Breadstuff* (1884-85, 1920), *Zuñi Folk Tales* (1901, 1931).

DALY, JAMES: "nomadic." Poem NMS.

DASBURG, MARINA WISTER: res. Taos; poet. *Fantasy and Fugue* (1937).

DAVEY, WILLIAM: res. Santa Fe and Carmel, Calif. Poems, sketches NMS.

DAVIES, W. T.: Welshman, studied at Yale; Santa Fe visitor. Sketch NMS.

DE HUFF, ELIZABETH WILLIS (Mrs. John David De Huff): b. S.C., 1886 (note: "born in the 'gay nineties' in Augusta, Georgia," A&W, p. 10); ed. Teachers Coll, NY; to NM 1916; writer, lecturer; juveniles, drama, nonfiction, poetry. *Taytay's Tales* (1922), *Taytay's Memories* (1924), *From Desert and Pueblo* (with Homer Grunn, 1924), *Five Little Katchinas* (1930), *Hoppity Bunny's Hop* (1939).

DELLINGER, E. S.: b. Mo., 1886; ed. State Teachers Coll, Springfield, Mo., NM Normal U; to NM 1920; teacher, railroad worker, writer; fiction about railroading.

DERLETH, AUGUST: Poems, sketches NMS.

DNEH BI'KIS: see Goudberg, Rev. William.

DORAN, GEORGE H.: b. 1869. His *Chronicles of Barabbas, 1884-1934* (1935) included: "only because written at Chamiza Plaza, Santa Fe - comes from the expression 'Now Barabbas was a publisher.' Unfortunate that he omitted the group of New Mexico writers from his book-for which omission he merits our disapproval" (MW&W, p. 28).

DOTY, KATE HORSLEY: Sketch NMS.

DOUGLAS, JOHN SCOTT: Sketch NMS.

DOUGLASS, VELDA: res. Flora Vista, NM. Poems, sketches NMS.

DOWLING, JOHN: res. Taos. Sketches NMS.

DRESBACH, GLENN WARD: b. Lanark, Ill., 1889; ed. U of Wis.; res. NM before WWI; efficiency expert, poet. *In Colors of the West* (1922), *The Enchanted Mesa* (1924), *Cliff Dwellings and Other Poems* (1926), *Star-Dust and Stone* (1928).

DUFFUS, ROBERT LUTHER: b. Waterbury, Vt., 1888; ed. Stanford; newspaper writer, magazine free-lancer; fiction, nonfiction. *The Santa Fe Trail* (1930), *Jornada* (1935).

DUGAN, A. G., JR.: res. Albuquerque. Sketches NMS.

DUNNE, BRIAN BORU ("Bee Bee"): b. Salt Lake City, Utah; ed. Benedictines in N.C., in Europe; to NM 1909; journalist, editor. *Cured, The Seventy Adventures of a Dyspeptic.*

DUNTON, NELLIE: b. Biddleford, Me., 1874; to Taos 1920, divorced from artist W. Herbert Dunton, to Santa Fe 1928; nonfiction. *The Spanish Colonial Ornament* (1935).

ELLIS, ANNE: b. Mo., 1875; raised and res. Colo., sojourned in Methodist Sanatorium, Albuquerque; autobiography. *The Life of an Ordinary Woman* (1929), *Plain Anne Ellis* (1931), *Sunshine Preferred* (1934).

EMERSON, ELIZABETH: res. Las Vegas, NM; playwright, poet.

ESPINOSA, AURELIO MACEDONIO: b. Carnero, Colo., 1880; ed. U of Chicago; UNM prof. 1902-10; professor, folklorist; monographs. *Los Comanches* (1907), *The Spanish Language in New Mexico and Southern Colorado* (1911), *España en Nuevo Méjico* (1937).

ESTABROOK, EMMA FRANKLIN: student of Edgar L. Hewett; res. Boston, summers in NM; monographs. *The Living Past* (1926), *Givers of Life: The American Indians as Contributors to Civilization* (1931).

EVANS, JOHN GANSON: b. Buffalo, NY, 1900, son of Mabel Ganson and Carl Evans; ed. Yale; married Alice O. Henderson, 1920, divorced, married author Claire Spencer, 1933; res. Taos; writer; fiction. *Andrews' Harvest* (1933).

E-YEH-SHURE': see Abeita, Louise.

FAUNCE, HILDA: b. Brooklyn, NY; raised Colo.; nurse; autobiography (life on Navajo Reservation). *Desert Wife* (1934).

FECHIN, ALEXANDRA (née Belkovitch, Mrs. Nicolai Fechin): b. Kazan, Russia; ed. Petrograd; emigrated to U.S. 1923, to Taos 1927, later res. Santa Fe; writer. *March of the Past.*

FELTER, WILLIAM: b. Kane, Ill., 1877; ed. Kan. "common schools"; to Des Moines, NM, 1915; res. Tucumcari after 1927; journalist; poetry, nonfiction. Compiled *New Mexico in Verse* (with John L. McCarty, 1935).

FERGUSSON, ERNA: b. Albuquerque, NM, 1888; ed. U of NM; res. Albuquerque; writer; nonfiction. *Dancing Gods: Indian Ceremonials of New Mexico and Arizona* (1931), *Mexican Cookbook* (1934,1940), *Fiesta in New Mexico* (1934), *Our Southwest* (1940).

FERGUSSON, HARVEY: b. Albuquerque, NM, 1890; ed. U of NM, Washington and Lee U; journalist, editor, writer; novels, nonfiction. *The Blood of the Conquerors* (1921), *Wolf Song* (1927), *In Those Days: An Impression of Change* (1929), *Rio Grande* (1933), *Followers of the Sun: A Trilogy of the Santa Fe Trail* (1936).

FICKE, ARTHUR DAVISON: res. Hillsdale, NY, and Santa Fe; poet. Various contributions NMS. *Mountain Against Mountain* (1929).

FIERLEIN, ELIZABETH: b. Muscatine, Iowa; ed. Mt. St. Joseph, Dubuque, Church School of Decorative Art, Chicago Art Institute; to NM 1936; nonfiction.

FISHER, IRENE: res. Albuquerque; editorial writer, poet; NMFWP.

FISHER, LOUIS W.: NMFWP. Poem NMS.

FISHER, REGINALD G.: b. 1906; res. Santa Fe; archeologist; monographs. *Archaeological Survey of Pueblo Plateau* (1930), *Santa Fe-Sub-Quadrangle A* (1931), *Some Geographical Factors that Influence the Ancient Population of the Chaco Canyon* (1934).

FITZPATRICK, GEORGE: editor of *NM Magazine;* nonfiction, drama, detective stories.

FLANAGAN, DOROTHY BELLE (Mrs. Levi A. Hughes, Jr.): b. Kansas City, Mo., 1904; ed. U of Mo., Columbia, U of NM; res. NM from 1932; writer; poetry, fiction, nonfiction. *Dark Certainty* (1931), *Pueblo on the Mesa: The First Fifty Years at the University of New Mexico* (1939), *The Cross-Eyed Bear* (1940), *This So Blue Marble* (1940).

FLETCHER, JOHN GOULD: b. Little Rock, Ark., 1886; ed. Harvard, U of Ark.; first visited NM 1907, frequent summer visitor, occasional res. Santa Fe; res. Little Rock; poet, essayist. *Breakers and Granite* (1921), *Preludes and Symphonies* (1922), *XXIV Elegies* (1935), *Life Is My Song* (1937), *Selected Poems* (1938, Pulitzer Poetry Award).

FLYNN, T. T.: sometime res. Santa Fe, Albuquerque; detective stories. "Also deserving."

FOSTER, BENNETT: b. Omaha, Neb., 1897; ed. NM Agricultural Coll; to Las Cruces, NM, 1916, res. Colfax Co., NM; teacher, writer; pulp fiction.

FOSTER, JOSEPH O'KANE: b. Chicago, 1898; ed. U of Wis.; to Taos early 1920s; writer; fiction, drama, nonfiction. *The Great Montezuma* (1940).

FOX, MARION L. ("M. L."): b. Asheville, N.C., 1865; ed. Tucson Coll, U of Chattanooga; to NM 1911; lawyer, newspaper editor, journalist.

FULTON, MAURICE GARLAND, Maj.: b. Oxford, Miss., 1877; ed. U of Miss.; to Roswell, NM, 1922; professor NMMI; monographs. Edited *The Authentic Life of Billy the Kid* by Pat F. Garrett (1927), edited *The Death of Billy the Kid* by J. W. Poe (1933), edited *New Mexico's Own Chronicle* (with Paul Horgan, 1937).

GALLAGHER, ESTHER: Poem NMV.

GARLAND, MARIE TUDOR (Marie Garland Fiske): res. Española. Poems, sketches NMS.

GAY, ROY: res. Hot Springs, NM. Sketches NMS.

GILLMOR, FRANCES: b. New Brunswick, Canada, 1903; ed. U of Chicago, U of Arizona; U of NM, then U of Ariz. English prof; novels, nonfiction. *Windsinger* (1930), *Traders to the Navajos* (with Louisa Wade Wetherill, 1934), *Fruit Out of the Rock* (1940).

GLASS, JULIA: Poem NMV.

GLIDDEN, FRED: res. Pojoaque. "Also deserving."

GLIDDEN, JOHN: res. Pojoaque. "Also deserving."

GOODWIN, ALICE PRESCOTT (Mrs. James W. Goodwin): b. St. Paul, Minn.; to Santa Fe ca. 1930; wrote fiction and articles under various pseudonyms. "Her books (that we found out about) were published under the name Alice Prescott Smith and although not New Mexican are well worth reading" (W&W, p. 54). *Montlivet* (1907), *Kindred* (1925).

GOODWIN, GRENVILLE: res. Santa Fe. Apache prayer translations NMS.

GOUDBERG, WILLIAM, Rev. (pseud. Dneh BI'Kis): b. Holland, 1887; ed. Calvin Coll and Sem, Grand Rapids, Mich., Lane Sem, Cincinnati, Ohio; missionary among Navajos; nonfiction for church periodicals. *The Upward Trail* (1935).

GRANT, BLANCHE CHLOE: b. Leavenworth, Kan., 1874; ed. Vassar, Boston Museum Art School, Pa. Academy of Art, Philadelphia, Art Students' League, NY; first visited Taos 1919, res. from 1920; artist, writer; NMFWP; nonfiction. *One Hundred Years Ago in Old Taos* (1925), *Taos Indians* (1925), *Taos Today* (1925), edited *Kit Carson's Own Story of His Life* (1926), *When Old Trails Were New: The Story of Taos* (1934), *Doña Lona: A Story of Old Taos and Santa Fe* (1941).

GRANT, EMIL (pseud.): refugee from Nazi Germany in 1937; settled in Taos; also student at U of NM; published *Worldstage*, a magazine of political commentary, in Taos, 1938. Commentary NMS.

GREENHOOD, DAVID: res. Santa Fe and NY. Sketches, poems NMS.

GRIFFIN, FRED: Poem NMV.

GUTHE, CARL EUGEN: b. Kearney, Neb., 1893; ass't dir. Pecos Expedition, Phillips Academy, Andover, 1917-21; archeologist; monographs. *Pueblo Pottery Making* (1925).

HAMMOND, GEORGE PETER: b. 1896; UNM prof. of history; monographs. *Don Juan de Oñate and the Founding of New Mexico* (1927),

Expedition into New Mexico by Antonio de Espejo, 1582-83 (1929), *The Story of New Mexico: Its History and Government* (with Thomas C. Donnelly, 1936), *New Mexico in 1602* (1938), *Narratives of the Coronado Expedition* (1940).

HARRINGTON, ELDRED R.: b. Cove, Kan., 1902, son of Isis L.; raised and res. Albuquerque; ed. U of S. Calif.; science teacher; scientific writing.

HARRINGTON, ISIS L.: b. Exira, Iowa, 1880; ed. U of S. Calif; teacher, writer; fiction, juveniles, poetry. *The Eagle's Nest* (1930), *Komoki of the Cliffs* (1934), *Nah-le Kah-de* (1937), *Told in the Twilight* (1938).

HARRISON, NAN HILLARY: b. Austin, Tex.; ed. Southwestern U; to NM 1931; res. Roswell; journalist, writer, painter; nonfiction, poetry. *Frontier Fighter* (with George Coe, 1934).

HAYWOOD, HELEN: Poem NMS.

HENDERSON, ALICE C.: see Corbin, Alice.

HEWETT, EDGAR LEE: b. Warren Co., Ill., 1865; ed. Tarkio Coll, Mo., Colo. Teachers Coll, Greeley, U of Geneva; res. Santa Fe; archeologist, professor, administrator; monographs. *Antiquities of the Jemez Plateau, New Mexico* (1906), *Ancient Life in the American Southwest* (1930), *The Chaco Canyon and Its Monuments* (1936), *Indians of the Rio Grande Valley* (with Adolph Bandelier, 1937), *Pajarito Plateau and Its Ancient People* (1938), *Landmarks of New Mexico* (1940).

HOGAN, RAY GWYNN: b. Mo.; to Albuquerque at age 5, res. Albuquerque; writer; nonfiction, primarily men's magazines.

HOGNER, DOROTHY CHILDS: res. Albuquerque; novelist; juveniles. *Navajo Winter Nights* (1935), *South to Padre* (1936).

HOLBROOK, CAREY: b. Bolivar, Mo., 1885; ed. U of Ark.; to NM 1922; res. Albuquerque; newspaper editor and columnist; nonfiction, poetry. *Life Goes On* (1937).

HOLLIDAY, W. T.: res. Santa Fe and Cleveland. Sketches NMS.

HOLTER, SAGE: res. Santa Fe. Sketches, poems NMS.

HOOD, MARGARET PAGE: b. Conn., 1892; ed. Simmons Coll; journalist, publicity director; nonfiction, poetry. Poem NMV.

HOOTON, EARNEST ALBERT: Harvard anthropologist. *Indians of Pecos: A Study of Their Skeletal Remains* (1930).

HORGAN, PAUL: b. Buffalo, NY, 1903; ed. NMMI, Eastman School of Music, U of Rochester; res. Albuquerque late 1910s, returned to Roswell, 1926; librarian, writer; fiction, poetry, drama, history. *No Quarter Given* (1935), *From the Royal City of the Holy Faith of St. Francis of Assisi* (1936), *The Habit of Empire* (1938), *Figures in a Landscape* (1940).

HORN, HART S.: res. Las Cruces, NM. Sketches NMS.

HOYT, HENRY F.: b. Minn., 1854; ed. U of Minn., Rush Medical Coll; doctor; autobiography; d. 1930. *A Frontier Doctor* (1929).

HUDDLESTON, BLANCHE: res. Rowe, NM. Sketches NMS.

HUGHES, DOROTHY B.: see Flanagan, Dorothy Belle.

HUGHES, JAMES F.: Poem NMS.

HULBERT, ARCHER BUTLER: b. Bennington, Vt., 1873; ed. Marietta

Coll, U of Chicago, U of Wis., Columbia, Harvard; history prof.; monographs. *Southwest on the Turquoise Trail (1933)*.

HUMPHREY, ZEPHINE (Mrs. W. W. Fahnestock): res. Dorset, Vt. Excerpt from her book on Carlsbad, *Cactus Flower*, in NMS.

HUNT, ROBERT: res. Santa Fe; poet, architect. "Also deserving." Edited *The Selected Poems* by Witter Bynner (1936), *The Early World and Other Poems* (1936).

HURT, AMY PASSMORE: b. Albuquerque, 1898; res. Albuquerque; journalist. *Missions of New Mexico* (1934).

HUXLEY, ALDOUS (Leonard): b. Godalming, Surrey, England, 1894; ed. Oxford; settled in Calif. 1930s, summer visitor in Taos with Frieda Lawrence, 1937; novelist, essayist. "Emperor Worship," NMS, 9 September 1937.

ICKES, ANNA WILMARTH (Mrs. Harold L. Ickes): b. 1873; politician; nonfiction. *Mesa Land* (1933).

JAMES, AHLEE: res. 3 years in San Ildefonso Pueblo; teacher; juveniles. *Tewa Firelight Tales* (1927).

JAMES, GEORGE WHARTON: b. Gainsborough, Lincolnshire, England, 1858; editor, explorer, lecturer; nonfiction; d. 1923. *New Mexico: The Land of the Delight Makers* (1920), *Our American Wonderlands* (1920), *A Little Journey to Some Strange Places and Peoples in Our Southwestern Land (New Mexico and Arizona)* (1921).

JEFFERS, (John) ROBINSON: b. Pittsburgh, Pa., 1887; ed. Occidental Coll, U of S. Calif. Med. Sch., U of Zurich, U of S. Calif.; res. Carmel, Calif., summer res. Taos, 1930s; poet.

JOHNSON, E. DANA: b. Parkersburg, W. Va., 1879; ed. Marietta Coll; to NM 1902; newspaper editor; d. 1937.

JOHNSON, WALTER WILLARD (Spud): b. Mt. Vernon, Ill., 1879; ed. Colo. State Teachers Coll, U of Colo., U of Calif.; res. Santa Fe, then Taos; editor, journalist, poet. *Horizontal Yellow* (1935).

KEECH, ROY A.: b. Milwaukee, Wis., 1895; ed. Mich. State Coll, Columbia, U of NM, U of Denver; res. Santa Fe; fiction, essays, poetry, juveniles. *Ruth Visits Margot, A Little French Girl* (1934), *Pagans Praying* (1940), *Children Sing in New Mexico* (1941).

KEITH, GENTRY: Poem NMV.

KERCHEVILLE, F. M.: UNM prof. of modern languages; monographs, textbooks. *Practical Spoken Spanish* (1934), *A Preliminary Glossary of New Mexican Spanish* (1934).

KIDDER, ALFRED VINCENT: b. Marquette, Mich., 1885; ed. Harvard; frequent field trips to NM; archeologist; monographs. *An Introduction to the Study of Southwestern Archaeology* (1924), *The Pottery of Pecos* (with C. Amsden, 1931), *Artifacts of Pecos* (1932).

KLOSS, PHILLIPS: b. Webster Grove, Mo., 1902; ed. U of Calif.; to Taos 1928; poet, musician; poetry, nonfiction. *Arid* (1932), *The Cloudburst* (1937).

KLUCKHOHN, CLYDE: b. La Mars, Iowa, 1904; ed. Princeton, U of Wis., Oxford, U of Paris, U of Vienna, U of Madrid; first visited NM 1923; UNM prof. of anthropology from 1933; nonfiction, monographs.

To the Foot of the Rainbow (1927), *Beyond the Rainbow* (1933), *Navaho Classification of Their Song Ceremonials* (with Leland C. Wyman, 1938).

KNIBBS, HENRY (Harry) HERBERT: b. Clifton (Niagara Falls), Ont., Can., 1874; ed. Ridley Coll, Ont., Harvard; sometime Santa Fe visitor, res.; writer; fiction, poetry. *Songs of the Trail* (1920), *Saddle Songs* (1922), *Songs of the Lost Frontier* (1930), *Tonto Kid* (1936).

KONOPAK, FARONA (Mrs. Lothar T. Konopak): b. Philadelphia, Pa., 1895; res. NM 1918-29, Harvey Courier, res. Toledo, Ohio, summers in Santa Fe; poet. *Adobe in Sunlight* (1935).

KROMER, JANET SMITH: res. Albuquerque; NMFWP. Report, interview NMS.

KUIPERS, CORNELIUS: b. Sioux Co., Iowa, 1898; ed. Denver U, U of NM; teacher; fiction. *Chant of the Night* (1934), *Deep Snow* (1934).

KUNTZ, EUGENE: Poem NMV.

LADD, HORATIO OLIVER: b. Me., 1839; clergyman, founder and pres. U of NM, 1881-89; fiction, nonfiction; d. 1932. *The Story of the States: The Story of New Mexico* (1891), *Chunda: A Story of the Navajos* (1906).

LA FARGE, OLIVER: b. NYC, 1901; ed. Harvard; frequent visitor, sometime res. NM, 1920s and 1930s; res. NYC; anthropologist, writer; fiction, nonfiction. *Laughing Boy* (1929), *All the Young Men* (1935), *The Enemy Gods* (1937), *As Long as the Grass Shall Grow* (1940).

LAMBERT, FRED: Cimarron sheriff. "To be added to next volume" (MW&W, p. 85).

LARKIN, MARGARET: b. Mesilla Park, NM; ed. U of Kan.; journalist, publicity agent, poet, playwright. *El Cristo* (1926), *The Singing Cowboy* (1931).

LAUGHLIN, RUTH (Mrs. William J. Barker, 1915-33, m. Dr. Alexander, 1934): b. Santa Fe, 1889; ed. Colo. Coll, Columbia School of Journalism; journalist; nonfiction. *Caballeros* (1931).

LAVINIA, ALICE: res. Santa Fe. Poem, sketch NMS.

LAW, LOIS (Mrs. Owen J. Mowrey): b. Clear Lake, Iowa, 1898; ed. U of Colo., U of Wyo., U of S. Calif.; to Albuquerque 1933; English prof.; monographs. *Readings in Language and Literature* (1930).

LAWRENCE, D. H. (David Herbert): b. Eastwood, Eng., 1885; ed. Univ. Coll., Nottingham; intermittent Taos res., 1922-25; writer; fiction, poetry, essays; d. Vence, France, 1930; cremated, reburied Kiowa Ranch, San Cristobal, near Taos, 1935. *St. Mawr* (1925), *The Plumed Serpent* (1926), *Mornings in Mexico* (1927).

LAWRENCE, FRIEDA (von Richthofen): b. Metz, Germany, 1879; accompanied husband to NM, returned to Taos after his death in 1930; autobiography. *"Not I, But the Wind. . ."* (1934).

LAWRENCE, HENRY: Poem NMV.

LAWSON, WILLIAM PINKNEY: "Has article in Scribner's 'Hell and High Water.' 1935" (MW&W, p. 50). *The Fire Woman* (1925).

LINDON-SMITH, CORINNA (Corinna Putnam Smith, Mrs. Joseph Lindon Smith, Raymond Otis's mother-in-law): res. Santa Fe and Dublin, N.H.; feminist, author. Sketch NMS.

LIVINGSTON, CARL: b. ML Ranch, Dark Canyon, w. of Carlsbad Caverns, NM; ass't state land commissioner, writer; "has published a good many yarns in the New York Times and the Wide World Magazine (London)" (MW&W, p. 50).

LOHLKER, MARGARET: res. Santa Fe; poet, editor. Poems NMS.

LONG, HANIEL: b. Rangoon, Burma, 1888; ed. Harvard; visitor to Santa Fe, 1920s, res. from 1929; English prof., writer, editor; poetry, nonfiction. *Atlantides* (1933), *Interlinear to Cabeza de Baca* (1936), *Malinche* (1939). *Piñon Country* (1941).

LUHAN, MABEL DODGE (Mabel Ganson Evans Dodge Sterne Luhan): b. Buffalo, NY, 1879; ed. private and finishing schools; to Taos 1916; *salonierre*, writer; nonfiction, autobiography. *Lorenzo in Taos* (1932), *Winter in Taos* (1935), *Edge of Taos Desert: Escape to Reality* (1937).

LUMMIS, CHARLES FLETCHER: b. Lynn, Mass., 1859; ed. Harvard; journalist, photographer, folklorist, traveler; nonfiction, fiction, poetry; d. Los Angeles, Calif., 1928. *A New Mexico David and Other Stories and Sketches of the Southwest* (1891), *A Tramp Across the Continent* (1892), *Some Strange Corners of Our Country: The Wonderland of the Southwest* (1892), *The Land of Poco Tiempo* (1893), *The Man Who Married the Moon and Other Pueblo Indian Folk-Stories* (1894), *The King of the Broncos and Other Stories of New Mexico* (1897).

MACLEOD, NORMAN: b. Salem, Ore., 1906; ed. U of Iowa, U of NM, U of Okla., Teachers Coll, Columbia; writer; NMFWP; fiction, poetry, nonfiction. *Horizons of Death* (1934), *Thanksgiving Before November* (1936), *You Get What You Ask For* (1939).

MALKUS, ALIDA SIMS (Mrs. R. H. Sims, Mrs. Hubert Malkus): b. Genosee Valley, NY, 1895; erstwhile res. Valley Ranch and Albuquerque, NM; journalist, writer; fiction, nonfiction, juveniles. *Racquel of the Ranch Country* (1927), *The Dragon Fly of Zuni* (1928), *Caravans to Santa Fe* (1928), *Stone Knife Boy* (1933).

MALONEY, MINNEE: res. Albuquerque; poet and short story writer.

MANN, EDWARD BEVERLY: b. 1902. *Gamblin' Man* (1934).

MASTERS, MARY: res. Farmington. Poem, sketch NMS.

MAZZANOVICH, ANTON: b. Dalmatia, 1860; to U.S. 1868; army in Ariz. and NM, 1881-82; autobiography. *Trailing Geronimo* (1926).

McCARTHY, CHARLES: Poem NMS. According to Long: "Mr. McCarthy is director of the Little Theater in Carmel, Calif. He spent part of the summer in Santa Fe, incognito" (19 September 1938).

McCARTHY, CLIFFORD: res. Santa Fe; sometime owner Villagra Book Shop. Poems NMS.

McCORMICK, MARGARET: res. Virginia, Neb. Poem NMS.

McCORMICK, WILFRED, Col.: b. Newland, Ind., 1903; ed. U of Ill.; res. Hagerman, NM; reserve commission, U.S. Cavalry; after 1930, fulltime writer of sports stories and westerns.

McGOVERN, JANET B. MONTGOMERY: b. Rome, Ga., 1881; ed. Oxford, U of Lorraine, Nancy, France; res. Albuquerque; interested in archeology and ethnology; nonfiction, poetry. *Heroic Lives* (1906),

Among the Head Hunters of Formosa (1923), *Butterflies of Taiwan and Other Fantasies* (1924).

MEREDITH, GRACE: b. Pa.; in Southwest from 1924, res. Santa Fe from 1928; poet; NMFWP. Poems NMS.

MERRILD, KNUD: Sketches of D. H. Lawrence in NMS.

MEYER, Fr. THEODOSIUS: b. Batesville, Ind., 1882; ed. Franciscan Coll and Sem.; in various NM churches from 1915: Roswell, Santa Fe, Lumberton, Park View; history. *St. Francis and the Franciscans in New Mexico* (1926).

MILLER, JUDITH: Poem NMS.

MILLER, MARY: "a New York poet [who] has spent several seasons here [in Taos] and written much about this country, which she loves. Her book, *Intrepid Bird* is perhaps her best known work" (Spud Johnson, *Laughing Horse* no. 21, December 1939).

MITCHISON, NAOMI: Poems NMS.

MONK, HARRIET (Jadwiga Monkiewicz): ed. U of NM; editorial writer; "conducting a column at present in the [Albuquerque] Journal called 'Tales from Taos' describing the artists of Taos" (W&W, p. 135).

MONTGOMERIE, ROSEMARY: res. Santa Fe. Sketch NMS.

MOON, CARL: b. Wilmington, Ohio, 1879; res. Albuquerque, 1904-7, of Pasadena, Calif., after 1914; photographer, collector, illustrator; fiction, nonfiction. *Flaming Arrow* (1927), *Indians of the Southwest: A Collection of One Hundred Photographs Taken among the Tribes and Villages of Oklahoma, New Mexico, and Arizona* (1936).

MOON, GRACE PURDIE (Mrs. Carl Moon): b. Indianapolis, Ind.; ed. U of Wis., Chicago Art Institute; artist, writer; fiction, juveniles, poetry. *Lost Indian Magic* (with Carl Moon, 1918), *Chi-Wee and Loki of the Desert* (1926), *Nadita* (1927), *The Magic Trail* (1929), *The Missing Katchina* (1930), *Book of Nah-Wee* (1932).

MOORE, DOROTHY: res. Des Moines, NM. Sketches NMS.

MORANG, ALFRED: b. Ellsworth, Me., 1901; to Santa Fe 1937; musician, painter, writer; nonfiction, short stories.

MORE, LUCY STURGES: res. Tesuque; poet. Poem NMS.

MORLEY, SYLVANUS GRISWOLD: res. Santa Fe; archeologist. "Also deserving."

MORRIS, ANN AXTELL (Mrs. Earl Halstead): b. 1900; archeologist. *Digging in the Southwest* (1933), *Digging in Yucatan* (1933).

MYERS, SUSANNA: res. Santa Fe; "has published in mimeograph form eleven plays dealing with Indian life. Was quite overjoyed to find that the youngsters in the Indian School at Santa Fe like to perform the plays written about them. . . . Specialist in plays and songs for children for campfire, scouts etc." (MW&W, p. 55). *The Giant Who Swallowed the Clouds* (Zuni, 1934), *Weaving Woman* (Navajo, 1934), *Stronghold House* (cliff dwellers, 1934).

NICKELS, SAM H.: b. Whitesburg, Ky., 1883; res. Lincoln Co., NM; cowboy, writer; westerns.

NUSBAUM, AILEEN O'BRYAN (Mrs. Jesse L.): b. Las Vegas, NM,

1889; ed. Sorbonne; res. Santa Fe; NMFWP; artist, writer; juveniles. *Zuni Indian Tales* (1926).

NUSBAUM, DERIC: b. Paris, France, 1913; ed. Harvard; still a student in 1934, studying archeology. *Deric in Mesa Verde* (1926), *Deric with the Indians* (1927)—both illustrated by his mother, Aileen Nusbaum.

OTERO, MIGUEL ANTONIO: b. St. Louis, Mo., 1859; ed. St. Louis U, Notre Dame; politician, writer; nonfiction, autobiography. *My Life on the Frontier* (1935, 1939), *The Real Billy the Kid* (1936), *My Nine Years as Governor of the Territory of New Mexico, 1897-1906* (1940).

OTERO-WARREN, NINA (Maria Adelina Emilia Otero, Mrs. Dawson Warren): b. Los Lunas, NM, 1881; ed. Maryville Coll of the Sacred Heart, St. Louis; county sup't of schools, 1917-29, with CCC and WPA; folklore, autobiography. *Old Spain in Our Southwest* (1936), with illustrations by her cousin, Aileen Nusbaum.

OTIS, RAYMOND: b. Chicago, Ill., 1900; ed. Yale; childhood visitor to NM, res. Santa Fe from 1927; writer; NMFWP; fiction, nonfiction; d. Santa Fe, 1938. *Fire in the Night* (1934; English ed., *Fire Brigade*), *Miguel of the Bright Mountain* (1936), *Little Valley* (1937).

PARSONS, ELSIE WORTHINGTON CLEWS (Mrs. Herbert Parsons): b. NYC, 1875; ed. Columbia; folklorist,anthropologist; monographs; d. 1941. *Notes on Zuni* (1917), *American Indian Life* (1922), *The Pueblo of Jemez* (1925), *Tewa Tales* (1926), *Hopi and Zuni Ceremonialism* (1933), *Taos Pueblo* (1936), *Pueblo Indian Religion* (1939), *Taos Tales* (1940).

PARSONS, PAMELA SHACKLEFORD: res. Santa Fe, was Harvey Courier. Sketch NMS.

PATCHEN, KENNETH: Poem NMS.

PAYTIAMO, JAMES: Acoma Indian. *Flaming Arrow's People* (1932).

PEARCE, THOMAS MATTHEWS: b. Covington, Ky., 1902; ed. U of Mont., U of Pittsburgh; res. Albuquerque; UNM English prof., editor; nonfiction. Edited *America in the Southwest* (with Telfair Hendon, 1933), *Lane of the Llano* (with Jim [Lane] Cook, 1936), *Southwest Heritage: A Literary History with Bibliography* (with Mabel Major, 1938), *Cartoon Guide of New Mexico* (1939), *The Beloved House* (1940).

PEIXOTTO, ERNEST CLIFFORD: b. San Francisco, Calif., 1869; res. NYC and Paris; artist, writer; nonfiction. *Our Hispanic Southwest* (1916).

PESONEN, ELEANOR: res. Santa Fe; sometime owner of Villagra Book Shop; poet. Poems NMS.

PESONEN, EVERETT A.: res. Santa Fe. Sketch NMS.

PILLIN, WILLIAM: b. Russia, 1913; to U.S. ca. 1929, to Santa Fe, 1933, returned to Chicago, res. Santa Cruz from 1938; poet; NMFWP; poetry, nonfiction. Essays NMS.

POTTER, JACK MYERS, Col. ("Lead Steer"): b. Prairielee, Tex., 1864; res. Clayton, NM, after 1928; cowboy, rancher, politician, journalist, writer; folklore, nonfiction. *Cattle Trails of the Old West* (1939), *Lead Steers* (1939).

POUSMA, RICHARD H.: b. 1892; Medical Sup't at Christian Reformed

Mission Hospital, Rehobeth, NM. *He-who-always-wins and Other Navajo Campfire Stories* (1934).

PRINCE, L. BRADFORD: b. Flushing, NY, 1840; ed. Columbia; Chief Justice of NM, 1878-82, Governor of NM, 1889-93; historian. *Historical Sketches of New Mexico from the Earliest Records to the American Occupation* (1883), *New Mexico's Struggle for Statehood* (1910), *A Concise History of New Mexico* (1912), *Spanish Mission Churches of New Mexico* (1915).

RAINES, LESTER F.: b. Ill., 1896; ed. U of Ill., Carnegie Institute of Technology, Harvard, Ohio State U; English and speech prof., NM Normal U; NMFWP; play production, articles on same.

RAYNOLDS, ROBERT: b. in the Palace of the Governors, Santa Fe, 1902, son of acting Gov. James Wallace Raynolds; ed. Princeton, Lafayette Coll; res. Newtown, Conn.; writer; fiction, nonfiction. *Brothers in the West* (1931, Harper Prize), *Saunders Oak* (1933), *Fortune* (1935).

REEVE, PAUL EATON: res. Santa Fe; NMFWP; poet. Poem NMS.

REICHARD, GLADYS A.: b. Bangor, Pa., 1893; ed. Swarthmore Coll, Columbia, U of Hamburg; anthropology prof. at Barnard Coll; nonfiction. *Spider Woman: A Story of Navajo Weavers and Chanters* (1934), *Sandpaintings of the Navajo Shooting Chant* (with Franc J. Newcomb, 1937), *Navajo Medicine Man* (1939), *Dezba, Woman of the Desert* (1939).

REITER, WINIFRED: res. La Jara, NM. Sketches NMS.

RHODES, EUGENE MANLOVE: b. Tecumseh, Neb., 1869; ed. U of Pacific, San Jose, Calif.; first moved to NM 1881, returned to Santa Fe, 1926, res. Alamogordo 1927-31; teacher, cowboy, rancher, writer; fiction, nonfiction, poetry, d. Pacific Beach, Calif., 1934. *Good Men and True* (1910), *West Is West* (1917), *Stepsons of Light* (1920, 1921), *Once in the Saddle* (1925, 1927), *Pasó Por Aquí* (1926, 1927), *Beyond the Desert* (1934), *Peñalosa* (1917, 1934), *The Trusty Knaves* (1931, 1933), *The Proud Sheriff* (1932, 1935).

RICHTER, CONRAD: b. Pine Grove, Pa., 1890; ed. through high school; res. Albuquerque; writer; fiction, essays. *Brothers of No Kin and Other Stories* (1924), *Human Vibration* (1926), *Early Americana* (1936), *The Sea of Grass* (1937), *The Trees* (1940).

RICKETTS, ORVAL: b. St. Louis, Mo.; to Farmington, NM, 1908, res. there since; newspaper editor, poet. *Sketches of Santa Fe* (1935), *Green Leaves and Gold* (1940).

RIGGS, LYNN: b. near Claremore, Indian Territory (Okla.), 1899; ed. U of Okla.; res. Santa Fe 1920s, frequent visitor after; playwright, poet. *Big Lake* (1927), *Knives from Syria* (1927), *A Lantern to See By and Sump'n Like Wings* (1928), *The Iron Dish* (1930), *Green Grow the Lilacs* (1931), *Russet Mantle and The Cherokee Night* (1936).

RINEHART, MARY ROBERTS: b. 1876; "not a New Mexico author but visited the state and remarked in *The Out Trail* 1923" (MW&W, p. 62).

ROBERTS, FRANK HAROLD HANNA (Jr.): b. 1897; archeologist. *Shabik'eshchee Village* (1929), *The Village of the Great Kivas on the Zuni*

Reservation, New Mexico (1932).

ROBERTS, FRANK HUNT HURD: b. Mt. Vernon, Ohio, 1869; ed. Ohio U, Kenyon Coll, U of Denver; res. Denver; pres. NM Normal U, 1910-21; nonfiction. *History and Civics of New Mexico* (with Ralph Emerson Twitchell, 1914).

ROBINSON, WILLIAM HENRY: b. Lexington, Ill., 1867; ed. Park Coll, Mo., Business Coll, Los Angeles; res. Chandler, Ariz.; engineer, writer; fiction, nonfiction. *Her Navajo Lover* (1903), *Yarns of the Southwest* (1921), *Under Turquoise Skies* (1928).

RUDHYAR, DANE: intermittent Santa Fe res.; astrologer, writer; fiction, nonfiction, poetry.

RYAN, RICHARD R.: res. Albuquerque. Sketch NMS.

SAUNDERS, SALLY FAXON: "A magazine writer just settled among us. More later when she tells us" (MW&W, p. 66).

SAWYERS, ALICE: Las Cruces High School student. Poem NMS.

SCOTT, LENA BECKER: b. Maytown, Ill, 1875; ed. U of Chicago, U of Calif.; res. Oklahoma City; educational and social service worker, writer; nonfiction, juveniles; d. 1934. *Dawn Boy of the Pueblos* (1935).

SCOTT, MARIAN GALLAGHER (Mrs. William Earl Scott): b. Wiley, Kan., 1893; ed. Columbia School of Expression, Chicago, Lyceum Arts Conservatory, Chicago; "she and her husband have offices downtown in Sena Plaza, Santa Fe and go to work as to any other business" (W&W, p. 113); pulp fiction. *Dead Hands Reaching* (1932).

SCOTT, WILLIAM EARL: b. Atkinson, Neb., 1892; ed. U of Neb., Lyceum Arts Conservatory; first came to NM 1919; actor, director, writer; pulp fiction, poetry. *Splashin' Sunlight and Shadows* (1926).

SEGALE, Sister M. BLANDINA: b. Cicagna, near Genoa, Italy, 1850; to U.S., 1854; Sister of Charity; autobiography. *At the End of the Santa Fe Trail* (1932, 1948).

SERGEANT, ELIZABETH SHEPLEY: b. Winchester, Mass., 1881; ed. Bryn Mawr Coll, Sorbonne, College de France; first visited Santa Fe 1920, res. Tesuque and NYC; social worker, writer; nonfiction. *French Perspectives* (1916), *Shadow-Shapes* (1920), *Fire Under the Andes* (1927), *Short as Any Dream* (1929).

SETON, ERNEST THOMPSON: b. So. Shields, England, 1860; ed. Toronto Collegiate and Royal Academy, London; res. Seton Village, Santa Fe; writer, illustrator, lecturer, founder Woodcraft League of America, co-founder Boy Scouts; juveniles, nonfiction, natural history. *Wild Animals I Have Known* (1898), *The Biography of a Grizzly* (1900), *Lives of the Hunted* (1901), *Two Little Savages* (1903), *Rolf in the Woods* (1911), *The Gospel of the Red Man: An Indian Bible* (1936), *The Trail of an Artist-Naturalist* (1940).

SETON, JULIA MOSS (Mrs. Ernest Thompson Seton, pseud. Julia M. Buttree): b. NYC, 1889; ed. "in America chiefly"; res. Seton Village, Santa Fe; writer, lecturer; nonfiction. *The Rhythm of the Red Man in Song, Dance, and Decoration* (1930).

SEWELL, LILLIAN: Poem NMV.

SEWELL, O.: Poem NMV.
SHANNON, OPAL: res. Santa Cruz. Poems NMS.
SHERMAN, EDGAR: Poem NMV.
SHUSTER, WILL: b. Philadelphia, Pa., 1893. Poem NMS. Haniel Long: "One of the most widely known and loved local figures, Will Shuster, came to Santa Fe March 4, 1920, to recover from the effects of being gassed in the World War. Thus 'Shus' is one of the earliest settlers in the artist-writer group. A painter, etcher and sculpter, his friends know him as a poet. He read the verses published on the page today at the Poets' Roundup last Saturday" (14 August 1938).
SIMPSON, WILLIAM HASKELL: b. Lawrence, Kan., 1858; ed. U of Kan.; res. Chicago and NM; with Santa Fe Railway from 1881; poetry; d. 1933. Along Old Trails of New Mexico and Arizona (1929).
SINCLAIR, JOHN L.: b. NYC, 1902; ed. in England, including Cambridge; to NM 1923, res. Santa Fe from 1937; cowboy, rancher, writer; fiction, nonfiction.
SMITH, DAMA MARGARET (Mrs. Charles Jerod "White Mountain" Smith, pseud. Dama Langley): b. 1893; nonfiction. I Married a Ranger (1930), Hopi Girl (1931), Indian Tribes of the Southwest (1933).
SNOOK, SIDNEY: "Cimarron," sketch in A&W, Taos section, p. 3.
SNORF, A. L.: Poem NMV.
SPENCER, CLAIRE (Mrs. John Evans): b. Scotland; ed. drama schools; to U.S. 1918; married Evans 1933, res. Taos; novelist. Gallows Orchard (1931), Quick and The Dead (1932), The Island (1935).
SPINDEN, HERBERT JOSEPH: b. Huron, S.D.,1879; ed. Harvard; anthropologist; monographs. Songs of the Tewa (1933).
ST. CLAIR, GEORGE WILLIS: b. 1880; ed. Whitman Coll, U of Calif.; UNM English prof.; essays, drama, poetry. Young Heart (1933).
STAMM, ROY: Poem NMV.
STEVENS, PHOEBE: res. Santa Fe. Poem, sketch NMS.
STEVENS, THOMAS WOOD: b. Oregon, Ill., 1880; ed. Armour Scientific Academy, Chicago; purchased Santa Fe house, 1925; playwright, pageant producer, poet, artist. Westward Under Vega (1938), The Entrada of Coronado: A Spectacular Historic Drama (1940).
STEVENSON, PHILIP: b. NYC, 1896; ed. Harvard; res. Santa Fe; writer; fiction, drama, poetry, nonfiction. The Edge of the Nest (1929), The Gospel According to St. Luke (1931), God's In His Heaven (1934).
STEWART, DOROTHY NEWKIRK: b. Philadelphia, Pa.; ed. Phila. Academy of Fine Arts, U of Pa.; artist; nonfiction. Hornacinas: Niches and Corners of Mexico City (1933).
STOBIE, RAMSAY: res. La Luz, NM. Poems, sketches NMS.
STODDARD, ALFRED HAZEN: res. Santa Fe. Poems NMS, A&W.
STULTZ, MARY: res. Hatch, NM. Poem, sketches NMS.
SULIER, LOUIS: res. Las Vegas, NM; writer.
SWAINE, RUTH: res. Ranchos. Sketch NMS.
TAYLOR, CARL N.: b. Milltown, Ind., 1903; ed. Central Normal Coll, Danville, Ind., U of NM; teacher, writer; nonfiction, fiction; d. Cedar Crest, NM, 1936. An Odyssey of the Islands (1936).

THOMAS, DOROTHY: "A short story writer, now a resident of Santa Fe, whose short stories are most enjoyable reading" (W&W, p. 118).

THOMPSON, JANICE DE KAY: res. Santa Fe. Poems NMS.

THORP, NATHAN HOWARD (Jack): b. NYC, 1867; ed. St. Paul's School; to NM during his teens, eventually res. Santa Fe, after 1935 res. Alameda; cowboy, collector of cowboy songs and stories, writer; NMFWP; folklore, poetry, nonfiction; d. Alameda, NM, 1940. *Songs of the Cowboys* (1908, rev. 1921), *Tales of the Chuck Wagon* (1926).

THORPE, W. H.: "Forgetfulness," a cowboy story, A&W, p. 12.

TITZELL, JOSIAH: res. Santa Fe. Poem NMS.

TOOMER, NATHAN JEAN: b. Washington, D.C., 1894; ed. U of Wis., CCNY; "his first visit to New Mexico was in 1925 in the interests of the Gurdjieff Institute, a trip made possible by Mabel Luhan" (A&W, p. 21), res. Santa Fe and Doylestown, Pa.; writer; nonfiction, fiction, drama.

TWITCHELL, RALPH EMERSON: b. Ann Arbor, Mich., 1859; ed. U of Mich.; lawyer, lecturer, historian; nonfiction; d. Santa Fe, 1925. *Leading Facts of New Mexico History* (1911-17), *The Spanish Archives of New Mexico* (1914), *Old Santa Fe: The Story of New Mexico's Ancient Capital* (1925).

UDELL, I. L.: res. Taos, then Leadville, Colo. Sketch NMS.

ULMER, SARAH D.: b. near La Grange, Ind.; ed. Northwestern U, Kings Coll of Oratory, Pittsburgh, U of Denver; res. Tucumcari; teacher, rancher, writer; poetry, songs. Poem NMV.

UNDERWOOD, JOHN CURTIS: b. Rockford, Ill., 1874; ed. Trinity Coll; res. Santa Fe; writer; nonfiction, poetry. *Trail's End: Poems of New Mexico* (1921), *Pioneers* (1923).

VAN STONE, MARY ROBERTA (Hurt): b. 1876; director-curator Art Museum, Santa Fe; nonfiction. *Spanish Folk Songs of New Mexico* (1926), *Los Pastores; Excerpts from an Old Christmas Play of the Southwest as Given Annually by the Griego Family, Santa Fe, New Mexico* (1933).

VAUGHN, JOHN H.: b. Dobson, N.C., 1880; ed. U of N.C., U of Tenn, U of Calif.; prof. of English and history, NM State Coll; nonfiction. *History and Government of New Mexico* (1921, 1927).

VESTAL, STANLEY (Walter Stanley Campbell): b. Severy, Kan., 1887 (original name Vestal, adopted by Campbell, mother suggested he write as Vestal); ed. Southwestern State Coll of Okla., Oxford; summer res. Santa Fe; U of Okla. English prof.; history, fiction, poetry. *Fandango: Ballads of the Old West* (1927), *Kit Carson, the Happy Warrior of the Old West* (1928), *'Dobe Walls: A Story of Kit Carson's Southwest* (1929), *Wine Room Murder* (1935), *Mountain Men* (1937), *Revolt on the Border* (1938), *The Old Santa Fe Trail* (1939).

VIDAURRETA, VALENTIN: Poems NMS.

WALEN, HARRY L.: res. Otowi. Poem NMS.

WALLACE, LEW, General: b. 1827, d. 1905. Arrived in Santa Fe, 1878, to become Governor of NM. Finished last chapters of *Ben Hur*

(1880) in the old Palace of the Governors; fiction, nonfiction. *The Fair God; or The Last of the 'Tzins* (1873).

WALLACE, SUSAN ARNOLD ELSTON (Mrs. Lew Wallace): b. Crawfordsville, Ind., 1830; to Santa Fe, 1879; writer; nonfiction. *The Land of the Pueblos* (1888).

WALTER, PAUL A. F.: raised in Pa.; to Santa Fe for health, 1899; newspaperman, editor, politician, lawyer. Founded *El Palacio, New Mexico Historical Review,* installed El Palacio Press in basement of Art Museum, helped found *New Mexico Quarterly,* and "wrote reams of archaeological and historical ephemera" (A&W, p. 6).

WALTON, EDA LOU (Mrs. David Mandel): b. Deming, NM, 1896; ed. U of Calif. Berkeley; NYU English prof., writer; NMFWP; poetry, fiction, nonfiction. *Dawn Boy: Black Foot and Navajo Songs* (1926), *Jane Matthew and Other Poems* (1931), *Turquoise Boy and White Shell Girl* (1933).

WARNER, EDITH: Sketch NMS.

WARNER, LOUIS H.: b. Williamsburg, Mass., 1875; ed. Boston U; to Santa Fe during early 1920s to work on Pueblo Indian land grants; lawyer; nonfiction. *Archbishop Lamy: An Epoch Maker* (1936).

WATERS, FRANK: b. Colorado Springs, Colo., 1902; ed. Colo. Coll; summers in Mora and Taos, late 1930s; various jobs, writer; fiction, nonfiction. *Fever Pitch* (1930), *The Wild Earth's Nobility* (1935), *Below Grass Roots* (1937), *Midas of the Rockies: Biography of Winfield Scott Stratton* (1937), *The Dust Within the Rock* (1940), *People of the Valley* (1941).

WESTLAKE, INEZ BARNES: b. Brooklyn, NY, 1883; to Silver City, NM, 1885; ed. NM schools, Silver City Teachers Coll; teacher, artist; nonfiction. *American Indian Designs* (1925-30).

WHITFIELD, RAOUL: b. NYC, 1896; ed. Lehigh U; res. Las Vegas, NM; journalist, writer; movie scenarios, drama, fiction, juveniles. *Wings of Gold* (1930), *Green Ice* (1931), *Death in a Bowl* (1931), *The Virgin Kills* (1932), *Danger Circus* (1933).

WILLIAMSON, JACK: b. Bisbee, Ariz., 1908; ed. W. Texas Teachers Coll, U of NM; to Llano Estacado of NM, 1915, Santa Fe res. 1940; science fiction writer.

WINNEK, MARIAN: "Marian Winnek has transplanted herself from New England and now lives in Santa Fe" (W&W, p. 132). *Juniper Hill* (1932).

WISTER, MARINA: see Dasburg, Marina Wister.

WITMER, EMMA: res. Santa Fe and Overbrook, Pa. Sketches NMS.

WOODS, CLEE (pseud. Lee Forest): b. W. Va.,1893; ed. U of Denver; to NM 1920; various jobs, writer; western fiction. *Riders of the Sierra Madre* (1935), *Buckaroo Clan of Montana* (1936), *Raiders of Lost River* (1937), *Rebels Rendezvous* (1937).

ZARRO, RAMON: "a most mysterious poet of Taos. No one seems to know who he is, but he keeps bobbing up all the time, both in verse and prose" (Spud Johnson, *Laughing Horse* No. 21, December 1939).

BIBLIOGRAPHIC NOTE

In 1963, an exhibition of 109 works by Taos and Santa Fe artists travelled between the Amon Carter Museum of Western Art in Fort Worth,. Texas, the La Jolla Art Center in California, and the Art Gallery of the University of New Mexico in Albuquerque. The exhibition catalogue by Van Deren Coke, *Taos and Santa Fe: The Artist's Environment, 1882-1942* (Albuquerque: University of New Mexico Press, 1963), is a milestone attempt to define these two centers of artistic activity in New Mexico. "Picturesque Images from Taos and Santa Fe," an exhibition sponsored by the First National Bank of Denver and the Denver Art Museum, January 12-March 17, 1974, included 139 works, but in its more lavish catalogue (Denver, Colorado: Denver Art Museum, 1974), curator Pat Trenton concentrates on individuals and specific works rather than the definition and dynamics of the art colonies. The same is true of *Light & Color: Images from New Mexico*, Masterpieces from the Collection of the Museum of Fine Arts, Museum of New Mexico (Santa Fe: Museum of New Mexico Press, 1981). Unpublished dissertations by James Mann Gaither, "A Return to the Village: A Study of Santa Fe and Taos as Cultural Centers, 1900-1934" (University of Minnesota, 1957), and Kay Aiken Reeve, "The Making of an American Place: The Development of Santa Fe and Taos, New Mexico, as an American Cultural Center, 1898-1942" (Texas A & M University, 1977), are more analytical and include some discussion of both writers and artists. Gerald D. Nash briefly covers both the artists and writers of Santa Fe and Taos in *The American West in the Twentieth Century: A Short History of an Urban Oasis* (Englewood Cliffs, New Jersey: Prentice-Hall, 1973).

Until recently, Taos has received the most scrutiny and publicity from "aesthetic" perspectives. Claire Morrill's *A Taos Mosaic: Portrait of a New Mexico Village* (Albuquerque: University of New Mexico Press, 1973) presents every aspect—setting, history, folklore, the three cultures, and various artists, writers and other notable residents. She appends a good bibliography. Two magnificently illustrated art histories—Patricia Janis Broder's *Taos: A Painter's Dream* (Boston: Little, Brown, for New York Graphic Society, 1980) and Mary Carroll Nelson's *The Legendary Artists of Taos: Expanded from the Pages of 'American Artist'* (New York: Watson-Guptill, 1980)—focus on individuals rather than their "colony." More modest predecessors to these volumes include Mabel Dodge Luhan's *Taos and Its Artists* (New York: Duell, Sloan & Pearce, 1947) and Laura Bickerstaff's *Pioneer Artists of Taos* (Denver, Colorado: Sage Books, 1955). Also notable are a special illustrated section of *New Mexico Quarterly* (vol. 21, summer 1951, pp.

135-80), entitled "Taos and Individualism: A Brief Résumé of an Environment" and edited by Mabel Dodge Luhan with the assistance of Frank Waters and Spud Johnson, and Helen Greene Blumenschein's *Recuerdos: Early Days of the Blumenschein Family* (Silver City, New Mexico: Tecolote Press, 1979). Mildred Tolbert Crews has recorded her recollections of the Taos art colonists in the autumn 1979 issue of *South Dakota Review*, which has also published Taos Valley reminiscences by Dorothy Brett in 1967 and I. L. Udell in 1969, among others.

Paul Horgan portrays "fourth century" Santa Fe and its tourists, art colonists and residents in "The Chronicler: 1915 and after," the final chapter of his impressionistic history, *The Centuries of Santa Fe* (New York: E. P. Dutton, 1956). Oliver La Farge's more chatty *Santa Fe: The Autobiography of a Southwestern Town* (Norman: University of Oklahoma Press, 1959) is drawn from the pages of *The New Mexican* between November 28, 1849, and December 2, 1953, and includes various notes and comments on the arts scene. Although not strictly contemporary with the period covered in this book, *The Man with the Calabash Pipe: Some Observations by Oliver La Farge*, edited with an introduction by Santa Fe poet Winfield Townley Scott (Boston: Houghton Mifflin, The Riverside Press, Cambridge, 1966), contains many relevant reminiscences and characterizations from La Farge's Sunday *New Mexican* columns between 1950 and July 1963. Rosemary Nusbaum's *Tierra Dulce: Reminiscences from the Jesse Nusbaum Papers* (Santa Fe, New Mexico: Sunstone Press, 1980) usefully supplements La Farge's writings. A collection of photographs taken during the 1930s by Ernest Knee, *Santa Fe, New Mexico* (New York: Hastings House, 1942), makes vivid the visual setting of the capitol and its environs. The only book devoted solely to the artists is Edna Robertson and Sarah Nestor's *Artists of the Canyons and Caminos: Santa Fe, The Early Years* (n.p.: Peregrine Smith, 1976), for which David Noble was photographic editor. Although the authors discuss their artist subjects in terms of local society, the book's usefulness is diminished because the text lacks references.

The standard literary reference, Mabel Major and T. M. Pearce's *Southwest Heritage: A Literary History with Bibliography* (Albuquerque: University of New Mexico Press, 1938, 1948, 1972), is in its third revised and enlarged edition. Other useful checklists include Richard W. Etulain's *Western American Literature: A Bibliography of Interpretive Books and Articles* (Vermillion, South Dakota: Dakota Press, 1972), for which a second edition is in preparation at the University of Nebraska Press; *Publishing in the West: Alan Swallow* (Santa Fe, New Mexico: The Lightning Tree, 1974), edited by William F. Claire; and *Southwestern American Literature: A Bibliography* (Chicago: Swallow Press, 1980), edited by John Q. Anderson, Edwin W. Gaston, Jr., and James W. Lee. Also consult John R. Milton's *The Novel of the American West* (Lincoln: University of Nebraska Press, 1980) and various articles in *The American Literary West*, edited by Richard W. Etulain (Manhattan, Kansas: Sunflower University Press, 1980).

Perhaps the most elegant bibliographer and commentator on Southwestern books, writers, printers, bookstores and literary ambience is librarian Lawrence Clark Powell. Many of his works are listed in *Voices from the Southwest: A Gathering in Honor of Lawrence Clark Powell* (Flagstaff, Arizona: Northland Press, 1976), assembled by Donald C. Dickinson, W. David Laird and Margaret F. Maxwell. The most notable of Powell's pieces in the context of this book are his essay collections—*Books: West, Southwest* (Los Angeles, California: Ward Ritchie Press, 1967), *Southwestern Book Trails: A Reader's Guide to the Heartland of New Mexico and Arizona* (Albuquerque: Horn & Wallace, Publishers, 1963), and *Southwest Classics: The Creative Literature of the Arid Lands, Essays on the Books and Their Writers* (Los Angeles, California: Ward Ritchie Press, 1974). Powell also contributed to *New Mexico Magazine*, and it is interesting to compare his list of "50 Good Books About New Mexico" (January 1960) with Saul Cohen's article on "The 10 Best Novels of New Mexico" (March/Arpil 1974), which includes a useful map locating and dating ninety-five novels set in the state.

INDEX